To Allan,

You can say you knew me when

Mike Walsh

Realizing the Potential of Computer-Based Information Systems

Realizing the Potential of Computer-Based Information Systems

Myles E. Walsh

Macmillan Publishing Company
A Division of Macmillan, Inc.
NEW YORK

Collier Macmillan Publishers
LONDON

Macmillan Publishing Company
866 Third Avenue, New York, N. Y. 10022

Collier Macmillan Canada, Inc.

Printed in the United States of America

printing number

1 2 3 4 5 6 7 8 9 10

Library of Congress Cataloging in Publication Data

Walsh, Myles E.
Realizing the potential of computer-based information systems.

Includes index.
1. Management information systems. I. Title.
T58.6.W327 1984 658.4′0388 83-26764
ISBN 0-02-949810-4

to marc

CONTENTS

PREFACE

THIS BOOK IS AN ATTEMPT by a middle manager to communicate some information to senior managers and executives. We, the publisher (Macmillan) and I, believe that the organizational function that is responsible for data (information) processing (computers) has become just as important a business function as finance, accounting, marketing, and operations. Our purpose is to provide senior managers and executives with that which they won't find anyplace else within a single set of covers.

Many of the presentations that are made to senior managers and executives today take the form of superficial, "Gee whiz, holy cow, can they really do all that?" seminars, slick and glossy promotional brochures, and fast-moving multimedia slide presentations. Coming away from these, senior managers and executives are likely to be asking themselves, "If it's all that good, why are we having so many problems in our organization?" In this book, we strive to avoid both the superficiality just described and the technical detail of the treatments found at the other end of the spectrum. The seminars, brochures, and presentations present the *potential* of computers and information systems. The technical treatments tell technicians how to implement the individual components (there are hundreds of them) that when integrated with one another make computer-driven information systems a reality. The information imparted from these treatments, as history and our current situation indicate, has not led to a *realization* of that potential. We intend to remedy that and show what needs to be understood and what needs to be done to realize that potential.

We are aware that we are competing for time from individuals to whom time is a scarce resource. Yet we believe that if our treatment were too brief, we would merely be repeating the superficiality that we are critical of and wish to avoid. So we have made comprehensiveness with simplicity of presentation our goal.

The book is primarily a tutorial. Chapters 1 through 8 are devoted to defining and describing basic information system and computer concepts and facilities. Chapters 9 and 10 are editorial. In those last two chapters and in the appendices we offer our observations, evaluations, and recommendations. They are cautious and conservative and to some they may even be irritating. We concede that we may be wrong on some of our evaluations and recommendations, but at the same time we believe we are accurate in our assessments most of the time. Overall it is our hope that senior managers and executives may get some benefit from the author's twenty-five years experience in the EDP/MIS field.

I wish to express gratitude to those who helped while the book was in preparation. Thanks go to Diana, a motivator; to Mary Ellen (Mel) Kalbacker and Fran Innocencio who prepared the manuscript on a Wang word processor. Special thanks to Tony Murljacic for providing the foundation for the sixth chapter. Gratitude is extended to professional associates, Mike McSweeney the Vice President of MIS for CBS Records; to Ted Bache, the Vice President of Finance for the same organization; and to my fellow directors, Frank O'Neill, Warren Stephens, Ed Samuels, Joe Hroblak, Ruth Alexeichik, and Art Nichols, who were helpful merely by their professionalism. They helped in many ways without even being aware of it.

EXECUTIVE SUMMARY

IT IS NOW COMMONLY ACCEPTED that information systems management, along with the other major business functions such as marketing, finance, accounting, operations, distribution, and personnel, has become an area requiring the attention of executives and senior managers. Information systems, actually an amalgamation of several technologies, have come from virtually nothing to their present form in approximately twenty years. This phenomenon has been chronicled in considerable detail in books, journals, and seminars too numerous to count. Senior managers and executives are aware that this phenomenon exists, and they are also aware that information systems are somewhat shrouded by the complex technologies which support them. Because of other priorities and the speed at which information systems and their related technologies have sprung up, these individuals sometimes find themselves at a loss dealing with what often appears to be a labyrinth of overlapping technologies. This book removes the layers of overlap by first separating the subjects of information, systems, and management and then by making further subdivisions under each of these major categories.

The book is divided into three sections; the first deals with information, the second deals with systems, and the third deals with management. Within the sections there are chapters that explain more fully the concept of information, the hardware and software, the procedures and practices of systems, and the art of management.

Section I contains two chapters, the first of which defines *information* and explains a subtle difference between what is meant by that term and what is meant by the term *data*. The difference between unstructured data (mainly text) and structured data (mainly numbers) is discussed. The fundamental data-processing concepts of *field*, *record*, *file*, *key*, and *database* are introduced. The fundamental concept of a *transaction*, the entity that triggers processing in an information system, is discussed and illustrated. Another basic distinction is made between the term *application* and the term *system*. The two major acronyms of information systems, *EDP* and *MIS* also receive some attention. The first chapter concludes with an explanation of how and why computers got involved.

The second chapter is a descriptive chapter. A distinction is made between computer hardware and computer software, subjects discussed in more detail in Section Two. The process of *computer programming* is introduced, as is the idea of a computer program performing a unit of work, sometimes known as a *task*. Distinctions between *primary storage* and *secondary storage* are made and are illustrated. A number of other concepts and facilities such as *operating systems*, *input/output*, *database*, *data communications*, and *data dictionaries*, though discussed in more detail in subsequent chapters, are introduced. The concept of *management information* as opposed to the concept of *information* in general is defined. In short, the second chapter is a survey of information processing and the technology that supports it.

The second section of the book is devoted to more detailed descriptions and explanations of the technology that is used to support information systems. This section contains five chapters. The first of these, Chapter 3, is devoted to the description of the equipment that is used to store, manipulate, retrieve, display, and transmit information. Computer and telecommunications equipment, that is, hardware, is given functional definitions, descriptions, and explanations. Components such as *processors*, *primary storage*, *secondary storage*, *terminals*, and *modems* are examined functionally.

Chapters 4 and 5 deal with software, that is, the sets of instructions (computer programs) that tell the equipment components what to do. Chapter 4 is a treatment of what is known as *systems software*, those programs that instruct the equipment in the performance of essential background operations that must be carried on in any computer configuration. Chapter 5 consists of discussions on what is known as *application software*, those programs that instruct the equipment to perform the specific jobs of the user of the computer configuration. Application programs use the facilities of systems programs in the performance of their tasks. For example, we all know how to read and write. The mechanics of reading and writing are system software tasks. The reading of specific transactions, such as invoices or time cards, or the writing of specific information, such as paychecks or inventory reports, are application tasks.

In Chapter 4, *operating systems* or *control programs*, *database/data communications systems*, *compilers*, and other system software products are defined and described. The technical support required for such products is discussed. The potential and the limitations of system software is also given treatment. Chapter 5 takes a look at application software. The evolution of computer programming is traced, and interfacing with the facilities of system software in order to develop applications is described. The chapter concludes with a commentary on the relative merits of the various ways in which application software can be developed.

Chapter 6 attempts to describe the contemporary applications of information technology. In terms of its potential, it's all coming together. The networks of terminals, large and small computers, the database/data communications systems, word processing, electronic mail, graphics—all are technologically possible. Bringing it all to fruition, realizing the potential, is a managerial task; the technology exists.

Chapter 7 examines other areas that are rather mundane from a technological perspective, but which are necessary for the potential of information systems to be realized. *Data dictionaries* and *security* are vital to a successful information system. A data dictionary is an automated documentation tool that can be used to keep track of the kinds of data that exist in an information system. Integrated with an organization's database/data communication system, it can serve as an essential controlling and stabilizing component. The potential of the technology of computers and database/data communication systems is such that out of control situations may develop if some inhibitions, such as those available in data dictionary products, are not used. Data dictionaries can be used in conjunction with other rudamentary security procedures to maintain control in an information system.

The third section of the book deals with management, management of information and systems, and management using information and systems. The first chapter in this section, Chapter 8, deals with managing the operating environments where information system processing takes place. These environments vary in size and complexity from very large data centers with several large-scale computers and storage capacity for information measured in billions of characters to single individuals with small microprocessor based business computers. The number and complexity of the management concerns varies accordingly. In this chapter the elements to be managed in a large data center are examined in considerable detail. Understandably, these considerations take up the bulk of the chapter, but the unique management concerns of small installations and of the single user small business computer are also covered.

Chapters 9 and 10 reflect an assessment and some recommendations. Chapter 9 explains the source of problems; problems with technology, problems with people, and problems for other reasons. Chapter 10 presents a crystallization of the global term *management*, and then makes some recommendations on how to realize the potential that information systems offer management.

There are several appendices at the end of the book. These are intended to demonstrate that *change* is constant in the world of information systems, technology, and management. Appendix A presents some guidelines to successful project management, coupled with professional and personal survival, two conditions which are not always in a cause-and-effect relationship. Appendix B tries to narrate in a somewhat humorous vein the evolution of MIS and to illustrate change and its effects on those involved in it. Appendix C offers an easily applied technique with a proven track record that can be used to plan activities in an operational environment for a twelve to fifteen month period of time. Appendix D contains some thoughts that cross the minds of managers from time to time when contemplating the contemporary information systems scene.

Realizing the Potential of Computer-Based Information Systems

SECTION ONE

I Is for Information

Three observations can be made about the acronym MIS. First, when originally coined in the mid-1960s, the initials MIS stood for management information systems. In this context MISs were supposed to be computer-based systems that would supply management with the information they required for strategic decision making. Second, in the late 1960s, the organizational function that included electronic data processing, computer programming, and systems analysis assumed the organizational designation MIS. That function was to be the catalyst that would build the systems to give management the information needed. In the fifteen or so years that followed, the potential of MIS was only partially realized. Third, the term management information systems and the acronym MIS are in descendency, being eclipsed by the shorter term information systems. It seems that now, as the potential is about to be more fully realized, the scarred and bloodied old terminology is to be replaced with a new and unscathed term. Consequently, within this book and in day-to-day usage, the terms management information systems and information systems and the acronym MIS are used somewhat interchangeably.

Three words make up the term management information systems. The intent of the term is to convey the idea that systems can be developed that can be used by management to store useful information and make it readily accessible. However, such a broad concept can easily convey different ideas to different individuals. Therefore, it is necessary to elaborate on the term to convey a more specific idea. This elaboration involves examining each word of the term. The first two chapters examine what is meant by the word information in its context within the term management information systems. The discussions found in these opening chapters range from a brief history to semantics, and from the abstract of logical data structures to the concrete of physical data storage. The involvement of computers and why they are necessary is presented. There is an explanation of the difference between logistical systems that require detailed information and strategic systems that work with summary information. Some of the discussion can be kind of "heavy" to wade through, and yet the crystallization of the basics contributes to improved communication among individuals both within MIS and those served by MIS. The vagaries and ambiguities of management create difficulty enough. There is no need to compound that difficulty by avoiding an examination of the specifics of information.

CHAPTER 1

Introduction to MIS and EDP

SOME OBSERVATIONS ON SYSTEMS AND COMPUTERS

> *O great! Here we go! This guy is into the alphabet soup before we even get off the first page.*

Please don't be dismayed. The use of acronyms from this point on is to be kept to a minimum. The two used in the title of this opening chapter are fairly well known, and understood, in general terms. MIS represents *management information systems*. The second acronym, EDP, represents *electronic data processing*. The scope of electronic data processing includes that somewhat nebulous and intimidating subject known as computers. One way to simplify discussions at the outset and at the same time get away from the acronyms is to use the word *systems* when referring to MIS in general terms and to use the word *computers* when referring to EDP in general terms. As the discussions progress, certain distinctions and clarifications are made so that more specific words may be used.

The pages that follow reflect an attempt to walk a fine line between superficiality and technological complexity. There is certainly no denying that computers and systems can be extremely complex in detail. At the same time a significant number of seminars and vendor presentations, put together for the benefit of senior and general managers, treat these subjects in a superficial way. Within a relatively short period of time, the "seminar makers" attempt to expose a group of rather busy and somewhat preoccupied executives to a great deal of information.* Most of these seminars and presentations show managers the *potential* of the technology. In effect, the managers come away from these seminars with the notion of what is possible with computers and systems technology. If they were not exposed to this, they would not be motivated to use the technology. However, the senior and general managers are rarely exposed to the functional requirements necessary to *realize* the potential. The seminars, because of the limitations imposed by time constraints, cover their subject matter by pointing up what can be done with computers and systems technology.

It is an unacknowledged fact of life that senior and general managers have many, often too many, matters vying for their attention. Those that appear to be the most important get attended to, those that appear to be less important get slight consideration or get ignored completely. The successful senior and general managers are those whose judgment on these matters conforms to reality. Until recently, computers and systems were relatively unimportant to senior and general managers. Rightly or wrongly, who is to say, these managers gave slight attention to or ignored computers and systems. More recently, however, they have attracted considerably more attention. This is due to several factors. First of all, the quantity of funds allocated to systems and computers is significant. Second, small computers and computer terminals are popping up all over the place. Third, it is being found that many organizational functions are to some degree dependent upon computers and systems, and could not operate effectively without them. These factors taken together have raised computers and systems to the point where senior and general managers are paying attention. These managers are asking questions, questions such as: "Why are we allocating so much money to computers and systems? A terminal or a work station at every desk, why is that necessary? Why does it take three to six months to make a small adjustment to the way totals are taken on my report? What's the difference between 'batch' and 'on-line' anyway? Why can't we get the information we want on a screen just like the operators in the order entry department? What do you mean, we can't enter orders because the computer is 'down?' Twenty-five million

*This is not intended to slight management seminars or those who develop them. They provide an important service in bringing current, relevant material to the attention of senior and general managers who have no other way of getting it.

a year we spend on computers and systems and you, the director of computer operations, can't tell me how many terminals have access to our data processing facility, why not?" These are just a sample of the kinds of questions being asked of computers and systems managers by senior and general managers. The reasons that they are being asked, why they are difficult to answer, and what can be done about the situations reflected by the questions are addressed in subsequent pages. By the time the last chapter is read, senior and general managers will have had some of their questions answered; they will have a grasp of what is required to realize the potential offered by computers and systems, and they will be able to make a significant contribution to the effective and efficient use of the computers and systems resources.

WHAT IS INFORMATION?

The word *information* is being used with increasing regularity these days. In addition to management information systems, we also see terms like information systems, information management, information explosion, and more recently, information overload. There can be little doubt that information in receiving more attention presently than it has historically. There are several reasons for this. The quantity of information is increasing exponentially. (This statement is made without comment on the quality of the information.) The demand for timely and accurate information is accelerating in our fast-paced, constantly changing business environment. Large organizations now have stored in computer files and databases significant quantities of information that has become both valuable and at the same time sensitive. Some percentage of that information (the percentage varies from one type of organization to another) is dynamic; that is, it is updated frequently. These large information files and databases require periodic copying so that they are backed up in the event they are damaged. And in one of the most diabolical paradoxes of history, portions of this information must be made readily accessible, yet at the same time, these same portions must be made secure (some say inaccessible). This paradox itself leads to some rather frustrating situations as we shall see later on. In any event, information has become an important organizational asset. Senior managers in business, government, and institutional organizations now realize that the information contained in their computerized files and databases is vital to their continued operation.

To give it a simple definition, *information* is a representation of reality. Groups of numbers, symbols, and letters or arrangements of words form representations. For example: In the United States, 091-30-2265 is a group of numbers and symbols that most people would recognize as a social security number. JERUSALEM is a group of letters that forms a word that is the name of the capital city of the nation of Israel. "A Playboy bunny is not a rabbit," is an arrangement of words to form a sentence which conveys an idea. So, information, in addition to being a representation of reality, is also a means of communication. As a matter of fact, there is an area of study known as *information theory* that concerns itself with the processes of communication and the transmission of messages.

WHAT IS DATA?

Data are also a representation of reality. The word data is often used interchangeably with the word information. In broad terms, it is perfectly acceptable to do that. The difference between the meaning of the two words is subtle. There may be some debate on this, but we are going to define *data* as unformatted information and *information* as formatted data. Figure 1.1 shows the difference between the two.

In Figure 1.1, the first example shows a social security number, in both hyphenated and nonhyphenated form. Without hyphens, it is a string of nine digits. In that form it is data. The same nine digits are transformed from data into information by the hyphens between the third and fourth and between the fifth and sixth digits. The last example shows some billing data as it might look stored in "memory" of some computer and also as it looks as information displayed on a formatted invoice. The middle example shows numeric coordinates as data, recognizable when displayed as information in graphic form. Graphics represent an extremely useful way in which to present information.

Distinguishing between data and information is a prerequisite to understanding the way data is processed, especially when computers are involved. Computers almost always process data, but they display information. When computers produce graphic displays and tabular information, it is generally the result of having processed data. When computers produce textual information, it is generally the result of having processed textual information. This latter type of processing is frequently known as word processing.

PROCESSING DATA AND PROCESSING WORDS

During 1979 and 1980, many systems (EDP) trade journals were carrying articles with titles such as: "Should the Data Processing Function Manage the Word Processing Operation?" and "Word Processing and 'Automated Office' Operations Are Not Data Processing Functions."

DATA	INFORMATION
091302265	091–30–2265

77, 1500; 78, 2000
79, 2200; 80, 1750
81, 1500; 82, 1550

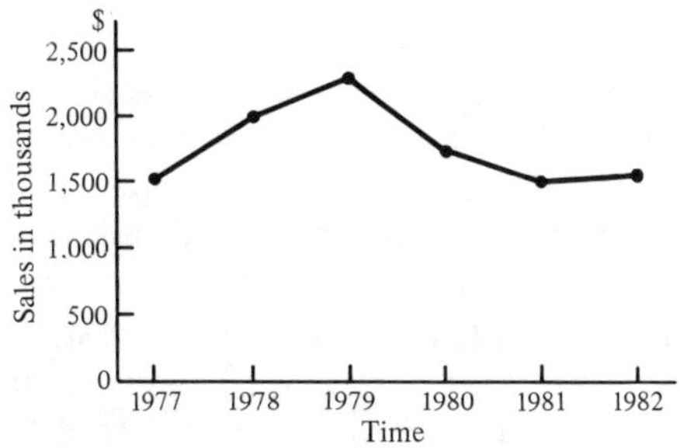

R&T PUMPS STORE #63 523ROUTE23 BUTLER NJ 0740563817 SHAFT 08 500079411732 VALVE 795004XR417 I MPELLER 2600002327Q2204195001R&T PUMPS CENTRAL OFFICE LANDIS AVE VINELAND NJ 08360

INVOICE

#60352

Ship To:
R&T PUMPS
STORE #63
523 ROUTE 23
BUTLER, NJ 07405

Bill To:
R&T PUMPS
CENTRAL OFFICE
LANDIS AVE.
VINELAND, NJ 08360

Part No.	Disc.	Pr	Qty.	Cost
63817	SHAFT	8.50	7	59.50
9411732	VALVE	7.95	4	31.80
XR417	IMPELLER	26.00	2	52.00
327Q220	SWITCH	41.95	1	41.95
			Total	185.25

Figure 1.1 Difference between data and information.

Two extreme positions were being taken and there were several less extreme positions between the two. On the whole, the articles made for interesting reading on the train and stimulating discussions over drinks or coffee among the intelligentsia of the data processing and word processing communities. While there are structural differences between *word* data and *nonword* data, to be discussed presently, any further distinction is artificial. From a management (senior, general, or middle) perspective, there is no distinction. Words or nonwords, it's still computers being used to process data and display information. To use just a bit of mathematical terminology and a little logic, word processing is a subset of data processing. Certain individuals in the word processing community may still object, but that does not invalidate the statement. Data are a representation of reality, so are words, therefore words are data. All words are data; all data are not words; therefore words are a subset of data. It then follows that word processing is a subset of data processing. The purpose of the preceding exercise is merely to show that word processing is just another form of data processing. The reason that the apparent distinction arose at all can be shown by considering the following interlude.

When the early electromechanical machines were applied to the processing of data, they had significant limitations in terms of speed, reliability and in the quantity of data that they could handle. Efficiency was the order of the day. Because of the limitations, the data that was to be processed was kept to a minimum. The benefit of this efficiency was most obvious in terms of the data storage medium, the eighty column card. One of the names for this storage medium was *unit record*. The machines that performed the processing read data from punched cards one card at a time. The analysts of that era made every attempt to design card layouts so that the information or data that represented some unit or some entity did not exceed eighty characters. Once that limit was exceeded, even to only 81 characters, there would be twice as many cards required and processing would be twice as long. If the number of characters exceeded the capacity of two cards, then a third card would be required. Each additional card increased the storage requirements and the processing time proportionately.

One of the ways analysts were able to introduce efficiency was through the use of codes. For example, six digit part numbers could be used to identify parts the description of which might run to twenty or twenty-five characters. Numbering schemes of one kind or another were able to achieve all kinds of efficiencies. In addition, numbers were more efficient for another reason. Eighty column cards employed a character coding structure that required two holes per column to be punched to represent alphabetic characters and sometimes even three holes to represent symbols. Numbers required a single punch. Figure 1.2 contains pictures of eighty column cards. One card is blank, that is, no information has been punched into it, while the other card has numbers, alphabetic characters and symbols punched into it. The row printed across the top of the card are the interpretations of what characters the punched holes represent. In the days when cards were used extensively to store data, the row of interpreted characters was rarely present, as it would have severely limited the speed of the operations to have them printed. Some operations, such as sorting, required double processing for multiple punches. This provided a further incentive to work with numbers. Something of a habit was formed and numbers and coding structures were used whenever possible. This continued for a time even after electronic computers replaced electromechanical accounting machines, even though the efficiencies were less important and in some cases counterproductive as they resulted in unnecessary complexity. In the 1970s some bright, creative individuals, unencum-

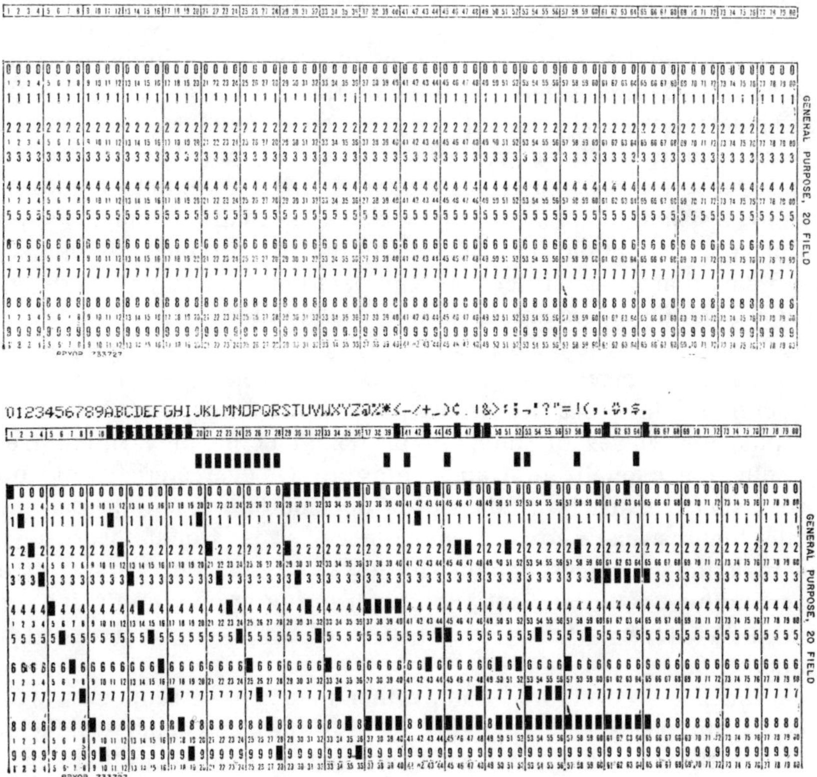

Figure 1.2 Example of a unit record—an 80-column card.

bered by old data processing habits, developed processing methodologies with computers that were oriented toward word and textual manipulation. Some genius decided to call it word processing.

So what we have with word processing is not a new function separate and distinct from data processing, but rather a broadening of the data processing function. We have been processing data, both words and numbers, for years; numbers we have been processing very well, words we have been processing not so well. As is frequently the case, some bright enterprising individuals observed the limitations in the data processing community and did something about it. And yet it cannot be denied that words are data and, as we shall see, the processing of words uses the same equipment and many of the same techniques, such as sorting and searching/updating, as those used in the processing of data that is largely numeric.

STRUCTURED AND UNSTRUCTURED DATA

While it is true that words are data and the tools and techniques for processing words are largely the same as those used for processing numeric data, it is also true that there are some differences. The terms *unstructured* and *structured* are frequently used to connote the difference. These terms are reasonably descriptive. All data, for it to be processed, has to be structured in some way or else it becomes random. However, to make a distinction, it is safe to say that word processing operates with data that is less structured than data that is largely numeric and that is generally stored and displayed in tabular form.

Let's look at the unstructured variety first. That type of data processing that is currently known as word processing works with unstructured data. Word processing works with words, sentences, paragraphs, and pages of data, all of which come in various sizes. Punctuation, capitalization, and syntax are also characteristics of word processing. Unstructured data does not conform to any preset templates that restrict its size or even a range of sizes. Even if it were possible to define the longest and the shortest word, sentence, paragraph, or page, nothing could prevent a longer or a shorter one from being produced. Whatever structure exists in word processing is provided by punctuation.

Turning to structured data, rather than words, sentences, paragraphs, and pages, we have fields, records, files, and databases. Fields, records, files, and databases are like predefined templates that can be superimposed on an array of digits, characters, and symbols to give them meaning, which would not be apparent or would be only partially apparent without the templates. Figure 1.3 illustrates. When working with computer storage or memory,* a conceptual template is used to define specific storage locations as for specific elements of data. For example, locations 503 and 504 might be defined as the locations where a two-character state code would be found. The definition is made by instructions within a computer program and the locations specified are used to house state codes for the duration of that program's execution. This may seem a bit vague now, but later chapters explain computer programs in more detail. The idea we're trying to put forth here is that of the conceptual template.

Understanding fields, records, files, and databases can be aided by an illustration familiar to most of us. Figure 1.4 is a picture of some file cabinets. Each one standing alone contains a file. Within the drawers of the file cabinet are the records that make up those files. The areas

*Computer storage or memory is that part of a computer where data or information and the executable instructions are stored. These storage components, as well as other computer components, are explained more fully in a subsequent chapter.

ARRAY WITHOUT TEMPLATE

6001195 – 375 AMERICAN HOME VIDEO CORP. 7200 DTC PARKWAY * ELMHURST NY 11373 MAGNE TIC VIDEO CORPORATION 23705 INDUSTRIAL PARK DRIV E PEQUANNOCK NJ 07440 VIDEO CONCEPTS WOODLAND H ILLS MALL SPACE 168 KINNELON NJ 07405 UPS REGUL AR PREPAID 142642 05268201 CASABLANCA06995 00200049534302 CASABLANCA0699500100049535303 GR EASE05995001000495340004 STAR TREK0799500400149503 0 E.T 07995005002495711.............

WITH TEMPLATE

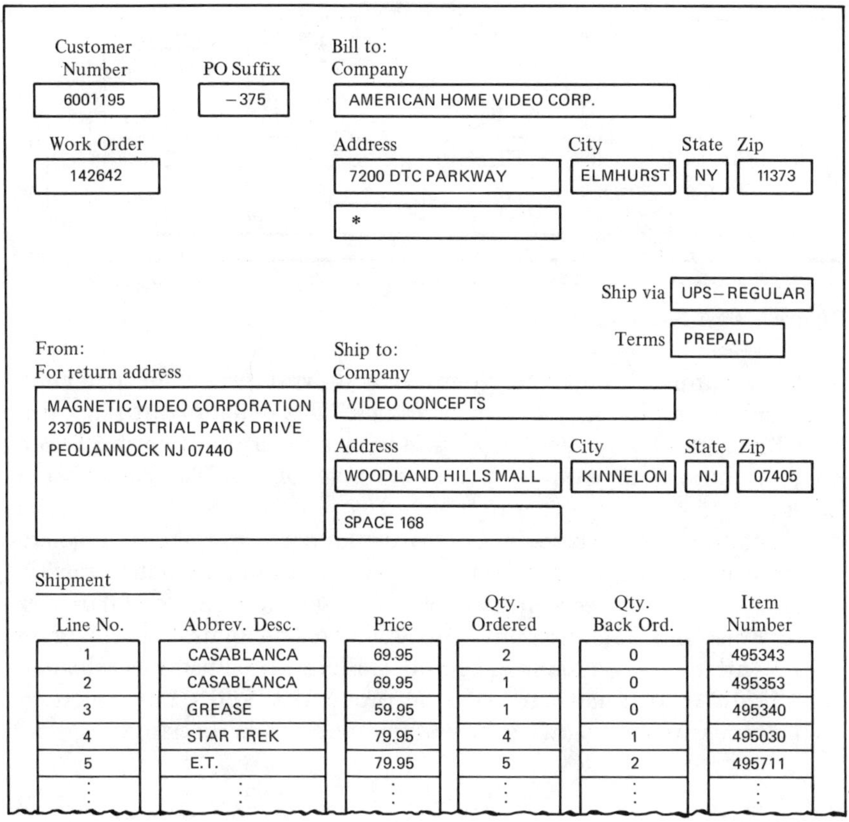

Customer Number: 6001195
PO Suffix: –375
Bill to: Company: AMERICAN HOME VIDEO CORP.
Work Order: 142642
Address: 7200 DTC PARKWAY / *
City: ELMHURST State: NY Zip: 11373
Ship via: UPS–REGULAR
Terms: PREPAID
From: For return address: MAGNETIC VIDEO CORPORATION / 23705 INDUSTRIAL PARK DRIVE / PEQUANNOCK NJ 07440
Ship to: Company: VIDEO CONCEPTS
Address: WOODLAND HILLS MALL / SPACE 168
City: KINNELON State: NJ Zip: 07405

Shipment

Line No.	Abbrev. Desc.	Price	Qty. Ordered	Qty. Back Ord.	Item Number
1	CASABLANCA	69.95	2	0	495343
2	CASABLANCA	69.95	1	0	495353
3	GREASE	59.95	1	0	495340
4	STAR TREK	79.95	4	1	495030
5	E.T.	79.95	5	2	495711
⋮	⋮	⋮	⋮	⋮	⋮

Figure 1.3 An array of data (without template), an array of information (with template).

blocked out on the records for specific information are fields. A database exists when there are relationships among the records or fields in one file with the records or fields in other files.

Data that is unstructured is generally put together so that it can produce documents, correspondence, letters, worded reports, or even

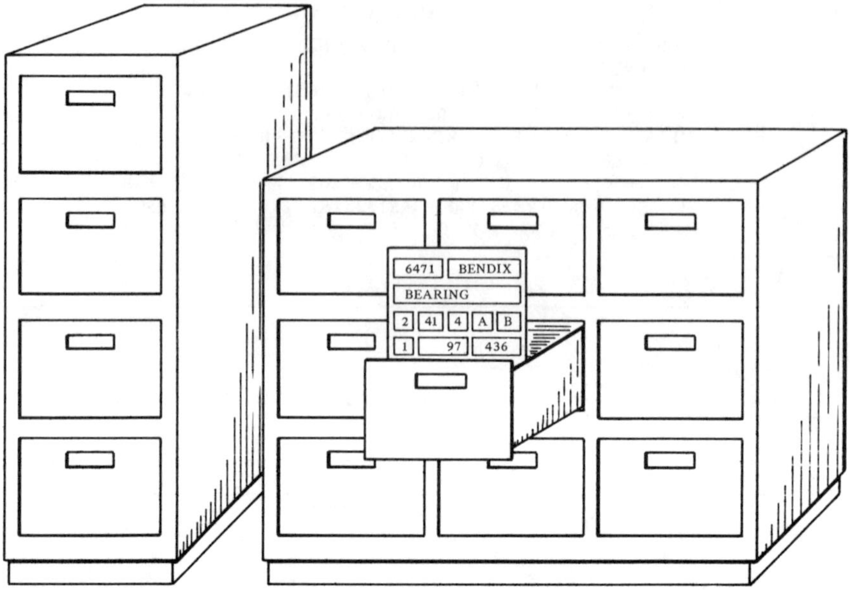

Figure 1.4 A file, a record, and fields.

books in manuscript form. A computer with word processing capability is a mechanism that facilitates this process. The data or words (text) are keyed into the computer, they are edited and printed, output is producted. There is no need for structure, in the form of files, records, and fields.

Data that is structured generally uses a computer as a storage and retrieval mechanism. Data processing with structured data generally produces formatted screen displays from selected data or tabular reports. Files and databases are also updated and maintained by computers with data processing capabilities. Figure 1.5 illustrates schematically both word (unstructured data) processing and data (structured data) processing flows, two different types of data processing.

KEYS

Keys are used to uniquely identify data records, to arrange data records in some kind of order or to search for records. A key is a field or a group of fields within a record. Figure 1.6 shows a sketch of a record from within a file of parts, components, and other supplies found in a maintenance warehouse. The fields that make up the key in this illustration are the three character product code and the seven-digit part number. These are contained in the product code and part identifier fields

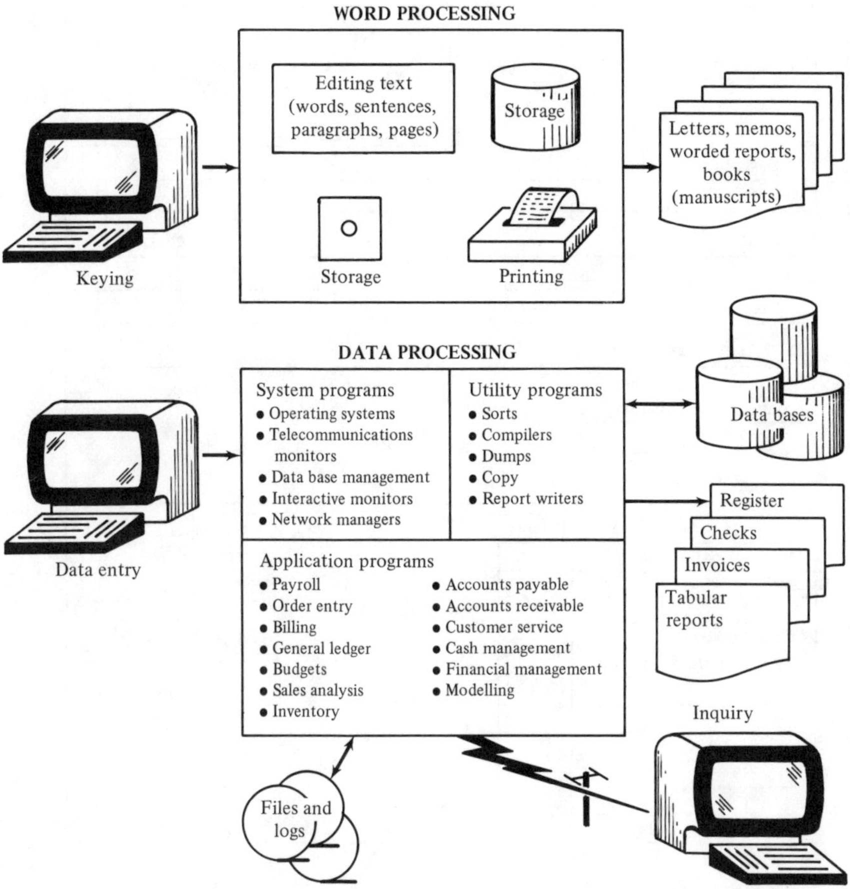

Figure 1.5 Word (unstructured data) processing and data (structured data) processing.

of the record. All the records of a file can also be arranged in order by means of the values in these two key fields. Ascending sequential, that is, lowest values first and highest values last, is one of the most common ways in which structured data records are arranged. There are other ways, which are examined in a subsequent chapter. Keys are also used to search. If, for example, somebody wanted to know how many of a certain type of valve were on hand, he or she could use the key to search the file and to retrieve the record on which that information was stored. There are many ways to search for data; these also are examined in a subsequent chapter. The concepts we are trying to explain here are the functions of keys to identify, arrange, and retrieve, in the context of structured data.

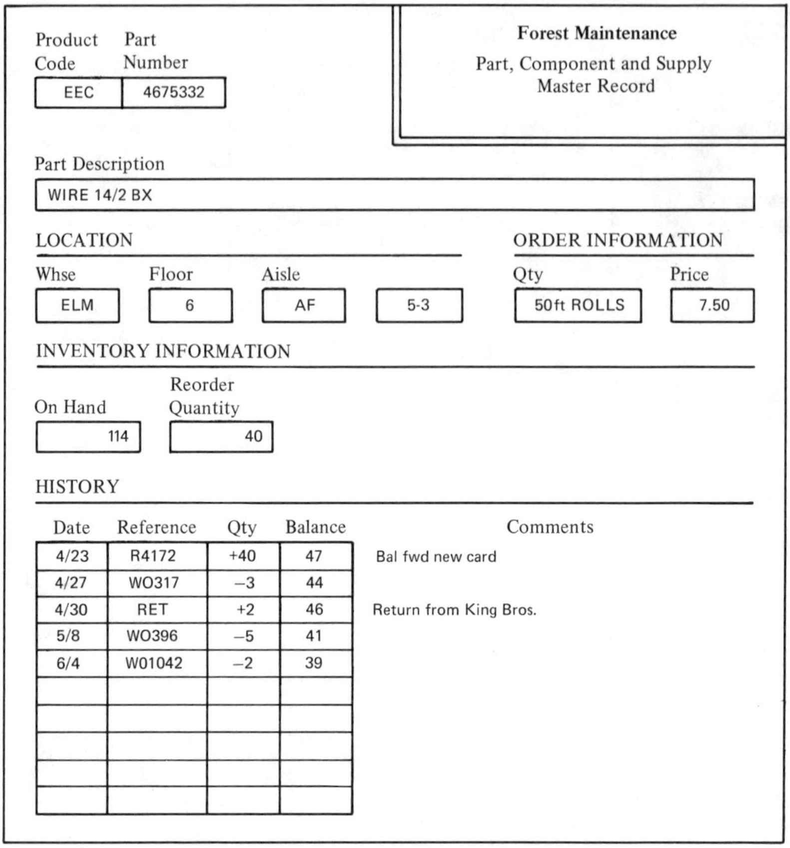

Product Code: EEC
Part Number: 4675332

Forest Maintenance
Part, Component and Supply
Master Record

Part Description: WIRE 14/2 BX

LOCATION
Whse: ELM | Floor: 6 | Aisle: AF | 5-3

ORDER INFORMATION
Qty: 50ft ROLLS | Price: 7.50

INVENTORY INFORMATION
On Hand: 114 | Reorder Quantity: 40

HISTORY

Date	Reference	Qty	Balance	Comments
4/23	R4172	+40	47	Bal fwd new card
4/27	WO317	−3	44	
4/30	RET	+2	46	Return from King Bros.
5/8	WO396	−5	41	
6/4	W01042	−2	39	

Figure 1.6 A record, fields, and keys.

TRANSACTIONS

A collection or grouping of data that triggers processing of some kind is called a *transaction*. Transactions may contain data that is to be processed, or they may merely cause processing to take place. A transaction may, for example, be an inquiry about some information in a file. "How many feet of 14 × 2 BX wire are in the Elmhurst warehouse?" is an inquiry transaction that causes an individual in the warehouse to check the 14 × 2 BX wire record in the file and respond to the question. Transactions may come in groups. For example, a truckload of supplies arrives at the Elmhurst warehouse. After the shipment is checked, the packing list is sent to the office and an entry is posted to the records that reflect the additions to stock in the warehouse as a result of that shipment. Each of the items on the packing list for which an entry is posted is a transaction. These transactions are processed serially; that is, part numbers are read by a clerk one at a time, records corresponding to those part numbers are retrieved from the warehouse file one at a time, and entries are made reflecting the additions to stock in the warehouse one at a time. Similar transaction processing tasks are performed when items are removed from the warehouse to fill work requests. A craftsman comes to the warehouse to pick up materials, say some 14 × 2 BX wire, a junction box, some toggle switches, and some duplex receptacles. In order to get these items, the craftsman must present an authorized work request. The warehouseman retrieves the items from the locations in the warehouse and gives them to the craftsman. He then sends a copy of the work request to the office so that the clerk can make the appropriate entries to the records reflecting the removal of these items from the warehouse.

This same basic collection or grouping of data, the transaction, is generally the trigger that commences activity in a computer system. Transactions such as those just described are found in contemporary computer based warehousing systems. Other transactions trigger activity in areas such as payroll, finance, accounting, marketing, order entry, and manufacturing.

In a sense, transactions are the things that computer systems are made of. Files are created to hold information. Procedures are developed to put information into, and to get information out of those files, to manipulate the information, and to present it in both tabular and display form. The entities that put specific units of information into or get specific units of information out of files, or trigger the manipulation or presentation of information, are transactions. A collection of transactions that are used for a specific kind of process and the programs which process them, say payroll, make up what is known a computer system or an application. In a computer application, the procedures that put, get, manipulate, and display information are called modules. Groups of modules are known as computer programs or, more simply, programs. A payroll system has a program to print checks; it has modules to calculate Federal, State, and Local taxes, and it has a file of records containing information (data) about each employee, all of which are part of a larger collection of programs, modules, and files that make up an application (computer system).

APPLICATIONS AND SYSTEMS

In the preceding paragraph, we used these terms somewhat interchangeably. This is a frequent practice. And yet, the term *application* is more specific than the term *system* or *computer system* which can have several meanings.

An *application* is a group of procedures that are followed to produce a defined set of results. Computers may or may not be involved. Examples of applications are: payroll, general accounting, finance, order entry, sales analysis, billing, accounts payable, and accounts receivable. Within specific organizations there are applications peculiar to those organizations. For example, airlines have their reservations applications, banks have their banking applications, and news organizations have their election estimating applications. While it is possible for the tasks of applications such as these to be performed without computers, it is in fact becoming less likely that they are, especially with the arrival of the small business and personal computers.

A system could also be defined as a group of procedures that are followed to produce of defined set of results. However, also included in a system are the tools needed to perform the tasks specified by the procedures. Furthermore, with the advent of computers, the term system implies the presence of computer equipment as part of an application. As a result, the term *system*, depending upon its context, has come to mean: an application, an application and the computer equipment configuration it uses, or a computer equipment configuration. Complicating the situation even further is the use of the word *system* in the names of certain types of computer program products that support the operation of elaborate computer equipment configurations. Terms such as operating system, database management system, and interactive system are examples. Each of these products and others like them are referred to as systems themselves. When the term system is used to refer to a complete configuration of computer equipment, implicitly included in the reference are the support products. Therefore, the expression, "the system is down," while it communicates the message that the computer *system* is temporarily unavailable, does not begin to communicate the reason for its unavailability. When a user of a computer equipment configurations cannot get his work done because the system is down, it could be for one of several reasons: any one of several components of computer equipment may have failed, any one of several support products may have failed, or a program or module within the application may have failed. The term *system* then is much broader in scope than the term application.

Within the term management information systems itself we again see the word *systems*. Management information systems are supposed to be systems or mechanisms that provide information to management. The management to whom MIS is oriented is senior or general management, the information they require is either a summary of historical information or estimates of future trends in sales and expenditures based on historical information. These latter are the facilities that MIS advocates were always promising but were rarely able to deliver until recently. While they are still potential, the technology necessary to make MIS a reality is available. This technology includes graphics, text editing and "word processing," database management, data communications and local area networking. The remaining requirement to make true MIS a reality is the proper application of this technology. Although we shall examine those various things which make up systems in the next section of the book, this short treatment is intended merely to provide some clarification in concepts and terminology.

THE ROLE OF THE COMPUTER

Processing data or information electronically and in large quantities began to become commonplace in the late 1950s. Up until this time, there had been limitations in both the amounts of data that could be stored internally and in the speed with which data could be processed by, read into, and written out of computers. Increases in the internal processing and in the reading in and writing out capabilities of computers together with the introduction of magnetic tape and magnetic disk as data storage media, as replacement for media such as eighty column cards and paper tape, significantly enhanced the potential of computers.

Why did organizations decide to use computers? Accuracy and speed were the motivating factors. A definite strong point in the use of computers is their ability to perform mathematical and logical operations accurately and quickly. While it is possible to misdirect computers by means of misleading instructions, it is a virtual certainty that a computer will never make an error that is has not been instructed to make. What it comes down to is this: computers or computer equipment configurations* have tremendous potential. Realization of that potential is the responsibility of a user or users of the computer or the computer equipment configuration.

The potential of computers was recognized and the early attempts to realize the potential were generally successful, although not without problems. The potential was often overestimated and oversold and the responsibility of the users were underestimated and underemphasized. Most of the commercial computer applications that were developed in the late 1950s and early 1960s were enhanced versions of those that had been implemented earlier on electromechanical office equipment, much of which used eighty column cards or a similar type of card as storage media. These applications included payroll, general accounting, budgets, accounts payable, accounts receivable, sales reporting.

*A computer is one of anywhere between a few and hundreds of pieces of equipment that make up a computer configuration. Subsequent chapters will clarify this further.

Other, more esoteric applications, rather primitive according to today's standards, using statistics, linear programming, and operation research techniques, were also developed. These types of applications, sometimes referred to as "number crunchers," differ basically from commercial applications in their data to computations ratio. The number crunchers are essentially scientific or mathematical/statistical and they perform a relatively high number of calculations and logical manipulations on a relatively small amount of data or information. They are, to put it simply, computationally based. Commercial applications, on the other hand, are data or information based. They perform a relatively low number of calculations and logical manipulations on a relatively large amount of data or information. This distinction was crystallized in the late 1950s/early 1960s time frame with the appearance of two computer programming language translators,* FORTRAN and COBOL.

FORTRAN is an acronym for the two words *for*mula *tran*slation. FORTRAN was developed for those individuals whose problems were generally expressed by means of mathematic/statistical formulas. It enabled mathematicians and statisticians to write programming statements that were very much like the mathematical/statistical expressions or statements they normally used in expressing relationships among variables. FORTRAN compilers were developed and provided that were able to convert these statements into instructions executable by a computer. COBOL is an acronym for the words *co*mmon *b*usiness *o*riented *l*anguage. It was developed primarily for commercial users of computers. Its merits have been debated within the EDP/MIS profession ever since it appeared. Despite all the criticism, COBOL is a programming language with which statements can be written in a form resembling English (or other) language sentence structures. As time passed new programming languages and compilers were developed, as well as a host of other tools, in an attempt to make computers easier to use.

But wait, let us pause here and ask: "Why were all these tools developed? Why were computers used in the first place? What caused individuals, both mathematical/statistical and commercial users to invest in computer technology?" All three of these questions have the same answer. Computer technology provides us with a tool that is able to store, manipulate, and retrieve information. It aids us in storing large quantities of information, in performing logical and mathematical operations

*Programming language translators, often known as compilers, are themselves computer programs whose functions is the translating of statements written by programmers into instructions executable by a computer. Compilers are explained more fully in a subsequent chapter.

on that information, and in retrieving either large quantities or single items of that information *accurately* and *quickly*. It has been stated that without computers, we could not have sent men to the moon (mathematical/statistical) and it was once estimated that the telephone companies of the United States would have required every high school graduate in the country, each year, to keep up with the clerical tasks being performed by computers (commercial). It seems therefore, to go without saying, that contemporary requirements for the storage, manipulation, and retrieval of information could not be met without computers.

SUMMARY

In this chapter we have attempted to provide a pragmatic explanation of information and data together with some introductory comments on systems and computers. The use of acronyms such as MIS and EDP was temporarily suspended, since they are an annoyance to the individuals this book is attempting to reach. We pointed out some distinctions between kinds of data, and some basic data structures were explained. The functions of keys, as identifiers, arrangers, and locators of data were discussed. We explained transactions, the units of data that trigger activity in systems, and we distinguished between the broad-scoped term *systems* and the narrower term *application*. Following that, it was shown that the quantity of computations and the magnitude of information in contemporary systems made the use of computers mandatory.

CHAPTER 2

Information Processing with Computers

THE GROWTH OF COMPUTER-BASED SYSTEMS

Between the late 1960s and the early 1980s, as nearly everyone is aware, computer technology became an integral part of commercial activity. Computers and the people who knew something about them went from being a minor consideration in business planning and operations to being a major concern. It is commonly accepted that a corporation of any significant size could not function in the contemporary business environment without computers. Why is this so? How did it all come about so quickly?

Essentially, it goes back to what was mentioned in Chapter 1. Computers are fast and accurate in arithmetic and logical operations, and in manipulating large amounts of data or information. Electronics technology kept improving computers so that they were constantly made faster and cheaper. It is possible today to purchase a computer for several thousand dollars that has the processing potential of equipment that fifteen years ago cost ten times as much. And yet, everything is not as it ought to be. Complaints are all to frequently heard about computers and MIS. "Modifications take too long," says one manager. "Can't get new applications developed," says others. There is a whole litany of gripes: "If they're faster and cheaper, how come my data center processing charges keep going up?" asks a financial vice-president. "Those MIS guys are always giving me reasons why I can't do something, instead of helping me do it," says an operations executive. The complaints are also heard from the MIS function. "Why can't those users decide what they want and then stick to it, why do they always change their mind?" asks an analyst. "Those computer and computer software product vendors make it all sound so easy, but they're not the ones who have to integrate their products into already tight operating environments," protests an MIS/EDP manager. So, what's the rub, and more importantly, what's the solution? Well, it has to do with potential and realization. That which vendors sell and users are led to expect is potential and that which the MIS/EDP function attempts to deliver is realization of that potential. To better understand the difference between the two, it is necessary that we examine some basics of computer technology.

BASIC DISTINCTIONS

There are two terms frequently used to make the first basic distinction in computer technology. The term *hardware* is used to indicate computer equipment, and the term *software* is used to denote both the data stored in, acted upon and displayed by the computer equipment and the sets of instructions, called *programs*, that direct the activity of the computer equipment. Further distinction can be made in that there are numerous types of hardware components and numerous types of software components. These hardware and software components are dealt with in some detail in subsequent chapters. At this point, however, a few more general distinctions need to be made so that data handling by computer equipment can be explained. Another distinction that ought to be made is that between a computer processor and storage or memory. These are two separate components, the processor executes instructions and memory holds data and sets of instructions. Generally speaking, processors fetch instructions from memory, serially unless the instruction directs otherwise, and execute them one at a time. These instructions cause data to be read into, moved around in, written out of, or otherwise manipulated within, memory.

The next distinction to be made is that between the hardware components of primary storage and secondary storage. It is these two components that are occasionally referred to as memory. From a conceptual or logical perspective,* storage is made up of a series of cells, each one of which can hold a single digit, character, or symbol, and each cell is identified by a unique address. Figure 2.1 shows a hypothetical section of computer storage in two states, empty and containing some data.

Primary storage is that which contains data that is immediately accessible to the processor. Secondary storage is that which contains data that is transferred to primary storage before it is immediately accessible to the processor. Figure 2.2 illustrates this concept. Notice that the illustration shows secondary storage to be significantly larger than primary storage. This is normally the case. Secondary storage capacity in large computer equipment configurations often exceeds that of primary storage in ratios of thousands to one.

This can be visualized by imagining an individual working at a desk. Think of the individual as a processor and the desk as primary storage. The materials on the desk at any one point in time are the data in primary storage. As the individual finishes with the material, it is stored in a file cabinet. If more material is needed, it is retrieved from a file cabinet. The file cabinets represent secondary storage.

COMPUTER PROGRAMMING CONCEPTS

Programs and Tasks

Computer programs are sets of instructions that direct the activities of a computer application in the completion of a unit of work. This unit of work is sometimes known as a *task*. The execution of programs is also

Figure 2.1 Computer storage, empty and containing data.

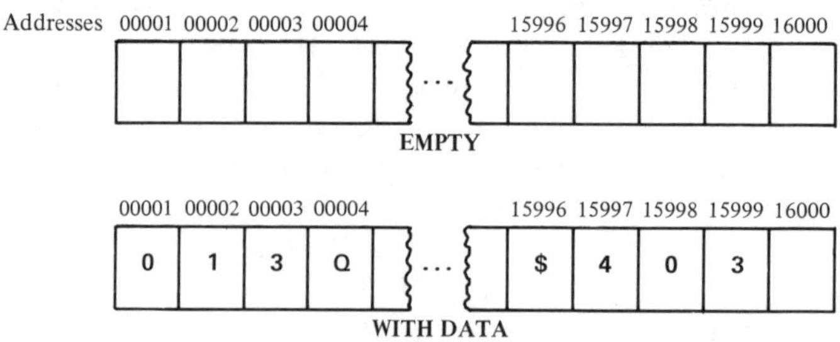

*Internally, computer storage, data, and addresses are made up of electronic circuitry and impulses. One need know nothing about this aspect of computers to work with them. Knowledge of the concepts of what the electronic circuitry and impulses represent is sufficient. Trade magazines that describe electronic components are for computer hobbyists and afficionados, not for executives, managers, and analysts who wish to use computers for commercial data processing applications.

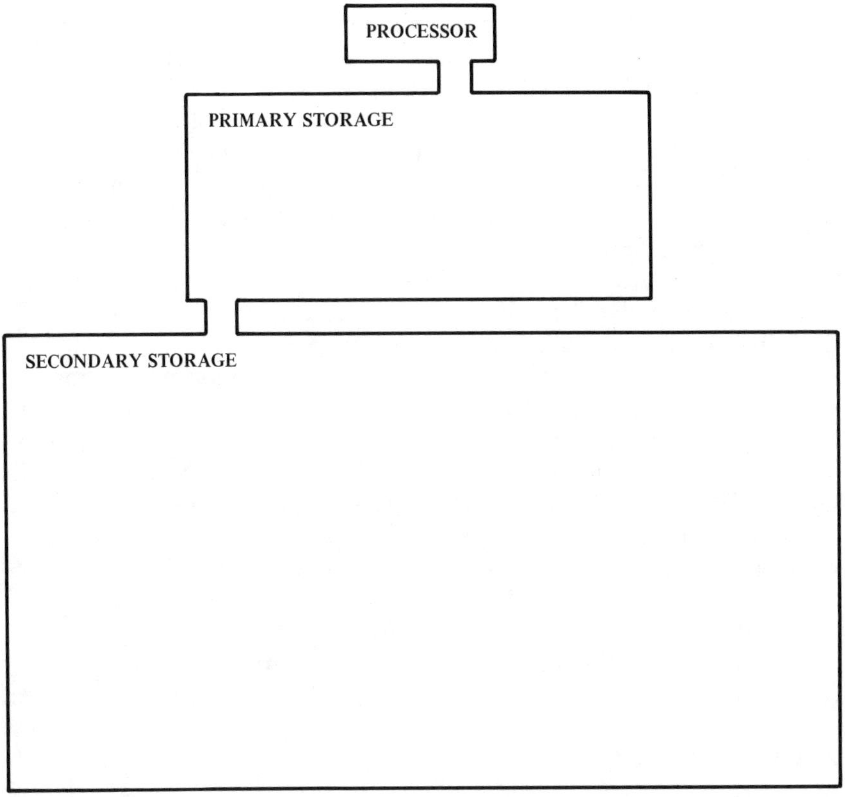

Figure 2.2 Primary storage and secondary storage.

analogous to the activities that could be performed by individuals working at desks. One individual might have the ability to perform essentially the same type of task repetitively on similar types of data, while another individual might be able to perform many different types of tasks on different types of data. A commercial example of the former would be the updating of multiple records in an inventory file, reflecting a day's activity in a warehouse. An example of the latter would be responding to a query about the sales activity for a specific product for a particular month, then being able to respond to a query about the inventory status of another product, and then being able to update a product master file by creating a record containing information about a new product. There is a different set of instructions followed by the individual to perform each of these tasks. If these tasks were to be transferred to a computer, a separate set of instructions (a program) would be required for each task.

Although computer programs are to be examined in more detail in later chapters, there is one significant factor worth mentioning at this point. There is a distinction between the preparation of a computer program and the execution of a computer program. The statements that are prepared by an individual developing a program are not the same as the instructions used by a computer in executing a program. The statements have to be translated into instructions before the program can execute. The translation process is sometimes known as *compilation*. However, it has become increasingly convenient lately, especially with small personal computers, to purchase programs or groups of programs that have already been *compiled*. These come in executable form; that is, they can be loaded into the computer and run. We'll talk more about programs and programming in a later chapter.

Broadly speaking, there are two types of programming statements: active and passive. The active statements are those which make something happen. Programming statements like READ A RECORD, SUBTRACT FED TAX FROM GROSS, and COMPARE QTYONHAND TO REORDQTY, once compiled into computer executable instructions, result in some action being performed by a computer. The passive statements are those which set up and define, among other things, work areas and files. Using the desk and file cabinet analogy once more, the passive statements define the size of the desk top and the organization and composition of the records in the file cabinet.

DATA DEFINITIONS FOR FILES

Programming languages, that is, the form and syntax in which programming statements can be written, are many and varied. There are what are known as problem-oriented languages such as BASIC and COBOL that have versions that allow their use on a number of different computers. There are also what are known as assembler languages. An assembler language is one that can be used for a particular computer or line of computers, but which cannot be used on computers outside of that line. For example, there is an assembler language that can be used on IBM 360, 370, and 3000 series computers, but it cannot be used on the computers of other manufacturers, or for that matter even on other IBM computers. However, no matter which type of programming language is used, it is necessary to prepare statements that contain specifications for the files that are to be accessed during the execution of the program.

Let's go back to our friends at the desks and their processing requirements. In most cases it is necessary for these individuals to retrieve data from file cabinets to perform their tasks. To find out what the sales for a specific product were for a particular month, for example, the record for that specific product would have to be retrieved from a file cabinet containing sales data. To retrieve such information, an individual would need to know the name of the file, the location of the file cabinet, the organization of the file, the key field or fields by which specific data can be identified, and whether the file has an index associated with it. In like manner, when a similar task is to be performed by a computer program, it is necessary for the program to have similar specifications supplied to it. Figure 2.3 shows this conceptually as a portion of secondary storage is specified to hold a file of records holding information. For a program to access records in this file, specifications indicating its size, location, record lengths, keys and indexes are necessary. These specifications are made by means of statements that are passive in nature. The statements merely specify an area of secondary storage at which a file is located or into which a file is to be written. They may also specify record lengths, key locations, file organizations, and indexes.

Figure 2.3 A sequential file in secondary storage.

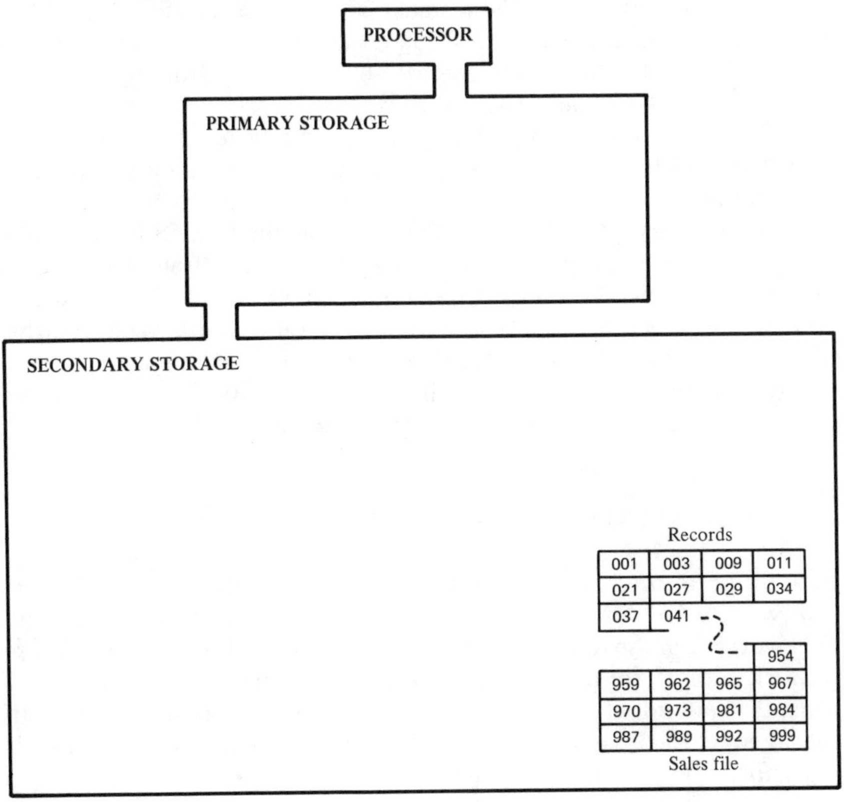

A typical data definition specification for a file might look something like this:

```
FILE NAME: SALES HISTORY
NO. OF RECORDS: 600
RECORD LENGTH: 312
KEY FIELD: 6,14
ORGANIZATION: IX SEQ
INDEX: SALES HIST IX
LOCATION: DISK VOLUME V60210, 416237
```

Of course, the format of this specification is entirely fictitious, but as an approximation, it illustrates what such a specification looks like. Most of it is self-explanatory. The name of the file is SALES HISTORY, the area set aside for it must be of sufficient size to hold 600 records of 312 characters each. The key field is in positions six through fourteen. Its organization is indexed sequential, which means that access to records is via an index that is arranged sequentially. The index is another file called SALES HIST IX which also requires specifications (not shown in the illustration). The file is located on a magnetic disk which is identified by a volume identifier of V60210. The beginning of this file is found at storage location 416237.

Since it is quite common for several programs to have access to the same file at different times, file specifications are frequently developed independent of the programs. They can be subsequently included with each program as it is developed. For instance, the SALES file might be accessed by several types of inquiry programs; in addition to a program used to update it, there might be another one that summarizes it and still another one that adjusts sales figures to reflect authorized returns. The specifications for the SALES file could be written once and included with each of the programs just mentioned. As new programs are written, the file specifications can also be included with them.

DATA DEFINITIONS FOR WORK AREAS

In addition to the specification for the file, a specification for the records within the file is required in the program. Once again, the individuals working at the desks require specifications for the records they are to work with. If, for example, there is a task for updating inventory records, the individual who is to perform that task must be familiar with the layout of the inventory record. The same is true for a program that is to perform the task in a computer.

The specification for the record includes the location of an area within a program where a record resides while it is being processed. Figure 2.4 illustrates. In addition to the allocation of an area for the records, a layout or map of the records must be specified. This map or layout, which usually specifies the fields in the records, allows the program to reference those fields as they are needed, just as individuals working at desks become familiar with the locations of the fields on the records that they use. A typical layout or map of a record might look something like this:

```
DEFINE AREA 55 POSITIONS, WHSEWKA
     PARTNO. 1,6
     DESCRPTN. 7,26
     UNIT 27,29
     PRICE 30,35
     QTYONHND 36,40
     BKORDER 41,44
     REORDQTY 45,49
     WHSELOC 50,51
     FLOOR 52,53
     ISLEBIN 54,55
```

This somewhat simplistic layout is for the kind of record that might be found in a warehouse. In a computer program, there are a series of statements to define first an area and then each of the fields. The statements above would reserve fifty-five positions of primary storage within a program to hold records as they were being processed. Whereas individuals working at desks would retrieve records from file cabinets and place them on desks, computer programs would contain an action statement something like:

```
READ FROM WHSEFILE TO WHSEWKA
```

Such a statement would result in a record being read from a file (WHSEFILE) in secondary storage to a work area (WHSEWKA) in primary storage.

Most programs require data from more than one file. Therefore, a work area would be set up to accomodate the records from each of those files. There would be several work areas set aside within the program. Also, in certain processing situations several records are transferred from a file in a single operation, rather than one record at a time. In those situations a work area large enough to hold several records would be defined.

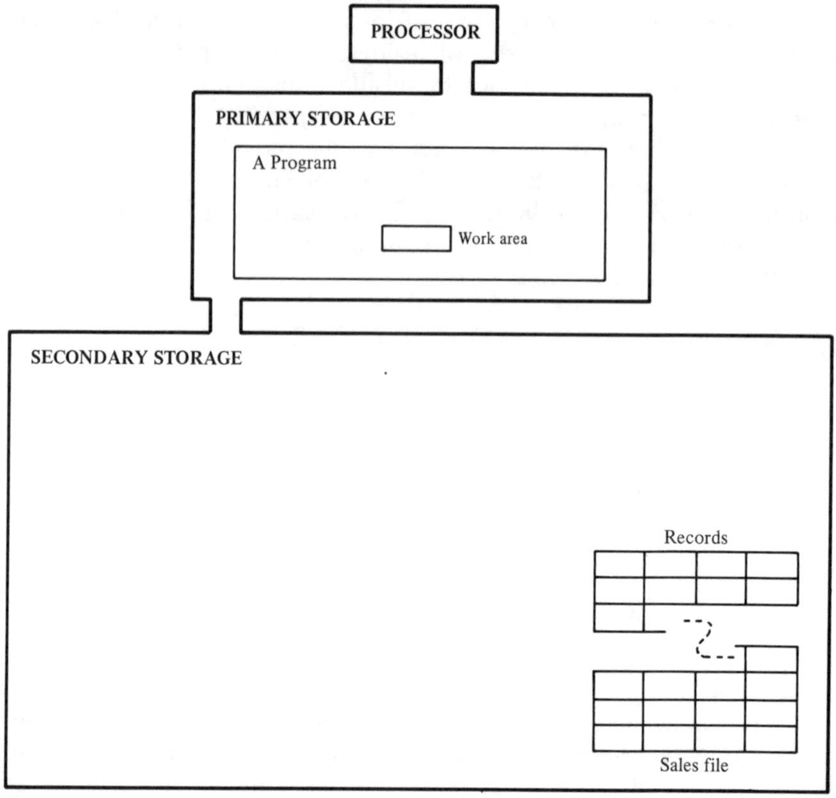

Figure 2.4 Records in secondary storage and in a work area.

WHY DATA HANDLING BECOMES COMPLICATED

One Program at a Time or Several Programs Concurrently

Up to this point we have attempted to describe the way in which data occupies both primary and secondary storage and to some degree how it is transferred between primary and secondary storage. Implicit in the foregoing explanations was the idea that a single computer program was operating on records from one or more files of data. The number of files operated on by a single program can vary depending upon the number of functions within the program. Most frequently the number of files used by a single program range between one and three, but there may be more. Single programs accessing more than three files tend to be complicated, and as the number of files used by single programs increases, so does the complexity of the programs. A trade-off can be made; complex programs may be able to accomplish a great deal when they execute, but they are also difficult to modify and maintain. A series of simple programs may take a greater amount of time to do the same amount of work as a complex program when executing, but they are easy to develop, to modify, and to maintain. In some of the smaller and less powerful (in terms of processing capabilities) computers, it is not unusual to see single programs, either simple or complex, executing one at a time. And yet, as computer configurations increase in size and in processing capabilities, it is not uncommon to see several programs operating concurrently within the configuration. A term sometimes used to describe this kind of activity is multiprogramming. While this type of processing is taking place, there may be tens or even hundreds of records from an equivalent number of files being processed by these programs. To visualize both the simple and the complex processing, consider a single individual at a single desk retrieving records from one, two, or three files, processing those records by perhaps correlating them, performing some arithmetic operations on them, putting some results in another file, then returning updated records back into the files from which they were originally taken. Then consider between twenty and thirty individuals with twenty or thirty desks working with records from a couple of hundred files in a single large room. Without some kind of overall plan, operating procedures, and supervision there would be pandemonium. In a computer equipment configuration, there is a supervisory type of program that directs the activity of all the other programs (the twenty to thirty individuals), allocates the resources (assigns desks), and sees to it that the transfer of records between secondary and primary storage (between desks and file cabinets) is coordinated and managed. This supervisory program is called either a *control program* or an *operating system*. We'll examine these in some detail in a subsequent chapter.

Directly Accessed Data or Batched Data

Transactions can be processed individually or in groups. Files can be structured so as to lend themselves to either individual transaction processing or to group transaction processing, or they can even be structured so as to lend themselves to both kinds of processing. Individual transaction processing triggers the performance of tasks which retrieve, store, or manipulate particular units of data on an immediate basis. For example:

> How many 3 × 3/4'' stove bolts are in stock?
> Calculate the latest estimate for the California Governor's race
> What are the outstanding orders for Consolidated Manufacturing?

Files that lend themselves to this type of processing are structured so that information can be quickly stored or retrieved. Such files are called direct access files.

Group transaction processing, sometimes called batch processing, involves the performance of the same or similar tasks repetatively on a series of the same type or similar transactions. The updating of a series of inventory records with a batch of transactions and processing a payroll from the inputting of a batch of time cards to the production of checks and registers are examples of batch data processing. Files that are used in batch data processing applications generally have their records in order according to a key. Such files are called sequential files. Under the management of an operating system or control program, it is possible for a computer equipment configuration, made up of processor, and primary and secondary storage, to be concurrently executing several programs. Some may be batch data processing programs, while others may be direct data accessing programs. Figure 2.5 illus-

Figure 2.5 Files and programs in secondary storage.

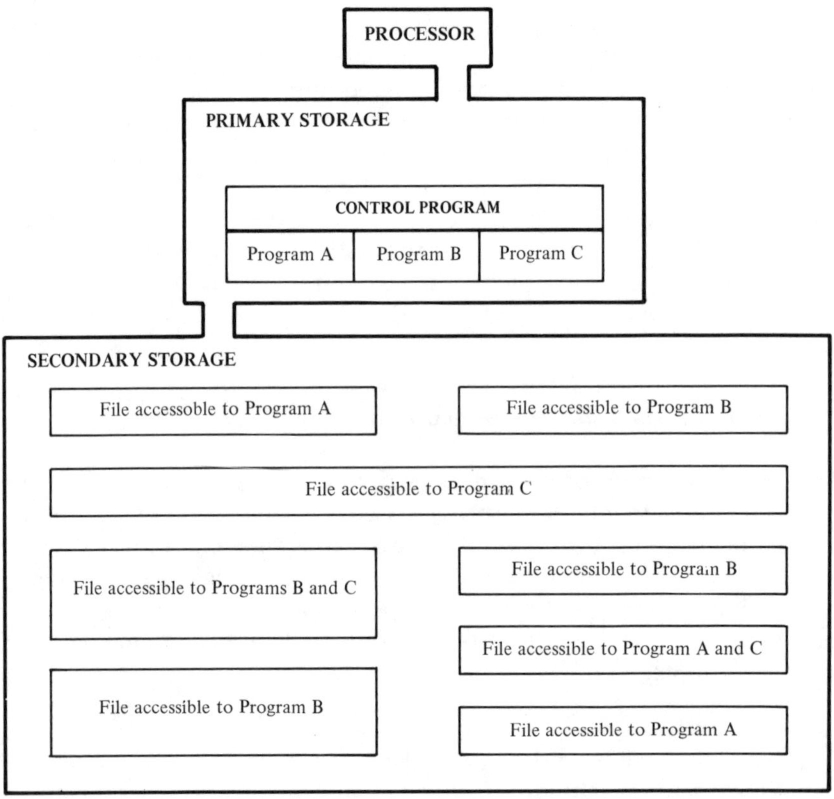

trates three programs and several files in secondary storage to which programs have access. The illustration also shows that a single file can be accessed by more than one program.

Data Communications and Teleprocessing

Contemporary computer equipment configurations include both hardware and software components that facilitate the transmission of both data and transactions among sites geographically remote from one another. Some of the examples used earlier, such as:

> How many 3'' by 3/4'' stove bolts are in stock?
> What are the outstanding orders for Consolidated Manufacturing?

could be inquiry transactions that an individual enters into a remotely located terminal device. This transaction would travel electronically from the terminal device across a communications line to a computer in some other geographic location. A program in that computer would access the appropriate record(s) in the appropriate file(s) and would fabricate a response in the form of a transaction to be sent back to the terminal device from which the inquiry had come. Figure 2.6 adds a couple of new elements to our basic illustration of a computer configuration. First, hardware is added. There is the terminal device and the data communications facility. Second, software is added in the form of what is known as a teleprocessing monitor. At the risk of oversimplification, we are going to define *data communications* as the facilities that make it possible to transmit information across communications lines, and *teleprocessing* is defined as data communications using computer equipment and under the control of computer software. Both of these technologies receive more detailed treatment in a subsequent chapter.

BUFFERS AND QUEUES

Using Figures 2.2 through 2.6, imagine an increase in the quantity of terminal devices, in the quantity of files, and in the quantity of programs. Visualize hundreds of terminal devices, hundreds of files, and hundreds of programs. This is what is found in a typical medium- or large-scale computer configuration. As a matter of fact, in a typical data processing center, housing several medium- and large-scale computer configurations, there may be thousands of terminals, thousands of files, and thousands of programs. To comprehend the complexity, just imagine the same thing in terms of individuals, tasks, desks, and file cabinets. The proper management of the traffic in records being transferred

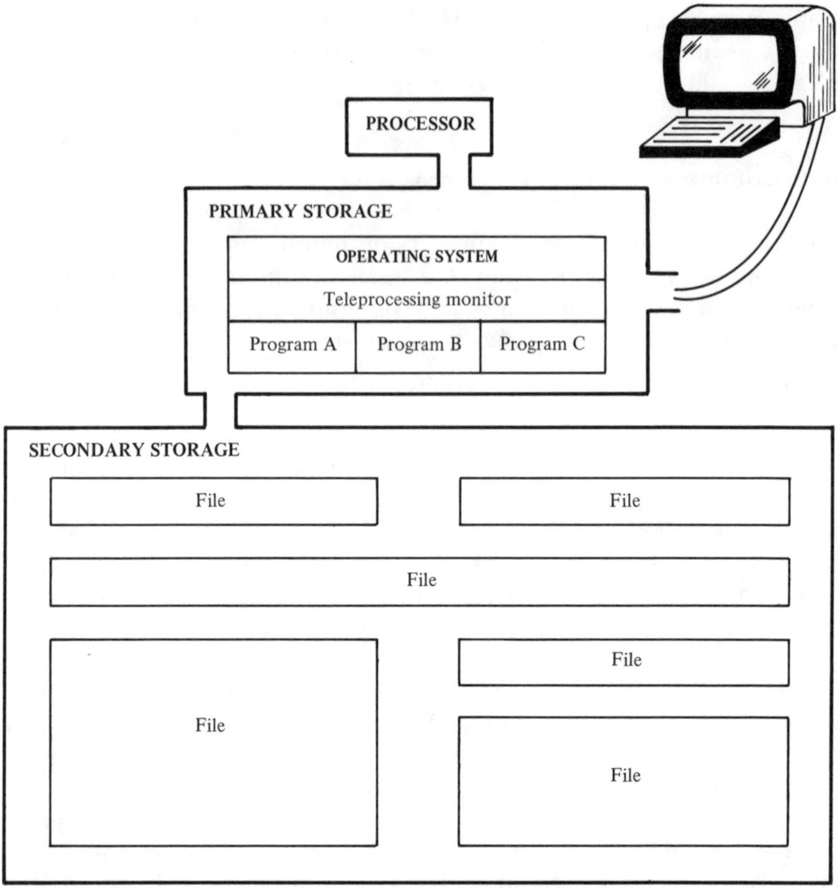

Figure 2.6 Files in secondary storage and programs in primary storage.

between primary and secondary storage and in transactions being transferred between terminals and the computers requires that a certain order be maintained. Control programs* and teleprocessing monitors have facilities which allow users to set up pools of primary storage into which records and transactions can be temporarily stored until resources are available to process them. The pools of primary storage for records are called buffers, and the pools of primary storage for transactions are called queues. The scarce resources in data processing with computer equipment are the processor and primary storage. Both of these components are involved in every transfer of information be-

*For the sake of readability, the software components known as either operating systems or control programs are from this point forward to the end of the chapter referred to as control programs.

tween primary storage and secondary storage and in every transaction that passes between primary storage and terminal devices. It is possible, through the use of buffers and queues, to balance the involvement of these two scarce resources in the transfer of information. Technical skill is required to maintain a proper balance in those installations where medium and large scale computers are in use.

A *buffer* is a staging area in primary storage in which several records can be stored. The actual physical transfer of information between secondary and primary storage involves the processor and takes time. In certain types of indexed and serial data handling, it is known ahead of time that a group of records is going to be needed. For example, if a batch of transactions is being used to update an inventory file and are being processed serially, it is known that after the first record is processed, the second one comes next, and then the third, and so on. Through the use of a buffer, it is possible to transfer several of those transactions from secondary storage into primary storage in one physical operation and process those several transactions without having to perform additional physical transfer operations. There is a saving of processor time. If it were an individual working at a desk, it would be the same as retrieving several records from a file cabinet and processing them all, instead of retrieving records one at a time. There is a trade off, however, as a greater amount of primary storage is used to hold several records than is required hold one record. In the case of the desk, it would be advisable to retrieve several records at one time only if the desk were big enough to hold the extra records. If the desk were too small, and the waiting records got in the way or got knocked on the floor, then the retrieval of several records would be counterproductive. Figure 2.7 shows the idea of a buffer. In complex situations where a computer configuration house control programs and significant numbers of applications programs, the applications often share common buffers. In these situations, the buffers occupy positions of primary storage apart from the application programs and are part of a control program facility whose function it is to transfer information between primary and secondary storage. Management of these buffers requires some elaborate software, and measuring and determining their impact on the overall performance of the computer configuration requires technical skill.

Queues are waiting lists used to hold incoming and outgoing transactions. In complex computer configurations, in which many terminal devices are sending and receiving transactions, there is a traffic management problem. There are basically two ways to handle traffic. One way is for the computer configuration to take in transactions up to a saturation point and from that point on to transmit a message to terminal devices that the configuration is busy and cannot take any transactions.

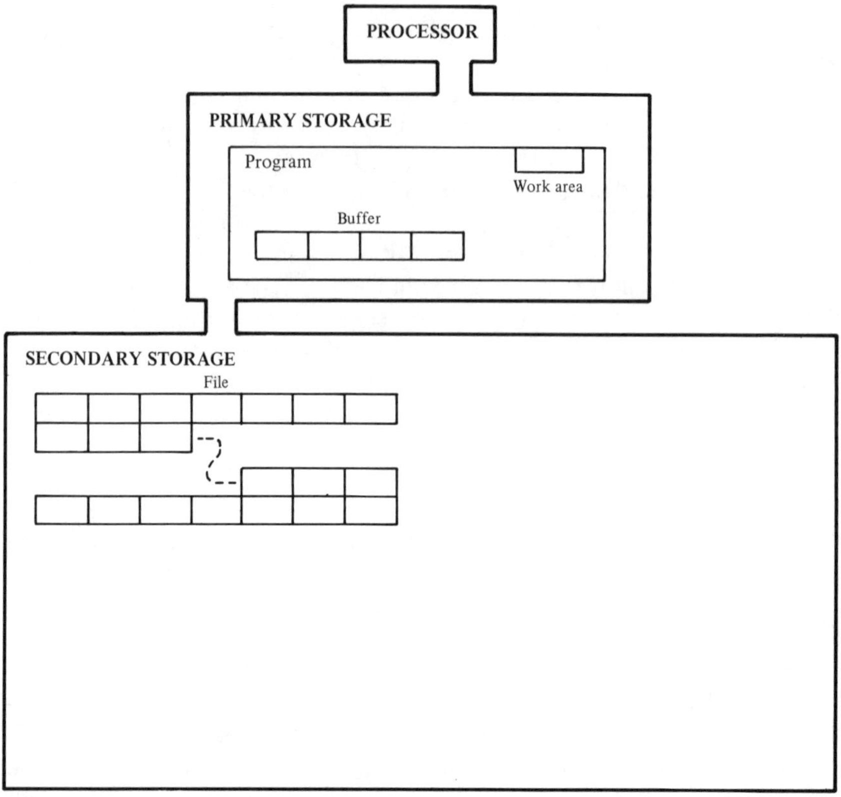

Figure 2.7 Concept of a buffer.

In this situation, the terminal device operator waits for a short period of time and then reenters the transaction. The second way to handle traffic is for the computer configuration to take in all transactions and to process as many as possible and to put the others on a waiting list. As traffic eases off, transactions are taken off the waiting list and processed. Similar waiting lists are also used to handle transactions going out of the computer configuration also. These transactions are put on waiting lists until the communication line is available to take it to the appropriate terminal device. In medium and large scale computer configurations that use them, elaborate software is required to manage the queues. Skilled technicians are required to support the software.

Transactions and records going into a computer are called input and transactions and records going out of a computer are called output. Buffers and queues are labeled input and output, depending upon whether they are used to handle transactions and records going in or coming out. The software, including the facilities for buffer and queue management, is examined in greater detail in a subsequent chapter.

DATA AGGREGATES AND DATA RELATIONSHIPS

Up until this point, we have considered data or information in terms of fields, records, and files. As we have just seen, handling large numbers of files and records can be a rather complicated operation. It can also be rather slow and cumbersome. There are, however, ways of storing, manipulating, and retrieving data or information that while even more complicated, are potentially faster and less cumbersome. The basic building block of what are known as data structures is an aggregate of data, which can be as small as a field, as large as a record, or somewhere in between. While the terms field and file commonly suggest the same idea to most people, the same can no longer be said for record and a multitude of other terms used as names for these aggregates of data. The more complicated, yet potentially faster ways of storing, manipulating, and retrieving information that we are referring to are known as *database management systems.* Made up of computer programs, database management systems themselves range in scope and complexity from the relatively simple, single-user products that can be used on small personal computers to the rather large, multiple-user database/data communication systems supported by large-scale computer configurations. In any event, some of the terms that might be found to describe aggregates of data include: segment, data element, data aggregate, record, tuple, and data unit.

When we defined the term record, we described it as a group of fields about a particular person, place, or thing. The card in the inventory file was used as an example. A record in computer storage would be made up of data fields related to one another by physical adjacency. When database management systems are used, the structuring of data records takes on a different form. Fields can be related to each other by physical adjacency making up a data aggregate, but data aggregates can be related to each other by means of pointers* as well as by physical adjacency. This capability of Database Management System technology creates the potential of not only relating data aggregates to one another within records of one file but of relating data aggregates to one another in relationships that transcend file and record boundaries.

DATABASE

The term database has been defined by numerous authors, speakers, technicians, and hardware and software vendors. The definitions range from the superficial to the in-depth. All the definitions are essentially correct, and yet some of them do not satisfy. For example: "A database

*This term will be defined a little later.

is a collection of data fundamental to an enterprise,"[†] is one of the more superficial definitions. It is certainly correct, and yet when we read it, we feel we are being told something that we already know. Nothing new is being added to our knowledge and understanding.

Another definition describes a database as consisting "of all the record occurrences, set occurrences, and areas that are controlled by a specific schema. If an installation has multiple data bases, there must be a separate schema for each data base. Furthermore, the content of different data bases is assumed to be disjoint."* This definition is also correct, but it includes technical terminology that immediately frustrates those of us whose day-to-day vocabulary does not include terms such as "set," "schema," and "disjoint." In addition, the term being defined—that is, "database"—appears twice, in slightly different form—(two words as opposed to one)—in the definition. There are many more definitions, but we'll refrain from listing them all.

Now, we are going to attempt one of our own, which rests only on what has gone before within this text. A *database* is a collection of data aggregates that are interrelated in such a way as to transcend record and file boundaries. Going one step further, a *database management system* is a collection of related computer programs that have the *potential* to transform a mere collection of data aggregates into a database and then to enable individuals to store data in, manipulate data within, and retrieve data from that database. The biggest single misunderstanding regarding database technology involves the idea of potential. Both database and database management systems have great potential. Realizing that potential is the responsibility of the individuals or organizations using them.

POINTERS

Interrelationships among data aggregates are established and maintained by means of pointers. A *pointer* is a mechanism that relates a data aggregate to one or more other data aggregates. Conceptually, this can be seen in Figure 2.8 It is possible for one data aggregate to point to one or more other data aggregates. There are different kinds of disciplines that govern the data aggregate structures of databases. Indexed, hierarchical, network, and inverted are the major disciplines that make use of pointers to relate data aggregates. Another discipline, called relational, does not use pointers in the conceptual structure. Figure 2.9 illustrates these disciplines.

[†]This definition is one of three that appears in an "IBM Data Processing Glossary," GC20-1699-5, p. 63.

*This definition was defined by a group known as CODASYL, or the Conference on Data System Languages, the same group that spearheaded the development of the COBOL programming language.

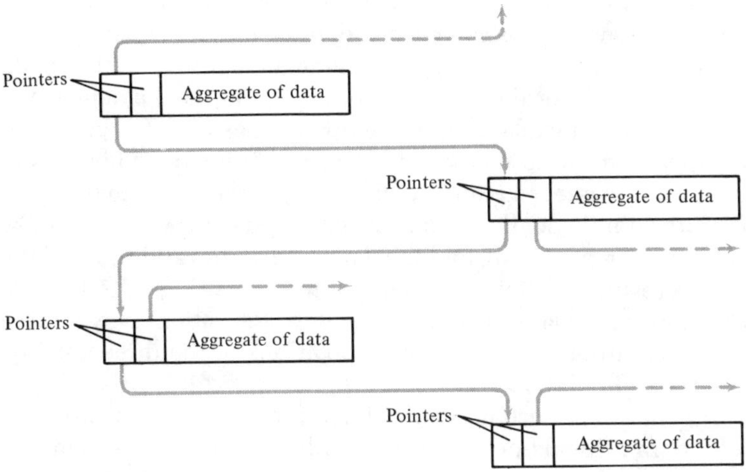

Figure 2.8 Concept of pointers.

Figure 2.9 Structures that use pointers (logical).

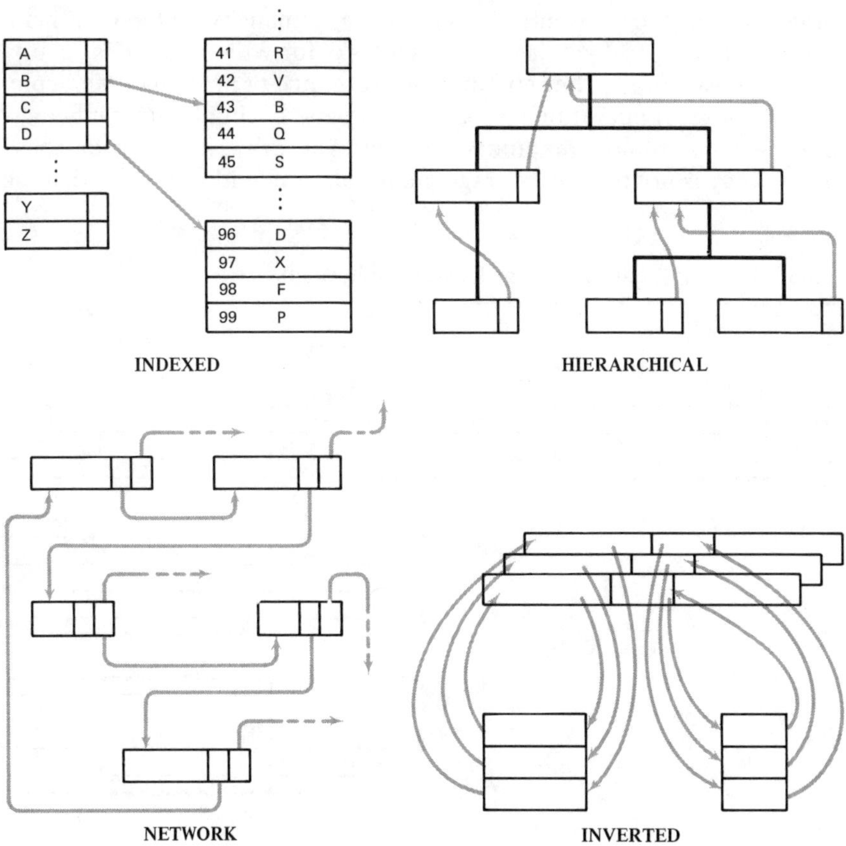

Conceptually, pointers are shown as arrows. In actuality, pointers are storage location addresses. When a data aggregate is being specified, there are facilities with a database management system that build in a field for each pointer that is required. For example, if a data aggregate that was to be interrelated to three other types of data aggregates was being specified, three fields would exist in it for the addresses of the those data aggregates to which it was going to relate. Once the specifications were completed, the structure generated (a process not unlike the compilation of a program), and the data loaded, the addresses of the other data aggregates would be in the pointer fields. Figure 2.10 illustrates. The data aggregate on the left of the illustration shows three pointer fields pointing to the beginning positions of the three data aggregates on the right of the illustration.

Pointers are the underlying mechanism for data relationships that go beyond the traditional field, record, and file data structures. Contemporary database management systems include programs which are able to create, maintain, backup, recover, and reorganize the complex databases that are built using pointer mechanisms. When individuals look at the complex structures and the potential data relationships of modern organization, they are intimidated by the immensity of the data management tasks. And yet, it is just such tasks for which computer equipment is best suited. The repetitive performance of arithmetic and comparative logical operations, so exhausting and boring to human beings, are the very things computers do well. The difficulty with database technology is not the data storage, manipulation, and retrieval—that the

Figure 2.10 Pointers as storage locations (physical).

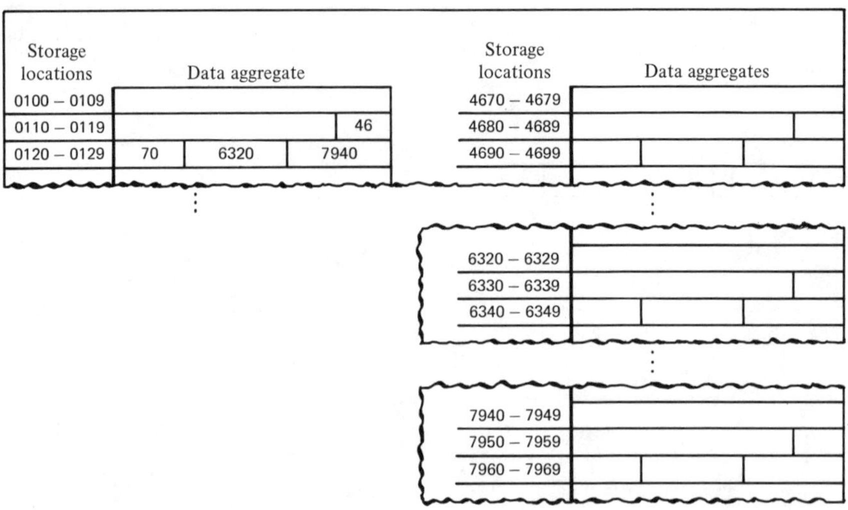

computer hardware and software can easily handle. The difficulty with database is determining the data relationships within an organization and getting responsible individuals to agree to those relationships. The theory of database is quite sound; putting it into practice can be quite another situation. From a technological perspective, implementation of database technology is practical. There are difficulties, but they can be dealt with. The real difficulties involved in database technology implementation are logistical, managerial, and political. The logistical difficulty is replacing existing technology with new technology without running up the costs. This is not a minor problem and cannot be overlooked. The managerial problem is the arriving at a consensus where data relationships truly reflect the needs of the organization. The political problem is caused by the perceived threat that database technology poses to entrenched MIS organizations and to department heads who prefer "going it alone" as opposed to cooperative efforts to bring benefits to the entire organization.

DATA DICTIONARY

Basic Functions

A data dictionary is a facility that, if utilized properly, forces an organization to document—that is, to identify and classify—and to be able to locate the data elements, fields, records, files, and databases that comprise an organization's data asset. Just as we use "Webster's" to define and describe the words we use in our day-to-day oral and written communication, we can use a data dictionary to define and describe the data structures that are used in our communications with the computer. We have all been exposed to terms like "information explosion" and "information overload." Well, there is no area where these terms are more descriptive of what is going on than in the area of information systems and computers. As quantities of information continue to increase and as computer equipment to store that information continues to proliferate, the task of managing it becomes more complicated. Identifying, classifying, and being able to locate that information is beyond the capability of men without the aid of technology. While it is theoretically possible to create and maintain a data dictionary using manual procedures and paper documentation, it is for all practical purposes impossible. There just is no way to keep that kind of dynamic information up to date and distributed without the help of a computer.

There are a number of data dictionary software products available. Such products are collections of computer programs that have the capability of creating files or databases into which descriptive information about organizations' data asset can be stored. This information can be subsequently manipulated and retrieved.

Data Dictionary System

When implemented, a data dictionary is composed of passive and active elements. The active elements are the programs that are used to load information into the dictionary, manipulate the information within the dictionary, and retrieve information from the dictionary. The passive elements are the files or databases which hold the information. Figure 2.11 is schematic of a data dictionary system.

Figure 2.11 Data dictionary.

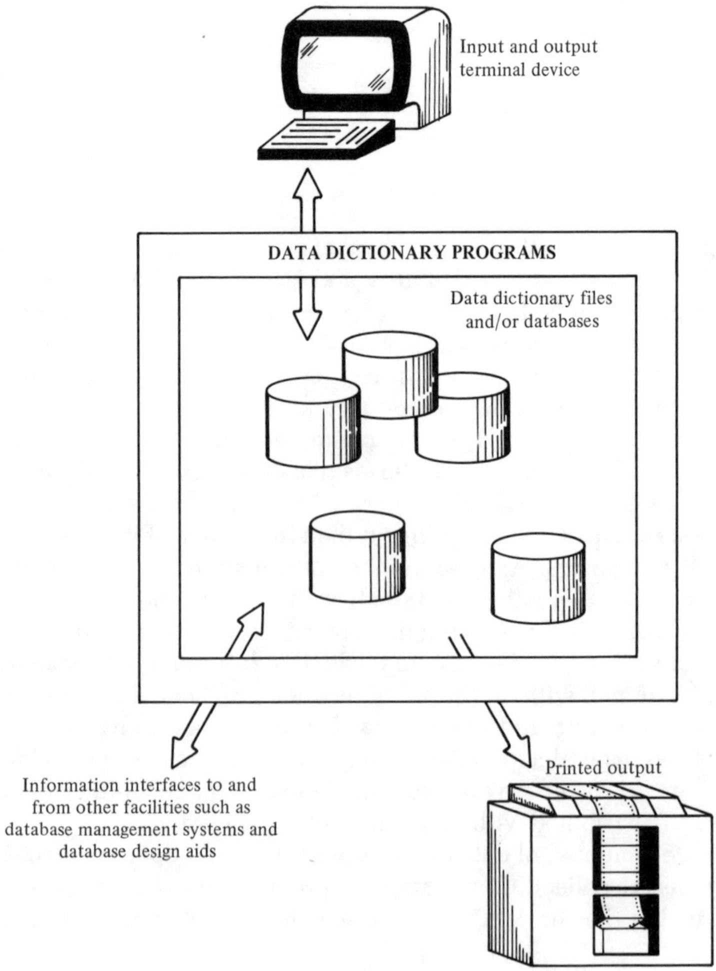

The real potential of data dictionaries lies in their ability to be used as a centralized repository for information describing not only the data asset, but also computer equipment, computer programs, computer applications, systems software products, and the various coding mechanisms found in many organizations. In those cases where a data dictionary makes use of the facilities of a database management system, correlations can be established among the elements and components described by the dictionary. For example, it would be possible to set up relationships within the data dictionary between programs and files, so that an individual could query the dictionary to find out how many programs used such and such a file. This type of query might be made to help determine the impact of a proposed modification to an existing file structure or layout. An equipment inventory could be set up and maintained using a data dictionary. Queries as to the quantities or locations of certain types of equipment could be handled. "How many terminal devices are located in the Elmhurst warehouse?" is a question to which many data dictionary products are able to respond.

The use of data dictionaries, relative to other technology seems to have been somewhat slow in getting started. This may have been due to some confusion not only in the minds of senior and general managers, but also in the minds of EDP/MIS managers, as to the distinction between data dictionaries and database management systems.* However, data dictionaries are extremely powerful tools, and whatever the reason for their slow start, that power is beginning to be recognized.

Operation and Function

Data dictionaries can function operationally as stand-alone systems or they can be integrated with database management systems. As stand-alone systems, they can be used as automated documentation tools in which it is possible to store descriptive information about fields, records, files, databases, programs, systems, and virtually any other component of the EDP/MIS repertoire. When integrated with database management systems, they can be used in the same way, but can perform additional functions, which we'll describe below. Before doing that,

*Speaking for myself, an information systems manager for a number of years, I was somewhat confused myself when first introduced to data dictionaries. At the time, I was reasonably familiar with the concepts of database management, and at first data dictionaries seemed just another term within the lexicon of new terminology of database technology. Only when I got into the operational aspects of database management did the distinction between the two crystallize. Database management systems store, manipulate, and retrieve information. Data dictionaries describe information (and as a by-product they can describe other things as well). Data dictionaries can and sometimes do use the facilities of database management systems to store, manipulate, and retrieve information about information.

however, it should be pointed out that there are varying degrees of integration. At one extreme, there are fully integrated database management/data dictionary products in which the functions performed by the data dictionary are automatically handled by the database management system. At the other extreme, there is integration that is user engineered. In such situations, users develop interfaces between the data dictionary and the database management system.

In addition to being a repository of information, a data dictionary can serve as a single central source of specifications to a database management system and can serve as a database design and development aid. Let's first look at the former. When a data dictionary product is integrated with or interfaced to a database management system, it either has or can be given the capability of feeding file and database descriptive information to the database management system. This function, alluded to in Figure 2.11, is more graphically illustrated in Figure 2.12. With an integrated data dictionary, file or database specifications are entered once. Once in the dictionary, they become available to the database management system. These specifications are transferred by means of an integration mechanism or a user engineered interface. File and database specifications being entered into a database management system, either from a data dictionary or by direct keying through a terminal, are called, in the jargon of database, *data description language* (DDL) statements. For these specifications to be used by applications programs in execution, they have to be translated into a form recognizable to the computer. They are compiled, just as a program is, into a form sometimes known as a control block* and stored in a file known as a library.†

Many data dictionary products can serve as development aids, since they are able to store several versions of a file or database layout. One of these layouts can be the most current production version of the file or database that being used by active applications. Other versions can be used for development and maintenance activities. Other software products are available that facilitate the efforts of file and database designers in development efforts. Known as design aids, these products take some of the tedium out of design work. Designers enter the variables, i.e., the input, output, and processing requirements of a proposed application, into a computerized design aid product. Out of it come reports that show the proposed data aggregates, estimates as to the frequency of use of the relationships, suggested structure of the

*A control block holds, in computer executable form, the specifics of a file or database such as its size, record lengths, and storage locations.

†There are many types of library files. Their function is to store information and sets of instructions (programs) so that they can be accessed when needed by a computer or by an individual.

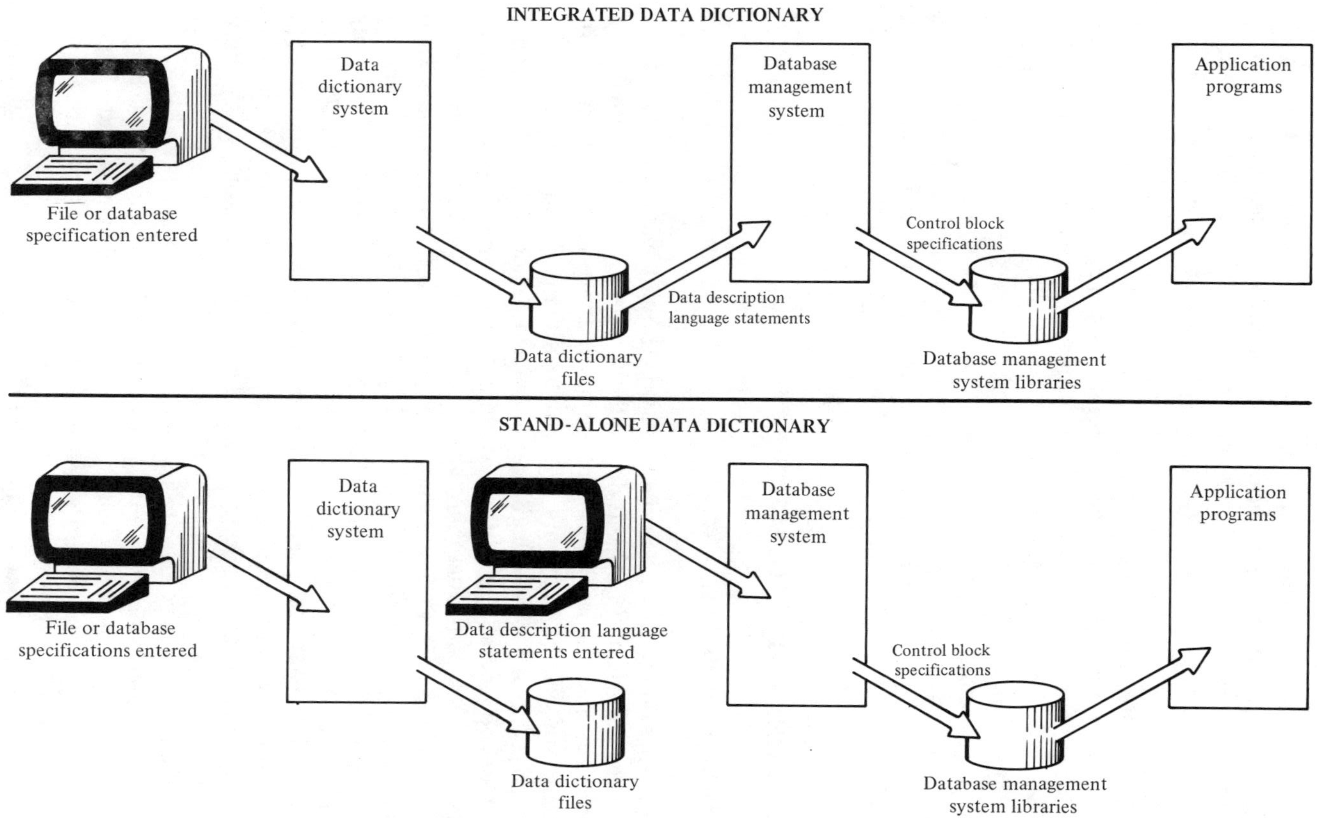

Figure 2.12 Integrated and stand-alone data dictionary data flows.

database, and suggested indexing schemes. In development work, designers frequently enter several sets of variables. A design aid product that is integrated with or interfaces to a data dictionary is able to directly transfer the output of design aid processes into data dictionary files.

Analysis of prototype databases is facilitated with another type of software product. Analysts can simulate the performance of alternative database designs by running a predefined set of test transactions and activity against the various structures housed in the data dictionary.

The point of all this is that there are several types of software products whose sole purpose is the performance of storage analysis and retrieval function on data descriptions and data relationships. This provides ample evidence that an era of information management is upon us.

MANAGEMENT INFORMATION

Detail Information

A vice-president of marketing once said, "I don't even want to look at a number that hasn't been rounded to thousands." At the other end of the spectrum lies the sentiment that supports the precise control of unit counts and dollars and cents. Both are legitimate, but each reflects a different point of view. A legitimate concern for detail exists in operational support and accounting systems. For example, in a shipping operation, a pick/pack document has to reflect a specific number of items. If a customer orders six videocassettes of "Star Wars," then six are picked, packed, shipped, and invoiced. Rounding to thousands just won't do in this type of an operation. In accounting, which reflects payroll among other things, an employee would be somewhat upset if a paycheck for $373.82 was rounded to the nearest thousand. The computer aided design/computer aided manufacturing (CAD/CAM) systems are engineering applications requiring extreme precision. Rounding to thousands would not work here either.

This is not an attempt to make dealing with summarized information look ridiculous. Summaries have the value also, and we'll look at them presently. Detail information handling, however, is quite important, not only for its own application, but also as the foundation upon which summary information rests.

Virtually all of the initial EDP/MIS applications that were developed were detail oriented. Accounting, order entry, inventory, and billing had requirements for exact "to the unit" and "to the penny" controls. Finance and budgeting applications were an exception, where rounding to tens or sometimes hundreds of dollars was permissable. Few of these applications could have been called Management Information Systems in the original sense of the term. A true MIS is a strategic system. It details in thousands, tens of thousands, or even millions of units or dollars. The initial applications would more aptly be called operational support systems or logistical support systems. (We'll not suggest an acronym for these since there are already too many of them already cluttering the EDP/MIS landscape.)

The information that is to be maintained, manipulated, and displayed in detail applications is very specific. A general ledger contains a detailed listing of every financial transaction that took place in an organization within a period of time (most often a month). Balance sheets and profit and loss statements, on the other hand, are summaries of an organization's position and earnings at some point in time.

Based on the assumption that they exist to sell things at a profit, a common process is found in most commercial enterprises. Starting with an order for merchandise, a process is begun whereby detail transactions are created that travel through a set of procedures causing activity to occur reflecting the impact of that transaction. Let's look at some indicative information and line items on an order to illustrate detail information and its flow through a set of applications of a typical commercial enterprise. An order contains a customer name and probably a customer number (remember numbers are easier to work with than alphabetic information), a ship-to address and a bill-to address, some shipping instructions, and a list of several items being ordered. In this particular scenario,* let's say videocassettes are the products being ordered. A transaction is created reflecting the indicative information, and line items consisting of product numbers, titles, and quantities ordered. This transaction is matched against the finished good inventory file, as pick/pack lists are prepared for the shipping operation. Inventory is relieved to reflect the shipment. When the order is picked, packed and shipped, a confirmation (basically a copy of the original transaction with additional information added) is sent to the billing department. An invoice is prepared and an accounts receivable is posted for the customer who ordered the videocassettes. When payment is subsequently received, the customer's account receivable is credited and the sale is booked by means of a similar transaction. At the end of an accounting cycle, most frequently every month or every four or five weeks, some journal entries are prepared to reflect, in dollars and cents, closing inventory, cost of sales (depreciation, selling, general and ad-

*The scenario set forth here is for the purpose of illustrating detail data flow. To avoid making the detail excruciating, a number of functions, including raw materials inventory, manufacturing, forecasting, back ordering, and returns are intentionally left out.

ministrative expenses), and so on. This information and the postings of the month's activity represented by the two transactions mentioned above and all the other like them, are used to prepare a detailed general ledger and monthly financial statements (summaries). In addition to the accounting and financial statements, monthly sales reports, inventory reports, manufacturing reports, both detailed and summary are produced. It is at the end of a cycle, a month, or a week, or a quarter, where a somewhat blurred distinction between the detailed data operational support systems and summarized data management information system begins to appear. This distinction is blurred because the managers, who are the potential benefactors of the information made available through a true MIS, are not only at different levels in organizations, but have different personalities and their various desires for the formats in which they wish to see data displayed are anything but standardized.

SUMMARY INFORMATION

As the information requirements of an organization grow, and applications proliferate, the actual quality of its information systems reflect more and more that organization's management of an earlier generation. In the operational support systems alluded to but only briefly described above, the data needs are generally detailed or summarized at an extremely low level. The following are examples. A manufacturing situation may occur where a process has stopped because a batch of components from a subcontractor has been found to contain a high percentage of defects. A first line supervisor or a manager needs to find out it there are any more on order and how soon they are scheduled for delivery. In another situation, a clerk in personnel department is required to post a change in the number of dependents for a specific male employee whose wife has just given birth to a child.

Until the late 1970s, senior and general managers were giving limited attention to information systems and computers, while middle managers, a high percentage of them from finance and accounting, gave quite a bit of attention to them. As a result, a large number of detail and low-level summarization applications were developed. Some of the middle managers made it to senior and general management, being familiar with both the potential and the limitations of information systems and computers. This familiarity, coupled with an awareness of the escalating costs being incurred to support them, shared with other members of senior and general management, is leading to a realization that information systems and computers have become a major consideration in all organizations: commercial, governmental, and institutional.

Senior and general managers require information with which they can make strategic decisions. The vice-president of marketing, alluded to earlier, was correct. They work with dollars in thousands or millions, with percentages and ratios. They work with truckloads of videocassettes as opposed to quantities on an order, with gross sales or gross sales per unit per month for a fast- or slow-moving item as opposed to a two-dollar discrepancy on a particular invoice, with gross inventory turnover as opposed to determining a reorder point for a particular type of bolt.

The current challenge to both senior management and the EDP/MIS community is to find an economical way to provide accurate summary information on a timely basis. In point of fact, this challenge is not different from the objective of MIS that was stated in the 1960s. But at this point there are a couple of differences. First, senior management is now interested, whereas in the 1960s they were not, and second, EDP/MIS technology presently has the potential to deliver what it was only able to promise in the 1960s. And yet, if we have learned anything at all from the past, we ought to be aware of the danger of artificially inflated expectations. Both senior and general managers and the MIS community must get beyond the "Gee Whiz! — Holy Cow!" superficiality of vendor presentations, glossy promotional brochures and slick advertisements, so that they share a common understanding of the basic concepts of information storage, processing, and retrieval. There is no need for senior and general managers to become programmers or operations technicians, but there is a need for them to become at least as familiar with the fundamentals of MIS as they are with the fundamentals of finance, accounting, marketing, and operations. The remaining chapters address those fundamentals.

SECTION TWO

S Is for Systems

This section of the book deals with what could be called the technology of information systems. There is what is known as hardware, computer equipment, and communications equipment. Then there is software, active and passive. Active software is the sets of instructions that tell the equipment what to do. Passive software is the data or information that is stored within, processed by, and retrieved from the equipment by the sets of instructions. From a management point of view, hardware is simple. There are a number of different types of boxes which perform functions. In Chapter 3, these boxes and their functions are explained. Software, on the other hand, is somewhat more complicated. Active software is the temporary man/machine interface. It is temporary, because hardware is continually being developed that replaces it. The ultimate computer equipment configuration, constantly approached but never reached, is going to consist of hardware instruction sets and data structures to house the constantly changing data which is a reflection of a constantly changing reality. Passive software is going to be with us for a while. The data, which is dynamic in both its form and its content, is causing a shift in emphasis from the processing aspect of data processing to the data aspect. The automated office, about which it can safely be said that when all is said and done much more has been said than done at this point in time, is the extension of the man/machine interface. The increasing sophistication of both hardware and software is making the technology of information systems more "user friendly."

The personal computing facilities of the large, medium, and small computer configurations are oriented toward the "nontechnical" individual or group. High-level programming languages, such as BASIC, word processing systems, menu driven control programs where users choose what they wish to do from a list of available options, automated spread sheets for financial analysts, and interactive graphics packages continually make computers more attractive and less intimidating. Bringing all the technology together, controlling, and managing it, creates the need for a tool to identify, classify, and describe the data in its various forms—databases, data elements, files, records, fields, and data interrelationships. This tool is known as a data dictionary.

Before getting into the functional examination of information systems technology, a few words on the term system are in order. It is a term that can mean different things at different times. Here are some examples:

- *A system is a computer equipment configuration.*
- *A system is a collection of programs that are run serially or in tandem in a computer equipment configuration to complete a specific set of tasks that make up a job. In this context a synonym for the term system is the term application.*
- *A system is a collection of procedures that defines and describes a set of tasks to be performed to complete a job. Computer equipment configurations may not be involved.*

The exact meaning can frequently be determined from the context in which it is found, but occassionally the meaning is not too clear. For example, when a computer operator at a remotely located data processing facility says over a telephone to a terminal user five miles away that "the system is down," three strong probabilities are present. First, the statement in and of itself means nothing; second, the operator is confirming what the terminal operator already knows, i.e., his or her terminal is not able to send or receive transactions; and third, the operator does not yet know exactly what the problem is.

CHAPTER 3

Computers

COMPUTER CONFIGURATIONS

Contemporary computer equipment configurations can generally be categorized into three basic groups: micro, mini, and large scale. The difference between the three is similar to the capacity difference between a pickup truck, a small local trucking company, and a comprehensive transportation organization, such as Federal Express. While functionally similar, the amount of material they can move and where and how quickly they can move it varies significantly. A pickup truck allows a single individual to move one payload at a time from one place to another. A microcomputer configuration generally provides its computing capabilities and the potential to store and retrieve relatively small quantities of information to one individual at a time. A small trucking company has the capability of transferring several payloads among multiple locations at the same time. A typical "minicomputer" configuration, or perhaps small business system* is a better term, pro-

*The term microcomputer was coined around 1970, probably by some marketing genius who knew that when you introduced a product that was less expensive but also technologically inferior to existing products of the same type, also knew that coming up with a catchy name would help. In 1970 minicomputer meant smaller, less expensive, less capa-

vides its users with computing, storage, and retrieval capabilities more comprehensive than those of a microcomputer configuration. Furthermore, these capabilities can be made available on a shared basis to more than one individual. A comprehensive transportation organization, such as Federal Express, with its fleet of airplanes, trucks, and vans has the capabilities of moving thousands of payloads among numerous locations at the same time. Similarly, a large-scale computer configuration has capabilities that permit interaction with hundreds of individuals who are able to store, retrieve, perform computations, and manipulate information at the same time.

In contemporary computer environments, there also exists a capability whereby computers communicate or talk to one another. This capability increases significantly the potential of computer configurations. There are installations where minicomputers communicate with large-scale computers, where microcomputers talk to minis and to one another; the combinations are virtually limitless. There are technical complexities involved in realizing this potential, but nevertheless, communications among mixed computer configurations is commonplace. Sketches of the three major types of computers are pictured in Figure 3.1.

COMPUTER DYNAMICS

Prefixes such as micro, mini, and large scale are somewhat imprecise, but they have a certain pizazz not found in words such as small, medium, and large. And yet, the terms micro, mini, and large scale, in reality, signify little more than is conveyed by the more mundane terms small, medium, and large. In addition, the terms microcomputer and minicomputer are used somewhat indiscriminately, because advances in electronics technology bring about changes, especially in the area of miniaturization of circuitry and components, that make it virtually impossible to be precise. For all practical purposes, computers referred to as *minicomputers* perform tasks in quantities that had been possible only by large scale mainframe computers a few years earlier, while *microcomputers* perform tasks that had been the domain of minicomputers a few years earlier. However, in spite of the lack of precision in differentiating computers by size and capability, there remains a functional similarity in all computer configurations regardless of size and capability. It follows, therefore, that all computer configurations

---

bility. Today it means nothing. Small business systems describe a configuration of computer equipment that falls in an area somewhere between a small, single-user microcomputer-based product and a large-scale computer equipment configuration.

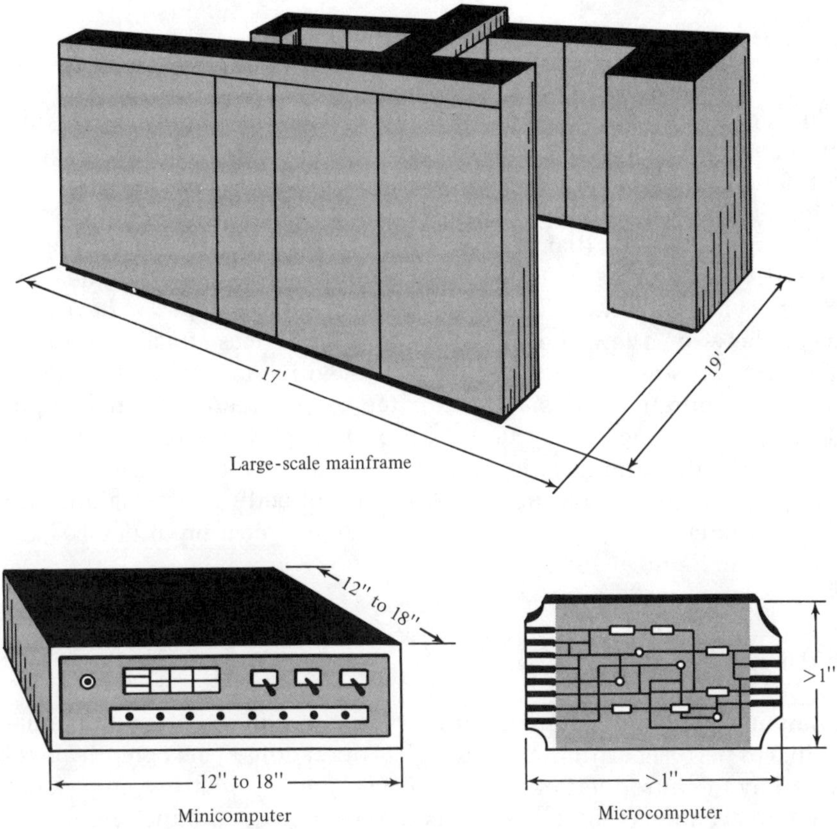

Figure 3.1 Computers—large-scale, mini, and micro.

have functional similarity and are able to perform a similar basic set of tasks.

COMPUTER CONFIGURATION FUNCTIONS AND COMPONENTS

There are five basic functions performed by all computers. The differences from one computer to another lie in the speed at which the functions are carried out and in the number of functions that can be performed concurrently. All computers have:

- An input function
- A processing function
- A control function
- A storage function
- An output function

INPUT

The input function, a combination of electronic equipment and circuitry and computer instructions, performs the tasks required to get information into a computer from sources external to the configuration. Although there are others, the most commonly used equipment components are keyboards that are part of CRT devices or typewriter terminals. A typical small computer (microcomputer configuration) has one input device, usually a CRT and a keyboard. Large computers have anywhere between a few and thousands of such devices attached to them. The circuitry and instructions are combined in various ratios in computer configurations. In small computers, where there is a single input device, the computer instructions are often part of the circuitry. In large computer configurations, there is a combination of circuitry and computer programs that performs the task of getting information into the computer from numerous devices. Some typical input devices are pictured in Figure 3.2.

PROCESSOR

Computer processors contain circuitry that provides them with the potential to perform arithmetic and logical operations. This potential is realized by the introduction of computer programs which are an ordered set of instructions that tell the processor what to do. Computer configurations may contain several processors. Some of these may be special-purpose processors and others general-purpose. Small computers generally have a single, general-purpose processor that is able to perform one task at a time in interaction with a single user. Larger configurations may have one or more general-purpose processors performing multiple tasks of numerous users, and also a number of special-purpose processors performing specific tasks such as initiating, moving, and stopping the transfer of information from an input device into the computer.

The arithmetic operations of a processor are generally quite straight forward. Add, subtract, multiply, divide, square root, and exponentiation are typical arithmetic operations that can be performed by processors. Processors vary in sophistication. More sophisticated processors have the capability, with electronic circuitry alone, of performing complex arithmetic operations. Less sophisticated processors can perform such operations only with an assist from software. In other words, a large-scale processor might be able to calculate the area of a circle by executing one instruction, while a smaller processor might have to execute divide and multiply instructions to perform the same calculation.

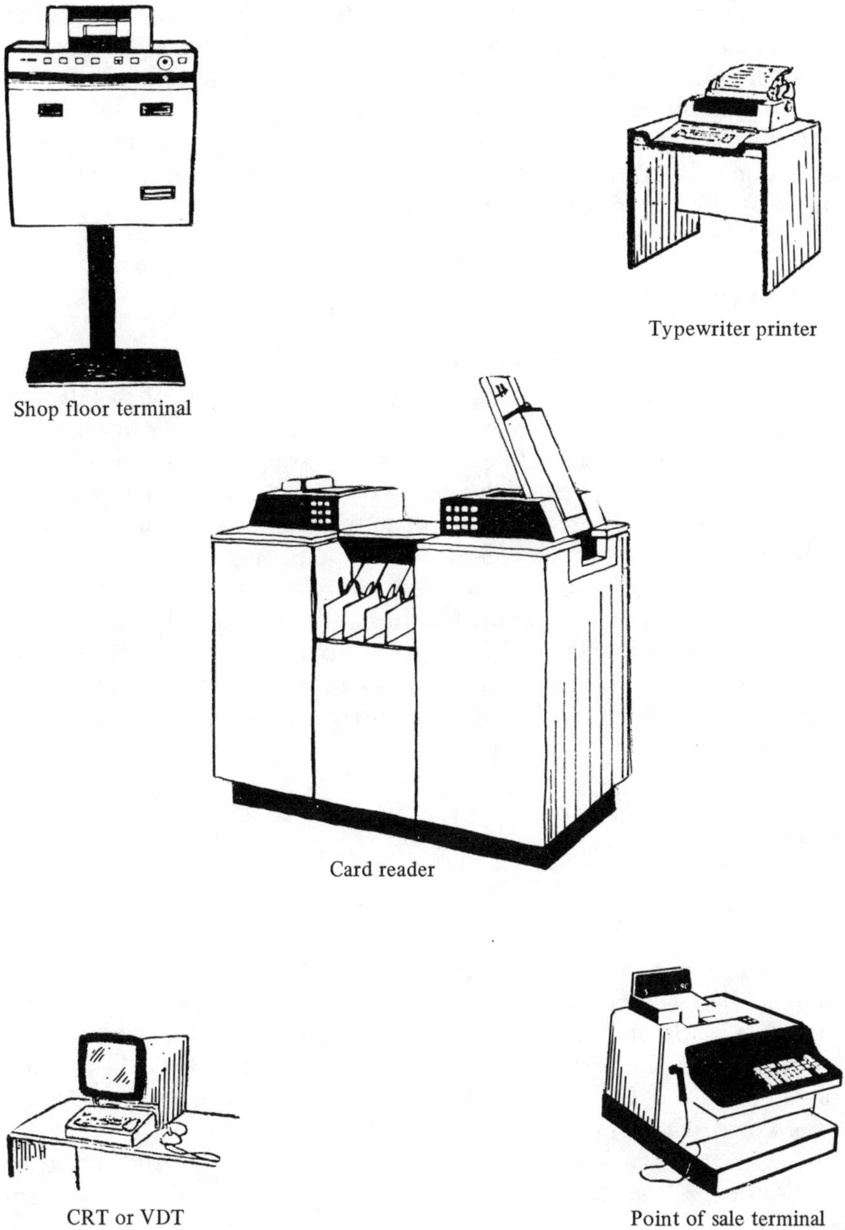

Figure 3.2 Input/output devices.

Logical operations involve comparisons and the taking of specific action based on the results of the comparisons. For example, compare A to B; if A is higher, do X; if A is lower, do Y; if they are equal, do Z. Again, the variation of the processor is a factor. A more sophisticated processor may have circuitry that facilitates a "table lookup" operation; that is, it has the capability to search for a specific value within a series of values and take action based on a finding of the value or not finding it. A less sophisticated processor might have to perform a series of compare instructions with each compare instruction followed by other instructions directing the processor to a set of instructions to be followed based on the outcome of the comparison.

CONTROL

The control function of a computer configuration coordinates the activities of the other functions. For instance, the control mechanism guides the processor in its execution of one instruction after another and directs the processor in its adjustments triggered by logical operations. The control function also may assure that information being entered into the computer does not prematurely overlay information that is being written out of the computer. In small computer configurations this coordinating function is relatively minor, while in larger configurations, it is enormously complicated. In small computers, it is sometimes fabricated as part of the circuitry of the processor. In large configurations it is a separate functional component. In all computers it is supported by a sophisticated set of computer programs, known as a control program or an operating system.

STORAGE

Overview

Computer storage is made up of primary and secondary elements. Primary storage is used to hold information that is to be made immediately available to the processor. This information includes instructions to be executed (computer programs) and data to be acted upon by the instructions. The processor can get information only from primary storage. Therefore, when a processor requires information that happens to be in secondary storage, instructions must be executed to transfer it to primary storage. Visualize a chef preparing a meal. Before the actual preparation commences, the various groceries, utensils, herbs, and spices must be retrieved from their various locations within the refrigerator, the pantry, and the cabinets. When all these have been retrieved and are within the chef's reach, they are in primary storage. While in the refrigerator, pantry, and closets, they are in secondary storage. In the trade, when information is in primary storage, it is said to be "in the computer." When information is in secondary storage, it is said to be "out on disk," or "on tape." Generally the computer is thought of as a combination of the processor, primary storage, and control components, while input/output devices and secondary storage devices are considered as peripheral or auxiliary equipment. The additional hardware interconnecting all these components are called buses on smaller configurations and channels on the larger configurations.

In a computer, or more precisely, within primary storage, information or data can be moved around or manipulated at electronic speeds, which is very fast. Transferring information between secondary storage and primary storage is a relatively slow operation. The speed and quantity of storage, both primary and secondary and the transfer rate are critical variables in evaluating the suitability of computer configurations for applications. Let's use a couple of extreme examples to illustrate. A small computer configuration would easily contain sufficient storage to hold the contents of the Bible,* while a significantly larger configuration would be required to contain the business data of a large organization.

Secondary storage mechanisms are of two basic types, magnetic disk and magnetic tape. There are others such as magnetic drum and mass storage, but they are merely variations of these two basic types. Magnetic disk has the advantage of making information directly accessible, while information on magnetic tape is only available serially. Since making as much information as possible readily available is a fundamental objective of information systems technology, magnetic disks in increasing quantities are used as the storage medium for current information, while magnetic tape is used for backup logs and audit-trail journals. Figure 3.3 has sketches of some secondary storage mechanisms.

Primary Storage

From a conceptual point of view, primary storage can be thought of as a set of grids. Each grid is uniquely identifiable, and each position within each grid is also uniquely identified. A combination of the number that identifies the grid and the number that identifies the position within the grid makes up what is known as a primary storage address. Figure 3.4 illustrates. Each position within the grid is able to hold one character of information. This is a correlation between the conceptual grid and primary storage as it exists in reality. Each grid contains 1024 positions or

*The Bible, in a couple of its versions serves as a good illustration of a database, as we'll show in a subsequent chapter.

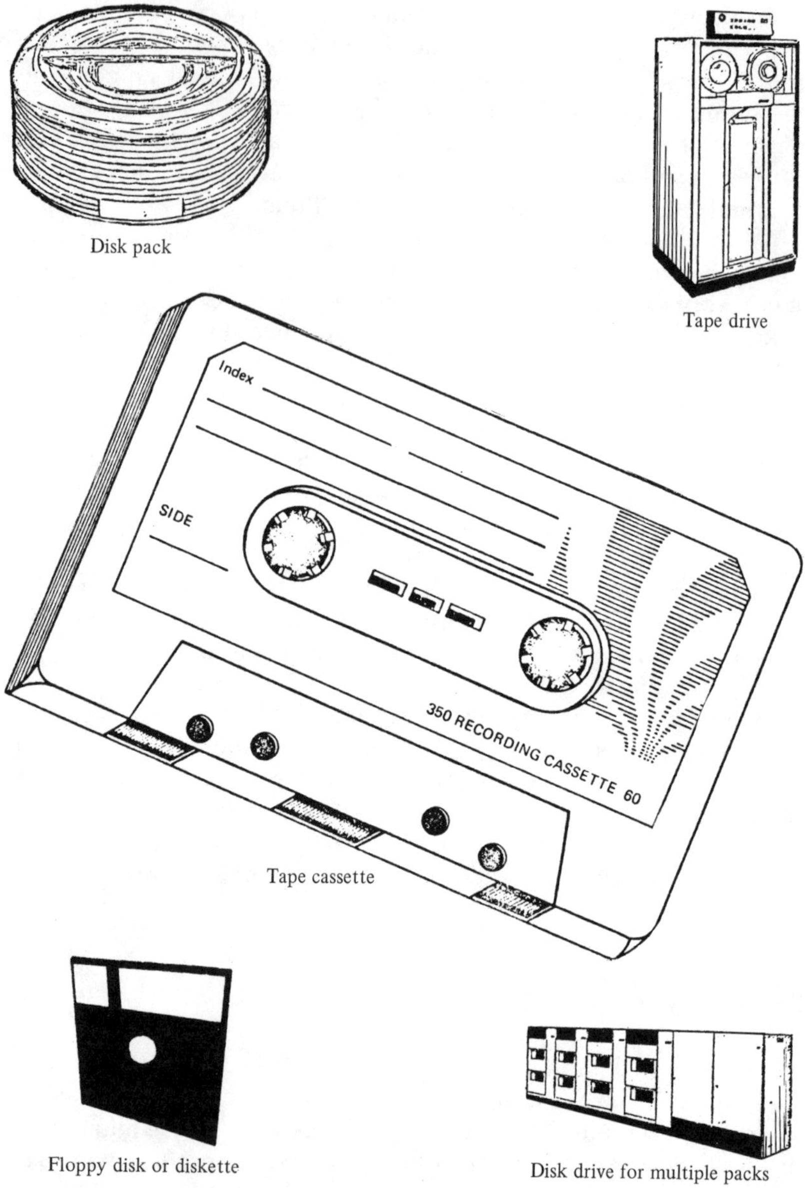

Figure 3.3 Secondary storage devices.

bytes of storage. One of the measures of the capacity of computers is the number of these grids. The letter "K" is frequently used to represent one grid. Therefore, a computer with sixteen of these grids would be referred to as a computer with 16K of primary storage or more simply as a 16K computer. Larger computers with thousands of these grids use the

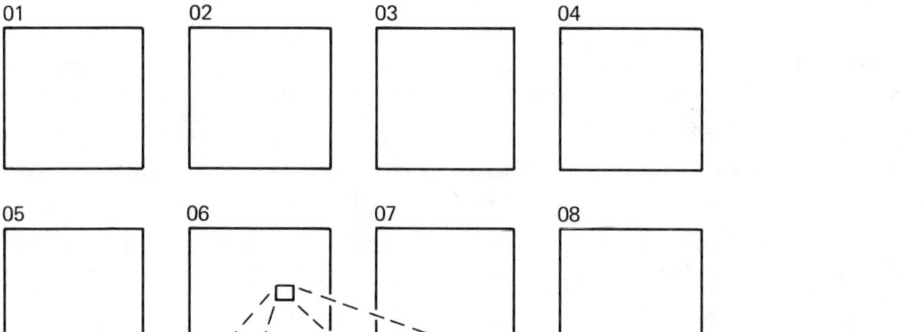

Figure 3.4 Concept of primary storage.

letter M or the term *MEG* to indicate primary storage capacity. A computer with eight thousand of these grids would be referred to as an 8MEG computer or as a computer with primary storage of 8M.

Contemporary microcomputers, rather than being labeled 64K or 256K, are most often called 8-bit and 16-bit. The term bit is a contraction of the words binary digit. When we get down to the basic way that a computer handles data, we're dealing with "on" and "off" electronic impulses, represented by "1" and "0," which are binary digits. Collections of bits, that is, a series of "0s" and "1s", or "on" and "off" impulses can make up the characters, decimal numbers, and symbols that we work with every day. One of the most common methods used where binary digits are used to represent characters is the 8-bit coding structure, where combinations of "0s" and "1s" in groups of eight make up characters, numbers, and symbols.*

*This particular structure is the extended binary coded decimal interchange code (affectionately known as EBCDIC, pronounced *eb su dic*). A single character, digit, or symbol is referred to as a *byte*. Eight *bits* make up a *byte*.

Each primary storage position can be envisioned as a pigeonhole capable of holding one character, number or symbol, i.e., one byte of information. An 8-bit computer has the capability of referencing 65,536 (64K) addresses or storage locations in primary storage, while a 16-bit computer can reference 1,048,576 (1M) addresses or storage locations in primary storage. Also, the 8-bit computer handles information in packages of eight bits, while the 16-bit machines handle information packages of sixteen bits.

Though there are accommodations that can "soup up" the performance of an 8-bit computer, the 16-bit machines have an edge over the long run. The potential of having one million positions of primary storage as opposed to sixty-four thousand gives the 16-bit machine the edge in terms of information immediately available to the processor. The ability to handle the 16-bit packages makes it possible for the computer to perform more unique internal operations than is possible with 8-bit packages. Information is moved more rapidly and instructions can be more powerful.

Secondary Storage Mechanisms

Magnetic disk also has an addressing scheme that facilitates direct storage and retrieval of data, but not at the level of detail as with primary storage. Whereas primary storage permits the processor to access data, a character at a time, transfers of data between a magnetic disk and primary storage take place a string at a time. The size of the string depends on the architecture of the disk device. Magnetic disk storage components and devices come in a wide variety of sizes. There are small flexible disks, called diskettes or "floppies" that can store hundreds of thousands of characters of information. At the other end of the spectrum, there are rigid disks grouped into components made up of one or more recording surfaces that are able to store billions of characters of information. Rigid disks are frequently referred to as hard disk to distinguish them from floppies. Components made up of several recording surfaces are called disk packs.

The recording surface of a magnetic disk is made up of a series of concentric circles called tracks on which data is stored. Figure 3.5A depicts this. On some magnetic disk devices, tracks are subdivided into sectors so that data is transferred between the disk and primary storage a sector at a time. Those disk devices whose tracks are not subdivided into sectors transfer data under the direction of software. In Figure 3.5B there are four sectors indicated.

Magnetic disk drives are the devices on which disk packs are mounted or into which single hard disks or floppies are inserted. While

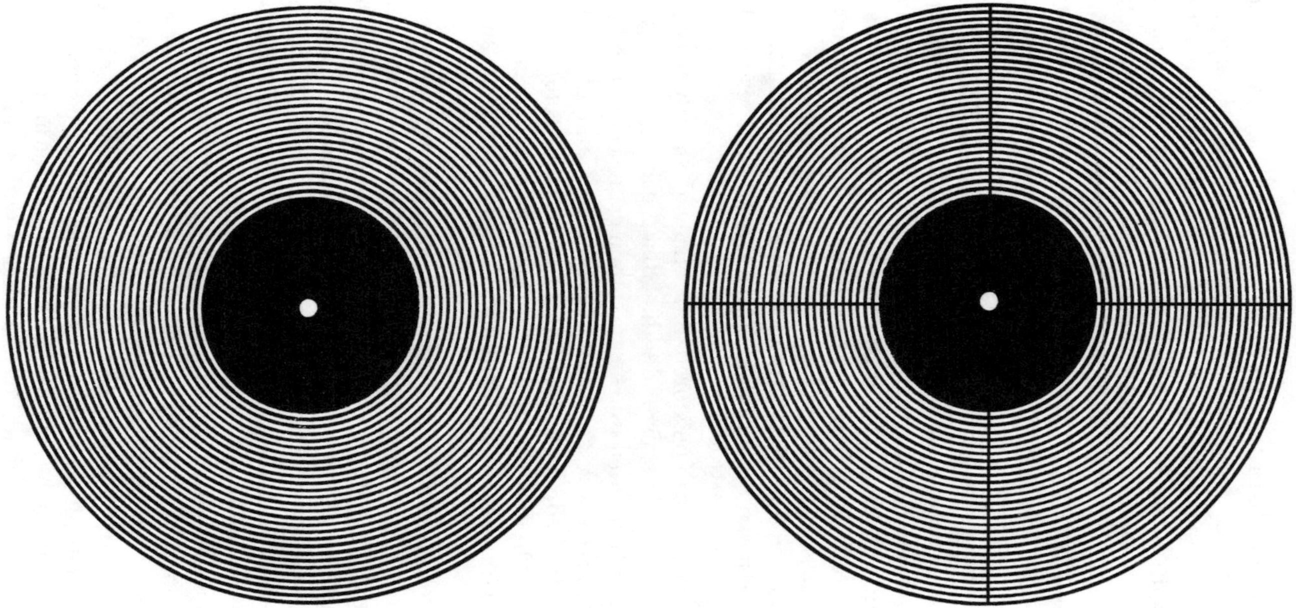

(A) (B)

Figure 3.5 Magnetic disk. (A) Tracks. (B) Sectors.

on these devices, the disks revolve on spindles at very high speeds. Read/write mechanisms are positioned on access arms a fraction of a centimeter above the surface and move back and forth across the tracks to record or pick up data. The devices that hold disk packs have a number of read/write mechanisms that move in parallel with one another; that is, when one moves, they all move. This movement of electromechanical access arms is extremely slow when compared to the purely electronic speeds at which data is moved around in primary storage. Much effort in both hardware and software design is expended attempting to minimize the movement of access arms. For example, when disk packs are used, data recording is done from one track to another in a perpendicular rather than parallel fashion; that is, when one track is filled, the next track used is the one below rather than the one next to the filled track. In this way, when moving to the next track, no arm motion is necessary. Data recorded in such a way employs what is known as a cylinder of data. Sets of tracks that are perpendicular to one another on a pack make up cylinders. A pack with surfaces that have 200 tracks has 200 cylinders.

Data stored on disk can be stored and retrieved directly because it can be located by an address. On individual disks, each track has an address. If the tracks are divided into sectors, then each sector also has an address. For example, track 37, sector 3, might have an address 0373. When stored or retrieved, the string of data on track 37, sector 3, would be read or written. On disk packs, each surface and cylinder has an address. For example, surface 13, cylinder 86, would have an address 13,086.

Data that is to be stored and retrieved directly can and often is kept on-line; that is, it is kept on disks or disk packs that reside permanently on disk drives that are wired to the computer. Whenever an update is made or a request issued, the required file or database record(s) can be retrieved from secondary storage to primary storage within a few seconds. Data stored on disk does not have to be kept on-line; however, disks, especially the "floppies" used on small computers, are inserted and removed from their drives on a regular basis. In a large- or medium-scale configuration, data is stored on disk so that it can be readily available when needed. Many configurations of this type are rarely turned off. They are kept running twenty-four hours a day, seven days a week. Data that does not have to be readily available can be stored on reels of magnetic tapes which can be removed from the machine and stored in a tape library. On the other hand, disks are used with small computers not only to make data readily available, but also to save it when the machine is turned off. Small configurations used by individual analysts or programmers are frequently turned off, and when they are off the information in primary storage disappears. Any information that is to be retained has to be written to secondary storage before the machine is turned off. Because of its superior reliability, the secondary storage frequently used with small computers is diskette. How disk storage is utilized depends on the application. Data can be stored and retrieved directly using disk, or it can be stored and retrieved serially using disk.

With magnetic tape, however, there is no choice. With magnetic tape, data is stored and retrieved serially. There are no tracks or sectors or addresses on magnetic tape. Data is stored in strings of contiguous records with small gaps between them corresponding to the size of the area (buffer) in primary storage from which the string was originally written. Updating of serially recorded data, in terms of updating (adding records), requires a complete recopying of the file, since there is no way to insert a new record between two contiguous records. In most situations, unless some conditions demand otherwise, most serial data recording is done on magnetic tape because it is less expensive than disk. Serial data recording is commonly used for sequential files.

Computer storage, both primary and secondary, is used to hold both sets of data to be operated on, and sets of instructions that tell the computer what to do with the sets of data. Both the sets of instructions and the sets of data (let's call them *data sets*) are transferred from secondary to primary storage as they are needed. For instance, a set of instructions (a computer program) to do gross to net calculations would be called into primary storage on, say, Tuesday nights, as one of a series of payroll tasks required to prepare paychecks, registers, and so forth. Employee data would also be brought into primary storage and the calculations would be performed on that data. Visualize a payroll clerk at a work station. No computer. Next to the desk is a file, a set of cards, with each card containing payroll master information for each employee. A file of employee time cards is brought to the clerk. Processing for this payroll would be done serially. Also, to facilitate things, the files are both sequentially ordered by employee number in ascending sequence, that is lowest number first, second lowest and so on up to the highest (00016, 00140, 00152. . . ., 99413). The clerk picks up the time cards one at a time sequentially, finds the matching payroll master, and using a calculator, computes a gross to net for each employee and prepares a check and a payroll register entry. A computer program processes data in a similar fashion. Input is a payroll master card or record and a time card or record, processing is gross to net and output is a check and a line on a payroll register.

OUTPUT

The output function is a combination of electronic equipment and circuitry and computer instructions that perform the tasks necessary to get information out of the computer in a format useful to those using it.

The equipment used for output is identical to that used for input with one exception, high speed line printers that produce printed reports, but that have no input capabilities. Output displays on CRT screens and the slower printouts on typewriter terminals are used primarily for interactive data entry and direct retrieval of information. In small computer configurations the CRT and its keyboard serve as a single input and output mechanism, while larger configurations include numerous CRT devices, typewriter terminals, and line printers. A line printer is pictured in Figure 3.6.

COMMUNICATIONS AMONG COMPUTER COMPONENTS

Communication links connect equipment components. These components may be geographically local or remote to one another. For instance, many computer configurations have their components connected to one another by means of a device known as a bus. There are a number of kinds of buses, but it is basically a subassembly into which the functional components are plugged. The bus becomes the communication channel among the processor, storage, and input/output devices. This kind of arrangement is local. In large-scale computer configurations there may be several bus type subassemblies that are often called channels. Such channels frequently have capacity for connecting a couple of hundred secondary storage and input/output devices to the

Figure 3.6 Line printer.

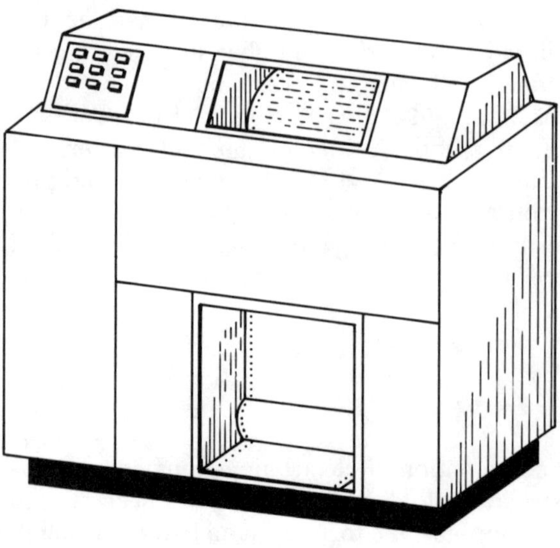

processor and primary storage. Within the channel itself, there is a small processor that initiates, regulates, and terminates the data flow between the secondary storage and input/output devices and the main processor and primary storage.

Remote communication accommodates links between computer configurations and components that are physically too far apart to be joined by buses or channels. Length restrictions for cabling by means of buses or channels vary, but where communication is required and cabling is impossible or infeasible, the facilities of a common carrier such as a telephone company line or a satellite may be used. Descriptions of the facilities offered and the technology afforded in the field of data communications can and has filled volumes. The objective here is to provide a brief survey. Terms like teleprocessing, telecommunications, data communications, and distributed processing frequently imply the facilities and technology associated with moving data and information among computer equipment configurations by means of common carrier facilities.

Basically, communication between two components geographically remote from each other, say a computer and an input/output terminal device, can be accommodated by means of a dedicated line or by means of a dial-up facility. Direct communication is an arrangement whereby the common carrier provides a connection between the input/output terminal device and the computer that is constantly present; that is, the terminal, for all practical purposes, can be thought of as "hard-wired" to the computer. Since there is often an incompatibility between the way common carrier facilities move data and the way computer equipment carries it, a device called a modem is often used to translate. The schematic in Figure 3.7 illustrates the place of a modem in a computer/communication configuration. Figure 3.8 contains sketches of some typical modems.

In those situations where the need for communication facilities is sporadic and the volumes of data are insufficient to justify the cost of a

Figure 3.7 A direct-line telecommunications arrangement.

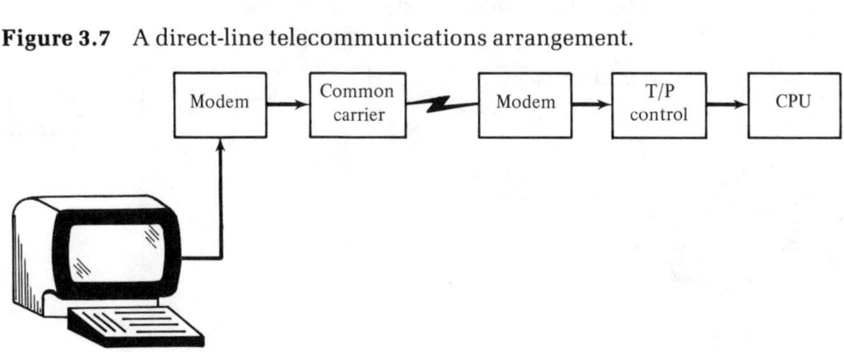

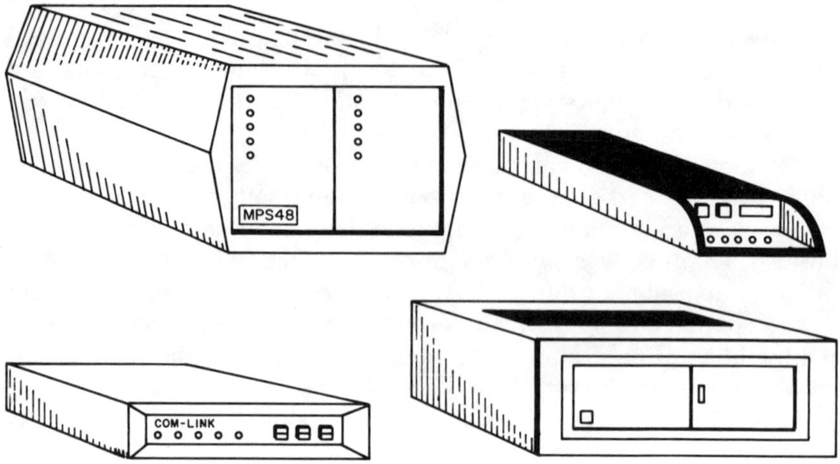

Figure 3.8 Modems in various shapes and sizes.

dedicated line, a dial-up arrangement can be used. A dial-up arrangement is one in which the common carrier makes available a connection between the input/output terminal device and the computer on an as-needed basis. For all practical purposes, it is just like a telephone call made from one individual to another. Quite often, telephone instruments are used to establish, maintain, and terminate the connection. Figure 3.9 illustrates this schematically.

The terminal devices used in communications arrangements are virtually identical to those described as input/output devices. The difference may be in some minor switch settings or wiring linkages within the device.

There is one more piece of equipment that is frequently found in configurations of equipment in which there are many terminals. Known as controllers or control units, these pieces of equipment are used as buffers and control mechanisms between the terminal devices

Figure 3.9 A dial-up telecommunications arrangement.

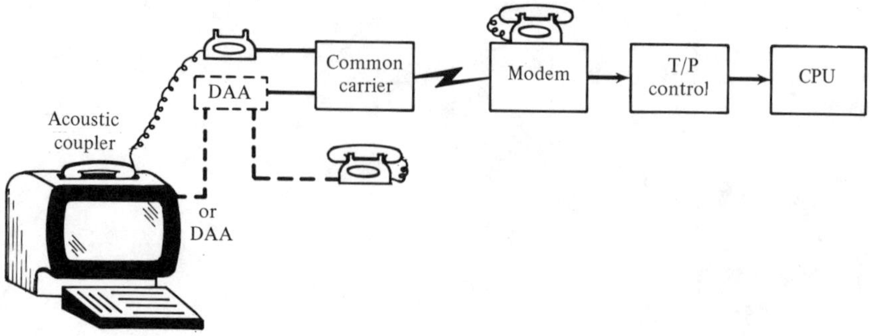

and the computer. Some types of controllers generally have a number of terminal devices attached to them, and they provide for an orderly flow of information between the terminals and the computer. Without controllers the flow of information would be haphazard, somewhat like a meeting without a chairman where everybody is trying to talk at the same time. In addition to the types of controllers having terminals attached to them, there are other types that act as buffers and control mechanisms between secondary storage devices, that is, disk and tape devices, and the computer. Still others are used between communications lines and the computer and perform the same buffering and control functions. These latter are often called teleprocessing control units, while the former are called, appropriately, tape controllers or disk controllers. Control units for terminals are called terminal control units.

HARDWARE AND SOFTWARE

The computer equipment just described is frequently referred to individually and collectively as hardware. Software is a term used to describe data stored on computer equipment and computer programs which are made up of sets of instructions that tell the computer configuration what to do. Stated another way, software is made up of data and the instructions which direct the computer configurations to store, retrieve, manipulate, and display information. Software includes computer files, programs to process payrolls, programs to produce checks, programs to relieve inventory, programs to enter orders, and programs to record journal entries. These are known as application programs. There are also programs to store records in files and databases and retrieve records from files and databases, to coordinate the activities of several concurrently executing programs within a computer, and to handle the information traffic coming in from and going out on communication lines. These are known as system programs. Subsequent chapters deal in detail with both types of software.

SUMMARY

This chapter has dealt essentially with computer equipment, hardware. We have shown that computer configurations—large, medium, or small—are made up of the same functions, with components varying in quantity, depending upon the size of the computer. The design and development of new computer equipment is constantly leading to newer, faster, smaller, and less expensive machines, making terms like minicomputer and microcomputer quite imprecise, if not irrelevant. Five essential functions, *input*, *processor*, *storage*, *control*, and *output* were explained, and the most commonly used components were mentioned and illustrated. Also receiving attention was communications equipment that is now commonplace as computers "talk to" one another.

CHAPTER 4

System Software

SOFTWARE IN GENERAL—HOW IT EVOLVED

This book deals with the realization of potential. In the first two chapters we looked at information and data, and in the third chapter we examined equipment, which is known in the vernacular of computers as hardware. Software, in the vernacular of computers, is everything but the equipment. Information and data—when transcribed to computer storage—and the sets of instructions that store, manipulate, retrieve, and display that information and data are both software. What makes the task of information systems so dynamic is the constantly changing nature of both the hardware and the software.

Primitive electronic computers were able to perform arithmetic operations on data where both the data and the instructions had been entered into storage by the engineers and scientists who had designed and built the computers. It was an extremely tedious task. There was nothing even resembling the software and input/output equipment we know today. Since electronic computers ultimately reduce everything to binary arithmetic, that is, to zeros (0) and ones (1), the individuals who developed the first computers had to enter data and instructions into the computer in binary by means of switches. The output produced by the computer was also in binary form, and the scientists and engineers were required to translate the zeros and ones into meaningful decimal information. At that point in time, the theoretical distinction between data (zeroes and ones) and information (decimal representation) was less subtle. It soon became obvious that unless better ways of interacting with them were developed, computers would never catch on despite their potential. Well, as the saying goes: "We've come a long way, baby!" Hardware improvements were made, but they were merely extensions of the electronic and mechanical engineering that had gone into computers themselves. The biggest improvements of all included the development of the transistor and semiconductor technology, but even these developments were merely extensions of the potential offered by the hardware. The most important strides made toward realizing the potential offered by the hardware were and continue to be in the area of software. No matter how fast, inexpensive, or small the hardware, it would be impossible to accomplish what can be done by manipulating zeros and ones. It is in the area of software that the man/machine interface has been improved to the point where anybody who has the interest can learn within a few hours how to interact with computers. The whole thrust of software is to make it easier for individuals to realize the potential of computers.

Software is a reflection of the minds of individuals. Data and information are representations of individuals' perceptions of reality. Computer programs, the sets of instructions that tell computer configurations what to do, are merely directions given to machines by individuals. Some data elements are relatively static, others are dynamic. Some computer equipment activities are repetitive and remain essentially the same, requiring fairly static sets of instructions that are executed over and over again, day in and day out. Other activities that a computer configuration might be required to perform are rather unpredictable and only periodically repetitive. Those that are repetitive and essentially the same are temporary because over time, they are replaced by hardware components. The repetitive sets of instructions make up what is known as systems software. The periodically repetitive sets of instructions make up what is known as application software.

To understand this a little better, let's go through a short and somewhat oversimplified historical narrative. The earliest computers were developed by scientists and engineers primarily for their computational ability. These early computers were able to perform rather complex calculations on relatively small amounts of data. At that point in time there was no distinction between systems software and application software. In fact, the term software had not yet been coined. The strain of human nerves that resulted from entering data and instructions in binary soon led the computer pioneers to develop what are known as mnemonic languages, assemblers, and compilers. With mnemonics, which take the form of letters and digits, it became possible to deal with computers using a more familiar and comprehensive set of symbols. For example, the letter A might mean add or the letter M might mean move. These were significantly easier to use than their binary equivalents, which would be represented as a combination of zeroes and ones. The assemblers were themselves sets of instructions (programs) which were used to translate the mnemonics of the scientist or the user into the binary representations required by the computer. After this came the more sophisticated compilers, which were able to translate statements in the form of mathematical formulas into the binary form executed by the computer. FORTRAN was one of the first compilers. It was so successful initially that it continues to be widely used. FORTRAN is an acronym for the two words *for*mula *tran*slation. The term software came into use and the distinction between applications software and systems software began to appear. Those who developed the programs made up of mathematical formulas that were then compiled into executable form and then executed to produce some desired result for an engineer or scientist were *applying* computer technology to something. Hence, the term application programming. Those who developed the compilers themselves were involved in improving the capabilities of computers by making them easier to use and by increasing the services of computers. This was and continues to be the thrust of systems software.

Prior to the early 1960s, most computers were able to hold and execute only one program at a time. When operating systems, or control programs as they are also known, came on the scene, all that changed. Hardware advances and software enhancements together made it possible; computers with operating systems were able to store and execute two or more programs concurrently. Following quickly after the emergence of operating systems, there came telecommunications, virtual storage, database management, and interactive systems. Those who labor at developing, maintaining, and supporting products of this type are known as system programmers. The development of systems software products has as its objectives, increasing the overall capability of computer configurations and making it easier to use computer facilities. For the remainder of this chapter, we'll examine system software in some detail. In the next chapter, we'll have a look at application software.

OPERATING SYSTEMS OR CONTROL PROGRAMS

Operating Systems in General

An *operating system** is a collection of programs that ties together, manages, and controls the interaction of the hardware and software

*For the sake of editorial simplicity and ease of reading, the one term operating system is used from here on out.

components of a computer configuration. An operating system is generally made up of two components: the monitor, sometimes called the supervisor or the executive, and the utilities. The monitor interfaces between application programs, the utilities, and the hardware. Application programs execute under the control of the monitor and in execution, they may use facilities of the monitor. The utilities provide services to application programs. For example, operating systems utilities frequently contain preprogrammed and precompiled routines which are able to transfer records between primary and secondary storage. When an application programmer is coding a program and comes to a point where a data transfer is required, he/she can prepare a statement containing a "READ" or "WRITE" operation instruction and a few parameters such as the name of the file, the name of the work area in primary storage where records are held, and the location within the records of the key. When the programmer is finished coding the program and it is being compiled, the compiler includes within the program the routines needed to transfer records. Figure 4.1 is a schematic showing the relationships among an operating system, application programs, hardware, and utilities.

There is a wide range in the scope, size, and complexity of operating systems. Quite obviously, the larger the equipment configuration supported and the greater the facilities offered, the larger and more complicated is the operating system. There are, however, functional similarities in all operating systems. All operating systems consist of a monitor, alternatively known as a supervisor or executive, and utilities. The monitor "owns" the computer configuration resources and provides the interface between the user, the hardware, and the application. The utility programs are provided to aid users in the development of applications and to facilitate the management of files and databases.

Figure 4.1 The essentials of a computer system.

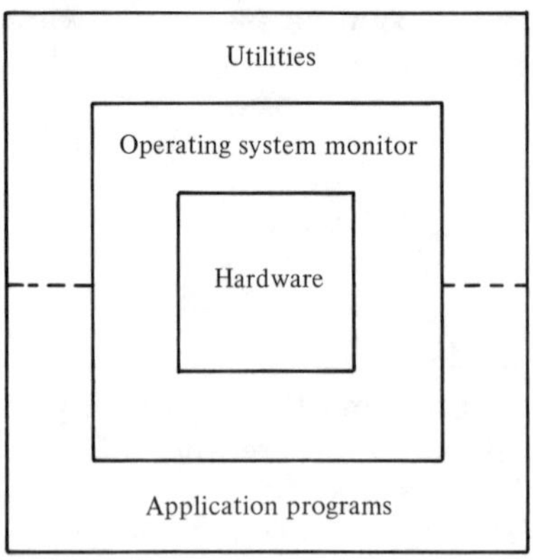

Operating Systems for Small Computer Configurations

Small personal computers often use relatively simple operating systems such as the one known as CP/M. The acronym stands for control program for microcomputers. While it is not the only operating system used on small personal computer configurations, it is one of the most widely known and used.

Small personal computers usually consist of a CRT and keyboard for input/output, a printer for output, one or more floppy disk drives and/or a tape cassette recorder to be used as secondary storage, and possibly a communications adapter for interconnections with other computers. Operating systems like CP/M consist of the two primary components, the monitor and the integrated set of utilities.

On a small personal computer, the monitor can be easily loaded. This operation is usually as simple as inserting the floppy disk containing the operating system into a drive and depressing a specific function key on the keyboard. A simple program called a bootstrap loader, or more simply, a boot, that is quite often part of the computer circuitry, reads the operating system from the diskette and positions it in primary storage. Once loaded, an operating system like CP/M "sets up house," so to speak, a process known as initialization and gets ready to initiate and control the execution of an application program and to prioritize and control input/output operations.

The utility programs of small operating systems like CP/M include those that aid in program development and those which provide for file management. Program development utilities include assemblers, compilers, linkers, editors, debugging aids, and interpreters. Assemblers and compilers translate entire programs from user statements into computer executable instructions. Linkers tie separate modules together, that is, an input/output routine joined to an application program. Editors are program statements and word processing syntax checkers. Debugging aids are used by programmers to isolate errors when developing and testing programs. Interpreters translate user statements, one at a time, into computer executable form as the program is executing.

File or data management utilities, those used for copying files, deleting files, renaming files, printing files, and checking status, are included in small operating systems like CP/M.

Operating Systems on Large-Scale Configurations

At the other end of the spectrum are the operating systems that are required to support large-scale computer configurations. Of these, the most commonly known is one of IBM's operating systems. It has been known by various acronyms, including OS, MVT, MFT, and most recently OS/VS or MVS. Given IBM's penchant for attempting to provide as many facilities as possible to as many users as possible through the use of generalized software, IBM's operating system may be the most comprehensive and complex of all.

In addition to providing the same type of facilities as CP/M, the IBM operating system makes it possible for a large-scale computer to perform several tasks (programs) concurrently. The IBM operating system is somewhat like a supervisor or a foreman in a factory/warehouse complex. The supervisor directs the activities that are taking place, such as the machine setups, the retrieval of new materials and components from the stockrooms, the placing of some finished goods into the warehouse, the shipping of other finished goods to customers, the handling of exceptional situations, and providing a channel of communication among the various functional departments within the complex. A number of tasks are being carried on concurrently within the complex that are partially directed, monitored, and controlled by the supervisor or foreman. It is the control program or operating system that partially directs, monitors, and controls the activity in a computer configuration.

The IBM operating system consists of three basic functions:

1. Job management
2. Task management
3. Data management

Using the factory/warehouse analogy, job management involves what the foreman does to get work done. For example, one job might consist of all the steps needed to put together, package, and load 100 carburetors onto a truck. Another job might consist of all the steps required to try out a newly developed process for testing voltage regulators. A third job might involve unloading a truck that has arrived with several kinds of subassemblies needed for the fabrication of other finished goods. The process that the foreman goes through to see that all these things are started, kept moving, and finished represent *job management.* In a computer environment, jobs might include: running a batch payroll process, from time card input to check and register preparation; the compilation, linking, and testing of a newly written program; and periodially updating an inventory master file with transactions reflecting activity taking place as operators make entries through CRT terminals.

Task management involves initiating and terminating the individual chores that must be completed to finish the jobs. In the factory/warehouse situation tasks include: machine setups and machine operations in carburetor construction, making sure the receiving area is ready to handle the incoming subassemblies and having men and equipment available to test the voltage regulators. In a computer environment tasks might include: making a space available on magnetic disk on which to sort payroll records that are to be used to print registers and checks, starting up processing region in main storage to handle the inventory updating transactions as they arrive and invoking the compiler for a program that is to be compiled.

Data management entails the transfer of needed elements between where they are stored and where they are needed. In the factory/warehouse, this might mean getting some linkages, screws, and flanges that are used to make carburetors, moving subassemblies from a truck to a storage location in a warehouse, and storing tested voltage regulators in boxes after they have been checked out. The management of data in a computer configuration consists of reading records from a payroll master file, storing a compiled computer program in a special data set called a library, and reading transactions containing inventory update information from a computer network.

In an elaborate operating system like IBM's, there are other features and facilities. For example, the *library* mentioned in the preceding paragraph is one of several found within an operating system. Their function is to store programs and procedures that are used periodically on a recurring basis. For example, a procedure to compile, link, and perform a test execution of a computer program is stored in one type of library, while the actual programs for doing the compilation and linkage are stored in another. Think of libraries as a set of cookbooks containing hundreds of recipes. As the chef needs a recipe, he retrieves it, executes the instructions contained in it, and then stores it for future use. A *catalog*, another facility of IBM's operating system, is simply a directory to the programs and procedures stored in the libraries, not unlike the card catalog found in an ordinary public library.

The equivalent of the file or data management utilities found in CP/M are the access methods found in IBM's operating system. The transfer of data between primary storage and secondary storage or I/O devices on communications networks is the function of *access methods*. Figure 4.2 helps to convey the concept. Access method, however, is an imprecise term. The software, that is, programs, comprising an access method can be numbered between several modules and hundreds of modules.* The basic instruction set for simple access methods is "READ" a unit of data and "WRITE" a unit of data. The read and write operation involves transferring a single unit of data, commonly known as logical record, between some device and primary storage or between secondary storage and primary storage. Examples of logical records include a payroll master record for a single individual, a sales record for a

*Module is a set of instructions to perform a specific task.

single point of sale transaction or a single line of information to be printed on a high speed printing device. Access methods that transfer single logical records are known as basic access methods. *B*asic *s*equential *a*ccess *m*ethod (BSAM), for transferring single records serially from or to a sequential file or data set, is an example of a basic access method. Others are *b*asic *d*irect *a*ccess *m*ethod (BDAM), *b*asic *t*elecommunications *a*ccess *m*ethod (BTAM), and *b*asic *p*artitioned *a*ccess *m*ethod (BPAM). BDAM is used to select specific records to be transferred to or from direct access files, BTAM initiates the transfer of records between devices in a telecommunications network and primary storage, and BPAM is used primarily to transfer records between libraries and primary storage. Access methods increase in complexity up to a point where they become data management or communications network management systems. These and their associated access methods handle records and transactions in groups, known as blocks or control intervals.

Figure 4.2 Access methods.

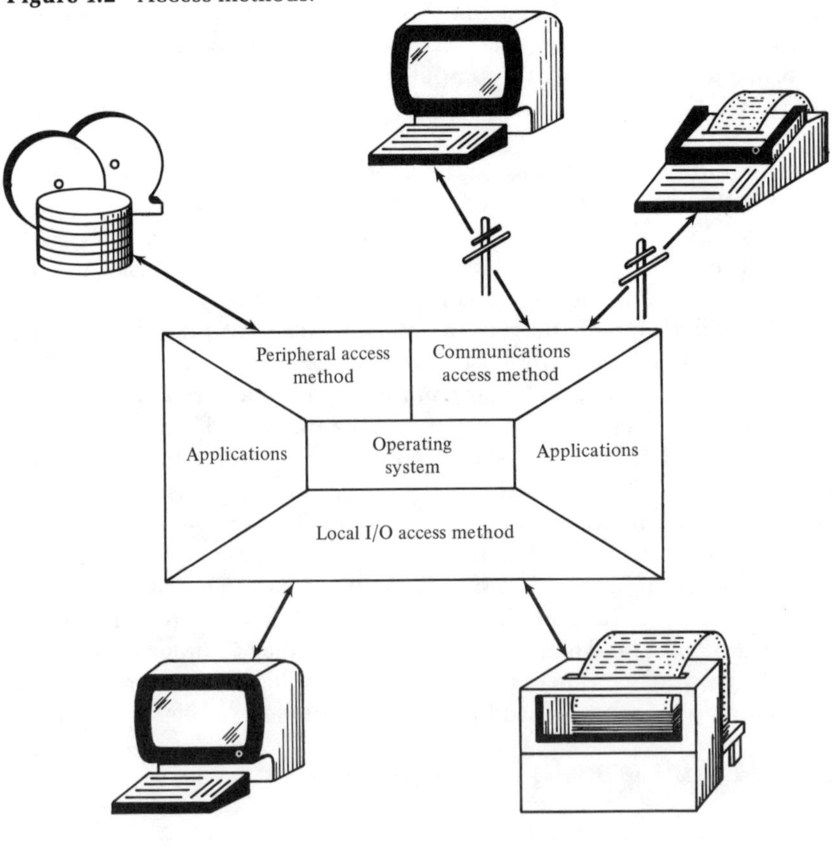

For IBM's operating system to function properly, it has to be given instructions. These instructions come in the form of job control language statements commonly known as JCL. JCL, while not the same thing as a computer program, is nonetheless a way in which individuals communicate with a computer. It is through job control language that a computer is told what programs are to be executed, the sequence in which they are to be executed, the files and data sets that are required, and to some degree what to do if certain criteria are not met when programs complete their execution. The difference between a set of program instructions and a set of JCL instructions is similar to the difference between the detailed instructions describing how to prepare veal parmigiana (a program) and the instructions on how to put on a banquet for a hundred people (JCL).

In addition to operating systems and their facilities, there are many other systems software products found in a typical computer installation. The quantity and the complexity of these products varies. Some products are found in virtually all installations, others in the more elaborate computer environments.

DATABASE/DATA COMMUNICATION SYSTEMS

Database, the Passive

The next area of system software we wish to examine is that of the combined technologies of database and data communications. Let's start with some definitions. In terms of software, a database is a passive element; it is acted upon. A database management system, on the other hand, is an active element; it acts upon the database. In Chapter 2, we defined a database as a collection of data elements among which there are relationships that transcend file and record boundaries. In other words, data elements that are part of one record can be related to data elements that are parts of other records, in other files. The relationships and the mechanics of database were also discussed in Chapter 2.

Within this chapter, we wish to describe database management system components and the mechanics of how these components are used by file and database design technicians, frequently known as database administrators.

Database Management System, the Active

Database management system products are made up of computer programs that enable users to: (1) define database structures and (2) store, manipulate, and retrieve information from those database structures. All database management systems have what are known as *d*ata *d*efinition *l*anguage (DDL) and *d*ata *m*anipulation *l*anguage (DML) facilities. It is these two separate facilities that are used to define database structures and to perform data storage, manipulation, and retrieval activities.

It all works something like this. A technically skilled individual, frequently known as a database administrator, defines database structures that are both global and specific, using the data definition language facility of the database management system product. The global definitions define an entire database, while the specific definitions define the portions of a database required by a specific program or application. The terms used to describe these two definitions are schema (global) and subschema (specific). The different definitions are like the blueprints for a building. The architect designs a complete building (schema) and yet there is a separate blueprint (subschema) for each type of craftsman. There's a blueprint for the plumbers, another for the electricians, another for the heating and air-conditioning mechanics, and yet another for the carpenters.

After the database administrators make their specifications, the specifications are compiled into a form recognizable to a computer. They are then stored in libraries, in both forms. Those in computer-recognizable form are incorporated (linked) into computer programs that must access the databases to get information for processing. The input/output instructions in those programs use the data manipulation language facility of the database management system to access the information in the databases.

Data Communications, the Immediate

Database management can function as a stand-alone batch processing facility, or it can be integrated or interfaced with a data communications facility and thereby acquire the capability to perform input/output activity directly against databases that are on-line. The integration or interfacing of database management and data communications facilities adds significantly toward realizing the potential of database technology, since it permits users to develop programs that can update or retrieve information in databases within seconds.

Data communications is very likely the most complex system software component of all. The programs within a typical data communications product have to deal with a communications network that may contain thousands of different devices of perhaps twenty-five or thirty different types. These devices may be attached to a few hundred communications lines that connect these devices to one or more computer configurations. In a distributed environment there may even be two, three, or even ten or twenty computer configurations interconnected by communications lines. The software that manages all the traffic that moves across all these lines between terminal devices and computers and between one computer and another is a data communications product. OK, so much for the "Gee Whiz, Holy Cow"; let's take a closer look at how such a product works.

The schematic in Figure 4.3 depicts a computer configuration in which the components of a data communications product are shown. The software of a data communications product (sometimes called a monitor) consists of several functions. Notice in the schematic that the traffic travels through the front-end computer (data communications controller), not directly between the host (main computer) and the terminal devices. For the sake of clarity, the two terminal devices pictured represent the hundreds or even thousands that may be present in a contemporary data communications environment. Also, for the sake of clarity, modems are not included in the schematic.

In a typical data communications monitor there is a function which causes the host computer to periodically poll each terminal device in the network to find out if it has anything to send. Appropriately enough this activity is called *polling*.

The *network control function* contains a list of all the devices that can send transactions to the host. The list includes the logical name of each device and its physical characteristics. The logical name is needed

Figure 4.3 A computer with data communications facilities.

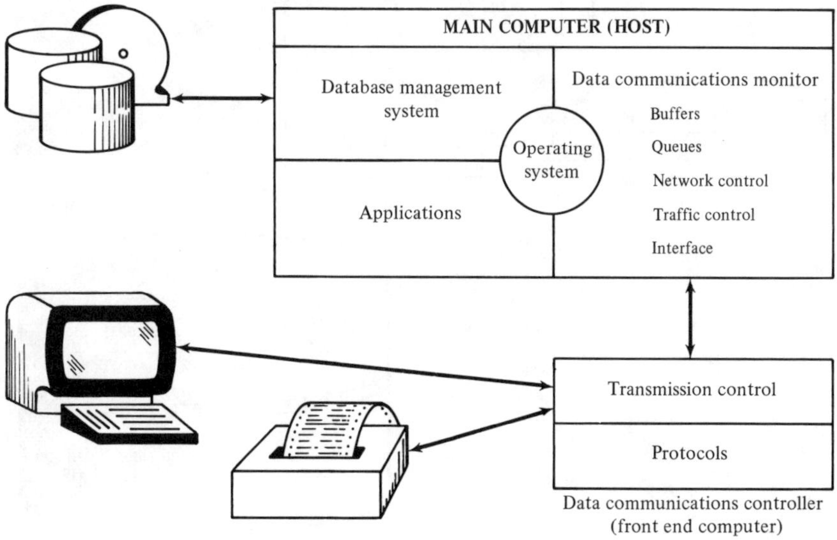

so that when a transaction comes in, the monitor can know where to send the response. This can be something of a complicated task, since it is quite likely that several hundred of the devices may be sending transactions at virtually the same time.

The traffic controller manages all the transactions coming in and going out. Since the host processor can only do one thing at a time, the traffic controller is obliged to manage queues. *Queues* are basically waiting lists that transactions enter when they are waiting to be serviced or waiting to be returned to devices. Incoming transactions are put on input queues, and the interface determines the application program that is needed to perform the activity triggered by the transactions. The interface initiates the appropriate application program and retrieves the transaction from the input queue and passes it to that program. Other programs within both the database management system and the data communications monitor have the capability of processing several transactions concurrently. Physical data records are retrieved from databases in secondary storage in response to the transactions and are stored in input buffers. Specific logical data elements are retrieved from the buffers for the transactions as they are needed. Figure 4.4 illustrates. Specific data elements that have been updated are placed in output buffers from which they are written back to secondary storage. Out-

Figure 4.4 The function of a buffer in data transfer.

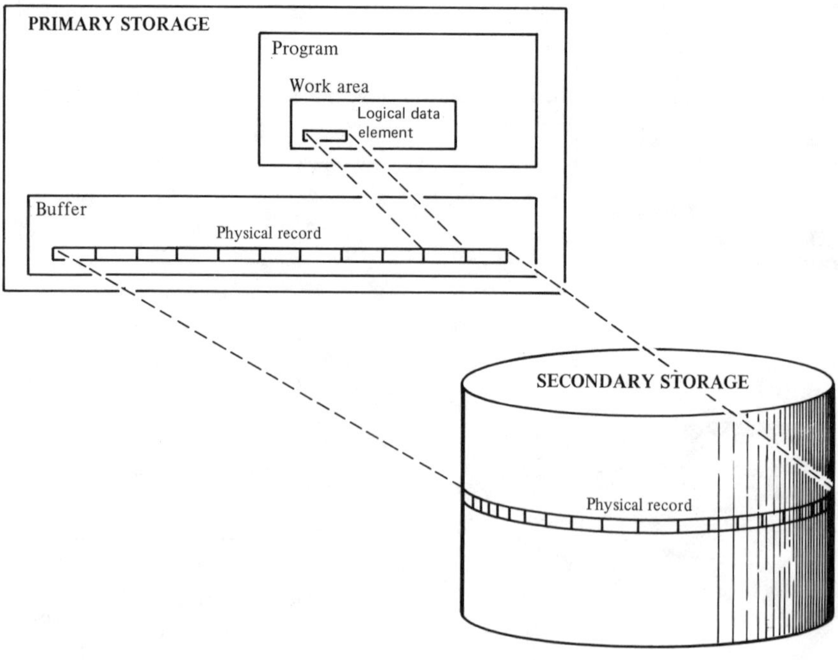

going transactions or messages are placed in output queues at an appropriate time determined by the traffic controller.

All of the activity just described goes on in the host (the main computer). There is other activity that goes on in the front-end (data communications controller) computer.

The transmission control component, in the front-end computer, works in conjunction with the traffic controller in the host. Basically, the transmission controller manages the traffic coming in and going out on the communications lines. Output, that is, transmission of response transactions, has priority over input, so that when polling takes place, the host and the front-end send responses before they accept input messages. Transmissions from an individual device, for example, are controlled by locking the keyboard after a transaction is accepted by the front end and the host. The keyboard is unlocked after a response is returned to the device.

Protocols are mutually agreed upon conventions that computer configuration components are obligated to abide by, if they are to communicate with one another. There may be several levels of protocol, including character structure, (e.g., seven-bit ASCII or eight-bit EBCDIC*), type of transmission, asynchronous or synchronous,† type of message format, and so on. These protocols are analogous to the conventions that individuals are obliged to follow when communicating with one another. For example, to place a telephone call to an individual in another state, it is necessary to dial or push ten digits on an instrument. In another situation, it might be necessary for two individuals from different countries to speak to one another in a commonly understood third language.

It remains tempting to say "Gee Whiz, Holy Cow," again, but, as they used to say in Brooklyn: "You ain't seen nothin' yet." The software necessary to support data communications with a single host and a few thousand terminal devices and a couple of hundred lines is, as you have just seen, rather complicated. However, suppose there are several computers, some of which communicate with one another and, on top of that, suppose that each of the several computers is to act as a backup in the event that one of the computers breaks down. And it's still not fin-

*ASCII is an acronym for American National Standard Code for Information Interchange, a standard code using a seven-bit code for characters. EBCDIC is an acronym for extended binary-coded decimal interchange code, a coded character set consisting of eight-bit coded characters.

†ASYNCHRONOUS is a method of data transmission where each character sent is individually synchronized, by the use of start/stop indicators. Synchronous is a method of data transmission where sending and receiving equipment components are continuously kept in synchronization by means of periodic checks and corrections. Asynchronous transmission is generally used by relatively low-speed devices, while synchronous transmission is employed by higher-speed devices.

ished. Add to this further complexity the fact that built into most data communications software products are a significant number of error recovery routines (programs). These are capable of giving a computer configuration the potential to recover from error conditions in such a way that the user of the system is unaware of what is taking place.

A Short Commentary on Database/Data Communications

By and large, database/data communications software products work and work well. Since they are extremely large in terms of function and number of instructions, they are developed and programmed by literally hundreds of individuals working in tandem. Specific modules are worked on and tested by individual analysts and programmers, all of whom are either employed by or contracted by the vendor of the product. As the individual analysts and programmers complete work on the specific modules assigned to them, a process of integrated development and testing begins. The specific modules are linked together by means of software interfaces and then tested as a unit. Depending upon the size and complexity of the product, there may be a few or several levels of integrated testing by a number of different teams of analysts and programmers. Eventually the process is complete. Because of the complexity of the products and also because of the virtually limitless number of combination of conditions that could conceivably occur, it is naive to assume that new database/data communications products or new releases of existing products are shipped to customers totally error-free.* Therefore, database/data communications products are shipped with errors (bugs) in them. However, in spite of the bugs, the products perform most of their functions according to specifications, and the combined efforts of the vendor's field support technicians and systems software technicians of the organization using the product are sufficient to either fix the errors as they occur or to work around them until they can be fixed.

The major difficulty in working with database/data communications products is not technical, it is managerial. Generally speaking, technical skills alone are insufficient to the task of maintaining a smoothly functioning database/data communications system environment. Other skills, administrative and organizational, are required. Ordinarily, those with technical skills are interested in employing those skills. There is also usually more than enough work to do with those

*Tracy Kidder's book *The Soul of the New Machine* is a fascinating narrative describing the development and testing of a new piece of hardware (a computer). Software development and testing is conceptually similar.

skills, and the administrative and organizational tasks are frequently minimized and given secondary consideration by technicians. Mundane tasks such as performing the necessary maintenance required to keep correlation tables current do not challenge system software technicians. And yet, this work has to be done. In any database/data communications system environment, some individual or group of individuals has to specify the relationships that exist in that particular environment. The database/data communications system product merely provides the potential for any user to use any device to access any application. The authorizations specifying who can use what device to access which application have to be specified by a database/data communications technician. Terms like "user ID" (pronounced *eye dee*), "password," "transaction ID," "terminal ID," are used to indicate the variables that must be specified and correlated in a typical database/data communications system environment.

INTERACTIVE SYSTEMS

Interactive systems are products that are interfaced with or are an integrated part of an operating system. They sometime include a problem-oriented programming language. The objective of interactive systems is to simplify the process of developing applications for computers.

Throughout the 1960s and the early 1970s, application programming involved the writing (coding) of program statements onto coding sheets, about twenty-five statements to a page. Depending upon the size and complexity of the program and the type of programming language used, the number of coding sheets required to complete a program may have been anywhere between half a dozen and a few hundred. As coding sheets were finished, they were forwarded to a keypunch operation where they were transcribed onto computer-readable media, such as eighty-column cards, or a little later on, magnetic tape. When an entire program had been transcribed, it was then read into a computer for compilation. Testing, debugging, and recompilations followed with the same series of steps: programmers wrote on coding sheets, keypunch operators transcribed the instructions to cards or tape, and so on. It was to counteract the inefficiencies of this methodology that interactive application programming development systems were introduced. These products are considered to be system software because they promote more efficient use of computer resources, and they require the support of system software technicians.

An interactive system allows programmers to code, test, and debug programs through a CRT or a typewriter terminal device. One of the most widely known interactive facilities is IBM's *t*ime *s*haring *o*ption of its operating system. Known by its acronym, TSO, this interactive system facilitates program development by making it possible for application programmers to code programs in whatever language they choose, Assembler, COBOL, PL/1,* FORTRAN, BASIC, and so on, using terminal devices and keyboards. The programmers are also able to access files (subject to security constraints), to create files, and to produce output, using terminal devices and keyboards. Development time is reduced, since the two extra steps of keypunching and reading the cards or magnetic tape into the computer have been eliminated.

Interactive facilities are constantly being improved, as are the compilers that they support. The programming language of BASIC serves as a good example. Originally developed as an easy-to-learn, easy-to-use problem oriented language, BASIC caught on quickly. As it became increasingly popular, enhancements were made so that it could be used interactively. BASIC has become one of the most used interactive problem-oriented languages, on large-scale, medium-scale, and small personal computers. In its more sophisticated versions, each statement is syntax† checked as it is written, so that when the program is completed, it can be compiled once and be free of syntax errors. In other versions, not only is syntax checked, but each statement can be compiled and tested individually. Amazing things, these computers!

Alas, all is not well in computerland. There are some costs to be incurred for all these enhancements. The first is the cost in resources. The old, inefficient method of coding sheets, keypunching, reading programs into the computer was not unlike a dam. When interactive systems were introduced, the dam broke. Handling the torrent became the task of the interactive system, but in order to do so, a lot more hardware was required. It was not that the interactive product itself required resources, but the fact that each individual programmer required a percentage of storage and a percentage of time on the processor. For each, the percentage was small, but resource (processor and storage) utilization climbs rapidly when fifty or sixty programmers all begin using the interactive system at the same time. Trying to control or restrict usage is virtually impossible. It's like putting fifty kids in a candy factory, giving them free samples to hold, but telling them not to eat any until Christmas.

Another cost is incurred when programmers or users develop programs that access files or databases that are currently in use by produc-

*PL/1 (programming language/one) is a problem-oriented programming language for IBM machines that combines some of the qualities of a problem-oriented language with some of the qualities of an assembler language.

†Syntax—in any programming language, certain conventions must be adhered to. If not, the statement cannot be compiled, since the compiler cannot understand it.

tion applications.[†] Interactive facilities have a tendency to degrade the performance of those applications. Again, an analogy: suppose you are doing an inventory on cosmetics and toiletries in a drug store and on the same day the management decides to run a sale on lipstick, deodorant, shampoo, eye shadow, and shaving cream. A bit extreme, perhaps, but you get the drift.

A final drawback, interactive facilities because of their ease of use develop lazy programmers. In the days of coding sheets, keypunching, etc., programmers, because of relatively slow test turnaround, performed a task known as desk checking. This involved going over a program at one's desk and attempting to isolate and correct as many errors as possible between each test run. With interactive systems, it's easier to let the machine do it. There are no statistics to prove it, but there is little doubt that many unnecessary test runs are invoked because it is easy and the facility is available.*

Other Products

The development of interactive system is a definite indicator of a trend to transfer work from people to machines. It is not surprising, then, that there has been and continues to be a proliferation of computer software in most organizations. In theory, at least, it is systems software that make computers easier to use and more accessible to individuals without technical skills. On top of that, system software is required to monitor and control overall computer performance within installations housing one or more medium or large computer configurations. In an earlier chapter, we pointed out that a data dictionary system is an additional systems software component that may be necessary to support a database/data communications product. Database design aids and database prototype simulators were also mentioned as suggested support products.

Well, there are other products that are found in typical computer installations. The following list describes briefly those types of products that enhance the overall performance of a computer installation. These products are found in virtually all computer shops where two or more

[†]Production applications are those applications that are currently supporting the day-to-day operations of the organization.

*Having been a programmer myself in the Dark Ages of EDP/MIS (early and mid-1960s) and now occasionally dabbling with interactive systems and talking to contemporary programmers, I can say, with some degree of assurance, that computer resources usage for testing and development has increased dramatically because of the availability of interactive systems.

large-scale computer configurations are present. Smaller shops may contain some but not all of them.

- *On-line performance and tuning monitors.* These products are interfaced with a major software component such as an operating system or a database/data communication system. They allow systems software technicians to examine what is going on internally with a large-scale computer configuration. More sophisticated versions allow the technicians to make "on the fly" adjustments to improve performance.
- *Space management utilities.* These products provide systems software technicians with tools so that they an analyze the way secondary storage space is being allocated. These tools are indispensable in computer shops where large quantities of direct access storage devices are in use.
- *Report writers.* Generalized in nature, report writers enable application programmers or users to prepare report specifications in the form of parameters, making it possible to produce tabulations and listings without writing a program.
- *Debugging aids.* These products are especially helpful to application programmers and analysts using problem-oriented languages, in helping them isolate problems caused in malfunctioning application programs. For instance, since causes often disappear before problems become manifest, one useful debugging aid allows a programmer to put a "trace" in a program which causes it to create a file containing an audit trail of "where the program has been and what it's done."
- *Management facilities.* Daily statistics about programs are kept by these products. Included are start and stop times and resources used, such as how often a disk was accessed, how often a tape was accessed, how many lines were printed, how much processor time was used. These statistics can be used for measuring application program performances, isolating unusual situations, and as input to the resource billing.
- *Resource billing.* Users of computer resources have to pay for them. Generally, rates are determined for the variables involved. There are rates for processor usage, disk accesses, lines printed, and so on. Volume discounts may be granted. The rate schedules of service bureaus may be quite complex and subject to change. Time-sharing facilities also have rate schedules. Payment for computer services is usually in terms of the variables mentioned above and others.
- *Security.* Software security can be provided by means of products that are installed in computer configurations. Such prod-

ucts provide security for files, databases, and in some cases for programs and procedures, according to parameters selected by applications analysts or users.

- *Scheduling*. In large installations where hundreds of jobs are run daily on the computer configurations, software products are available that can assist the operations department by making some of the job scheduling functions automatic. For example, job 65327 is to be executed if and only if job 65326 completes successfully. Instructions for such a situation can be specified to scheduling products and they will be followed, unless overridden by an authorized individual.
- *Application development systems*. These products are made up of the skeletons of programs to which can be added specifications for a particular application. The results are applications developed without the skills of application programmers.

There are other products frequently found in typical computer installations. Included are:

- *Generalized sort/merge* for sorting or merging files.
- *Dump/restore* for backing up files and restoring them if necessary.
- *Inquiry facilities* for information inquiries against on-line files and databases.
- *Interactive training facilities* for preparing and using training material that is "on the computer."
- *Tape library managers* for managing a magnetic tape library.
- *Data reduction facilities* for reducing actual data stored, by means of encoding for storage and decoding for retrieval.

The types of product listed above represent the major system software facilities found in most medium- and large-scale computer environments. There are others, but mentioning and describing them all would be tedious. The objective here is to provide you with a feeling for the type of software that resides in contemporary computer installations.

SOFTWARE SUPPORT

Generations and Testing

Without software, computer equipment can do nothing. Therefore, software is a necessity. However, software requires support. The amount of support varies from one product to another, depending upon the flexibility of the product. Products that can be adjusted and fine-tuned to meet changing environmental conditions require more support than those products that cannot be adjusted and fine-tuned. Some products require a rather elaborate and involved installation and testing process, while others can be put in place rather quickly. Let's have a look at a couple of examples.

First, suppose we have an installation consisting of several large scale computer configurations including an operating system, two database/data communications systems, an interactive testing and development product, and about forty other products similar to those mentioned. Let's further suppose that a new release* of one of the database/data communications system products has been announced, ordered, and delivered. Systems software technicians are to install it.

Installing a system software product such as a database/data communication system is a process known as a system definition or a system generation. In the jargon of the systems software technicians, the process is known as a SYSGEN (pronounced *sis jen*) or more simply as a GEN (*jen*).

A GEN process begins when the database/data communications systems features arrive at the installation on a reel of magnetic tape. A set of installation manuals comes with the product. The initial steps in the GEN process have the systems software technicians copying the system from magnetic tape to disk, selecting from a list of options those features that are to be installed, and then compiling those selected features. The selected features make up the fixed portion of the database/data communication system. Following that, the dynamic portion of the system is GENd. This includes the specifications for databases, database views for particular programs and devices supported by the system. Interfaces, that is, the software bridges between the database/data communications system and other software such as the operating system, are established.

This is all followed by a period of vigorous testing in which the new release is thoroughly shaken down. All this activity is taking place while the current release of the product is in operation supporting the production requirements of the business. When the testing is completed to the satisfaction of the systems software technicians and their management, a target date is set, users are notified, and the procedures for cutover to the new release are put into place. Finally, cutover is completed. This entire process, in an environment consisting of several large scale computers and the required software support, could easily

*Complex system software products are constantly being improved and enhanced. New releases are announced periodically. An installation wishing to stay up to date and to continue receiving vendor support is obliged to install the new release.

take a couple of months. A single systems software technician could handle most of the work, interacting with others along the way.

The type of product whose installation was described in the preceding paragraph, is the type that has flexibility and lends itself to adjustments and fine-tuning once it is installed. Such products generally require a relatively long and elaborate installation process.

In our second example, let's look at the type of product that is "What you see is what you get." This type of product, once installed, is not adjustable or tunable. Some database/data communication products are of this type, so are most report writers and application development systems. The trade-off is that their installation process is relatively straightforward and simple. Quite often, the vendor sends a technical representative to install the product. This representative talks to a systems software manager, perhaps one or two of the systems software technicians and the operations manager, determines the appropriate interfaces, and then installs the product. The entire process can frequently be completed in half a day. The result is a product that performs according to specifications, but is not adjustable or tunable. If it is found that the product appears to be unfavorably impacting overall configuration performance, no "on the fly" adjustments can be made to the product to remedy this. On the other hand, the more elaborate products can often be adjusted to meet changing environmental conditions.

The Tasks of a System Software Technician

Systems software technicians are highly trained, skilled individuals whose area of expertise is in the internal workings of systems software products. It is possible, though somewhat arbitrary to divide system software support into five major categories, (1) operating systems, (2) networking or telecommunications, (3) database management, (4) interactive systems, and (5) distributed processing. While there is overlap among the categories, it is not uncommon to find systems software technicians with expertise in one, two, or three of them. It is rare that a systems software technician has in-depth experience in all five, because systems software technicians tend to specialize and most frequently their expertise is in one or perhaps two of the categories. The basic tasks of the systems software support function in all five areas is quite similar, but the particulars are very different. For instance, all system software products have to be GENd, yet the options for an operating system are different from those of a database management system, and both are different from those of telecommunications monitors.

Let's look a little closer at the tasks of the systems software technician. When systems software initially became a requirement, back in the mid-1960s, operating systems were the first product of their kind to be seen. At that time, the whole concept was new, nobody had any in-depth experience with the products, and the whole GEN, test and installation process was traumatic for the systems software technicians, for the computer installation manager, and for the users of the computer facilities. Trial and error, up and down, it was a time that all who were involved would like to forget. Things have improved substantially since then. Currently, the process of GENing, testing, and installing software products, though time consuming and detailed, is somewhat routine and can usually be performed alone by a journeyman or even by a junior system software technician, with some supervision and assistance from a senior person.

In addition to the GEN, test, and installation tasks, systems software technicians are required to perform other duties, some requiring a great deal of technical knowledge, others requiring organizational skill. Technical skill is required to perform the following tasks:

- Troubleshooting, i.e., responding to performance problems as they occur, isolating their causes and initiating corrective action
- Handling technical questions that come up from application analysts and programmers and from systems software technicians in other areas
- Assisting application analysts in developing and implementing procedures for backup, recovery, and restart requirements
- Enhancing the overall performance of the computer facility through interaction with other systems software technicians to continually seek out better ways of doing things (tuning the system)

Organization skill is required to perform tasks somewhat less technical, but no less important. These tasks include:

- Gathering of performance statistics on a daily basis, storing them in an orderly fashion, keeping them for an appropriate period of time, and summarizing them into management reports
- Integration of usage statistics and their extension with rates so that computer users can be charged accurately and in a timely manner
- Maintaining the integrity of the system libraries that are used to hold programs, procedures and data sets that make up the installation's systems software products repertoire (housekeeping)

When performed properly, these tasks, both the technical and the organizational, go virtually unnoticed by the users of a computer installation. When not, everyone notices, as overall computer installation performance deteriorates.

System Software: The Potential, the Constraints

To get an idea of how far we have really come in terms of system software since the mid-1960s, let's turn for a moment to the personal computers. We can go to a computer store and for a few thousand dollars we can purchase a computer configuration and some software. The software includes, at the very least, an operating system and some packaged application software (to be discussed in the next chapter). The operating system comes on a floppy disk which is inserted into a disk drive and loaded into primary storage by the mere depression of a key on the personal computer's keyboard. Once loaded, we can begin to interact with the computer. Depending on what that operating system includes, we may be able to write a program, create a file, or copy the data on one floppy disk to another. The application software gives us further capabilities.

As these small personal computers increase in capacity, it is possible to acquire and load more system software and application software into their primary storage. There are database management systems, communications monitors, and interactive systems. They can be used to communicate with larger systems, to other small business computers, and or to large-scale systems. There are certain incompatibility problems from one computer to another, but these continue to be overcome as quickly as they occur through systems software and hardware enhancements. The potential, from a technical perspective, is unlimited.

There are, however, some constraints, and they are economic and managerial/political. Let's look first at the managerial/political. Historically, it has turned out that those organizations having their information asset stored in computers have it stored in what are now known as medium- or large-scale computers. This data is essentially accessible only to what could now be called traditional computer programs. When most of the files containing this information were established, the technology available at the time was used. For its time, it was adequate. Current technology, however, is constrained by traditional file structures and retrieval mechanisms. While it is technically possible to access information with current retrieval mechanisms, the unfavorable impact that would be made on existing operations makes it somewhat impractical. The technology, the systems software, is available to give senior management the kind of summary information that it needs. The information is available, but not in a format that makes it readily accessible. Senior management is faced with a choice: (a) go after the information and retrieve it from the files in which it currently resides and in doing so, bring its operational support system to a virtual standstill, or (b) make a relatively small investment in current technology but an even greater investment in an effort to convert the traditional information file organizations into database structures that can support both the detailed requirements of the operational functions and the summary requirements of those making executive judgments and decisions.

Economic constraints are also a factor to be reckoned with. There are invariably costs for systems software products. Except for a few microcomputer aficionados, nobody is giving away systems software. Some of the costs of systems software are subtle, others are direct.

The direct are the easier to detect and control. When a systems software product is leased or bought, it has a price. If leased, maintenance is generally included in the lease price. If bought, maintenance is usually extra. Some lease arrangements specify that the product is leased for a single installation, or a single computer configuration. If that is the case and if it is to be used in more than one installation or on more than one computer configuration, then an addition charge is incurred for each additional installation or configuration. However, these costs are tangible and decisions can be made whether to incur them or not to incur them.

The more subtle costs are the additional hardware costs that are incurred when systems software is added. In private conversations, some equipment vendors have confided: "We push the software, the hardware takes care of itself." It is not uncommon for systems software products to require between 50 and 75 percent of a computer's capacity. That leaves twenty-five percent for applications. Unfortunately, few individuals, especially executives and senior managers, are aware of this.

With large- and medium-scale computers, incremental costs relative to software are in terms of thousands of dollars. With small personal computers, these costs are in terms of hundreds of dollars. However, caution is recommended in both situations. Budgets made in terms of thousands of dollars can be exceeded in terms of thousands of dollars, and budgets in hundreds can be exceeded in hundreds. The results can be equally devastating. Those large or medium system users who exceed budgets by thousands of dollars, unless it can be justified, may find their bonuses cut or their jobs in jeopardy. The users of personal computers may find themselves with equipment that they cannot utilize the way they expected because they cannot spare the funds to purchase the required software products.

SUMMARY

In this chapter we have dealt in some depth with system software. We have attempted to make a point, namely that system software and computer hardware provide users with *potential*. Realization of that potential comes with use with applications, discussed in the next chapter. The chapter began with a short narrative describing how software came to be. We then took a look at the foundation of all software, the operating system. Following that, there was a discussion of database management and data communications. Interactive systems were explained, and there was a brief survey of other types of system software products. Systems software product support and the tasks of those individuals who install the products were examined. Finally, there was a discussion of the managerial/political and economic constraints that must be dealt with if systems software is to be used effectively.

CHAPTER 5

Application Software

OPENING COMMENTS

In the first two chapters, we discussed data and information that we wish to store, manipulate, and retrieve. In the third and fourth chapters, we looked at computer equipment and system software, the tools that give us the capability or the potential to store, manipulate, and retrieve data and information. In this chapter, we are going to examine application software, that with which we can realize the potential of the equipment and the system software.

The process of application development using computers began in earnest in the early 1960s. Prior to that time, except for some primitive commercial applications, computers had been used primarily in university laboratories or by governmental agencies. Their principal users were mathematicians and scientists. For the most part, computers were used by the same individuals who designed and built them. Applications prior to the early 1960s were almost all mathematical or scientific. These applications involved a relatively great amount of computational activity on a relatively small amount of data. Those early computers had rather primitive input/output capability, so that they were ideally suited to these applications. Commercial applications, with their relatively high input/output requirements and relatively low level of computational activity, were serviced by electromechanical accounting machines, as the computational capabilities of computers were not necessary. Data was stored on 80 column (or some other variation) cards.* The accounting machines and their peripheral equipment, such as punchers, sorters, collators, and calculators (and some of the first commercial computers), processed the data from the cards, producing reports, invoices, checks, and other commercial output. These machines also produced more cards, as each update of a record required a new card to be produced. There is no need to go into the application development process as it existed prior to 1960. Nostalgia would be served, but little else.

With the coming of the 1960s, significant advances were made in the input/output capabilities of computers, making them more viable as tools to be used on commercial applications. Magnetic tape and magnetic disk gradually began to replace cards as a storage medium for data. The speed and economy of storing, manipulating, and retrieving data with computers and magnetic media were quickly perceived to have an overwhelming advantage over the use of cards and electromechanical accounting machines. And so, the transition to computers began around 1960. The first applications to use commercial computers were essentially conversions of the card/accounting machine applications. As such, their processing was sequential in nature, they used magnetic tape as their storage media, and since their activity was generally processed in groups or batches, the term *batch processing* was coined to describe these applications generically. Many of these applications were virtually copied from their accounting machine versions. In essence, the computers were used as faster accounting machines. The idea was to speed up processing and to save money, which was done in most situations. Applications that had taken days with accounting machines were now completed within hours. Within a few years, all the accounting machine applications had been converted. Some individuals had recognized that the potential of computers far exceeded their function as "souped up" accounting machines, and enhancements had even been added. Then, in 1963/1964, it happened, not suddenly, but gradually; multiprogramming and operating systems arrived on the scene and EDP/MIS as we know it today was born. Although others had done it earlier, when IBM introduced them on their newly announced 360 line of computers, operating systems and multiprogramming were universally accepted in commercial circles.

*The 80 column card was by and large the most universally used of several types. It and others are still in use today, but are gradually being phased out as interactive capabilities of computers increase.

Those individuals who were growing up with the computer were aware of the fact that the internal processing speeds of computer processor and primary storage far outstripped the speeds of input/output devices. It was apparent to them that using a computer to process batch jobs one at a time left the processor and primary storage idle more then 90 percent of the time. They began to work on ideas to capitalize on that unused capacity. The results were control programs or operating systems, and as we have seen in Chapter 4, other software followed. Let's now look at application software in a contemporary environment.

PROGRAMMING, THE TOOL FOR DEVELOPING APPLICATIONS

From Bits to Compilers

In Chapter 4, we traced the evolution of software. We pointed out that the individuals who programmed the earliest computers used binary digits, both to enter data and to code instructions. As can be imagined, this was extremely tedious. A better way had to be found, and it soon was. Mnemonics* were developed that were made up of groups of binary digits. A number of different groupings emerged, but by the 1960s the two most universal were the seven-bit group, the American National Standard Code for Information Interchange (ASCII) and the eight bit-group, Extended Binary Code Decimal Interchange Code (EBCDIC). The seven-bit ASCII combinations allowed for 128 different characters, while the eight-bit EBCDIC allowed for 256. The tables in Figures 5.1 and 5.2 depict the ASCII and EBCDIC characters and their binary representations.

Using mnemonics to write programs became known as machine language programming. This, of course, was something less than precisely accurate, since true machine language is binary. However, circuitry of computers allows for the execution of instructions made up of groups of bits, so what we now refer to as machine language is reasonably descriptive.

However, even with mnemonics, computer programming remained somewhat mysterious to the uninitiated. Most users were still scientists and mathematicians. Commercial users were few and far between. The next breakthroughs came with the introduction of assembler macro instructions and compilers. These developments were not dramatic and sudden. They began in the late 1950s and continue right

*Mnemonics are memory aids. For example, in a given computer processor, the circuitry may be manufactured to execute an ADD when the bits 1000001 (an ASCII "A") are encountered. Remembering A is easier than remembering 1000001.

ASCII

		Control Characters		Graphic Characters					
	Col.	0	1	2	3	4	5	6	7
Row	Bits	000	001	010	011	100	101	110	111
0	0000	NUL	DLE	SP	0	@	P	\	p
1	0001	SOH	DC1	!	1	A	Q	a	q
2	0010	STX	DC2	″	2	B	R	b	r
3	0011	ETX	DC3	#	3	C	S	c	s
4	0100	EOT	DC4	$	4	D	T	d	t
5	0101	ENQ	NAK	%	5	E	U	e	u
6	0110	ACK	SYN	&	6	F	V	f	v
7	0111	BEL	ETB	′	7	G	W	g	w
8	1000	BS	CAN	(	8	H	X	h	x
9	1001	HT	EM	)	9	I	Y	i	y
10	1010	LF	SUB	*	:	J	Z	j	z
11	1011	VT	ESC	+	;	K	[	k	{
12	1100	FF	FS	,	⟨	L	\	l	¦
13	1101	CR	GS	–	‡	M	]	m	}
14	1110	SO	RS	○	⟩	N	^	n	~
15	1111	SI	US	/	?	O	_	o	DEL

Figure 5.1 ASCII character bit configurations. In ASCII, the letter K is 1001011, as shown by circled bits.

EBCDIC

Bits 0 and 1 →	0 0				0 1				1 0				1 1			
Bits 2 and 3 → / Bits 4, 5, 6, and 7	00	01	10	11	00	01	10	11	00	01	10	11	00	01	10	11
0000	NUL		DS		SP	&	-									0
0001			SOS				/		a	j			A	J		1
0010			FS						b	k	s		B	K	S	2
0011		TM							c	l	t		C	L	T	3
0100	PF	RES	BYP	PN					d	m	u		D	M	U	4
0101	HT	NL	LF	RS					e	n	v		E	N	V	5
0110	LC	BS	EOB	UC					f	o	w		F	O	W	6
0111	DL	IL	PRE	EOT					g	p	x		G	P	X	7
1000									h	q	y		H	Q	Y	8
1001									i	r	z		I	R	Z	9
1010		CC	SM		¢	!		:								
1011					.	$	,	#								
1100					〈	*	%	@								
1101					(	)	_	'								
1110					+	;	〉	=								
1111	CU1	CU2	CU3		|	¬	?	"								

Figure 5.2 EBCDIC character bit configurations.

up to the present. The use of assemblers and compilers involves some additional work performed by the computer between coding a program and executing a program. Macro instructions represent a methodology of writing programs that lies somewhere between using an assembler language and using a compiler. As we progress through the remainder of this chapter, the distinctions are clarified.

Machine Language

Programming in machine language is rapidly becoming a lost art, except for systems programmers and computer aficionados. But, it does provide a good place to begin describing programming. We have pointed out in Chapter 2 that both instructions and data reside in primary storage at the same time. When programming in machine language, the instructions are written in the form in which they are executed by the processor. In such form, they contain an operation code and one or more operands. The operation code is like a verb in a sentence; it denotes action to be taken. The operands are in the form of storage locations, the contents of which are acted upon. Computers execute instructions serially, that is, one after another, unless that serial processing is interrupted by an instruction that tells the computer not to execute the next instruction, but rather to begin processing at an address specified. In problem-oriented languages the instruction often takes the form of GO TO. In assembler languages it takes the form of a BRANCH (to). A GO TO or a BRANCH instruction may be unconditional or conditional. For example: GO TO STEP4 (unconditional), or IF A = B GO TO STEP6, OTHERWISE GO TO STEP9 (conditional).

In machine language the addresses specified in the GO TO or BRANCH instructions need be resolved and determined by the individual writing the program. Programmers are required to lay out or map the exact locations in primary storage of the instructions and data work areas. For GO TO STEP4, a programmer would have to know at what address STEP4 was located and would code say B6723, where B was the mnemonic for GO TO and 6723 was the location of STEP4.

The storage locations themselves may be single positions or multiple positions called words; that is storage address 0401 may define a single position able to hold a single character or byte of information, or it may define a word of several positions able to hold several characters or bytes of information. The hypothical machine instruction M05721538 could mean MOVE the contents of position (or word) 0572 to position (or word) 1538. An ADD instruction might look like A49635277, a MULTIPLY like X34779142, a GO TO like B5739.

Since computers unaided by software are extremely stupid, they follow one instruction at a time as directed, a limitation of machine language immediately becomes manifest. When writing a program of any length, all the instructions have to be entered contiguously. It is commonly accepted that programs are rarely written correctly in their initial form—there are invariably errors. Going back and recoding to fix errors in machine language with mnemonic operation codes and actual addresses can be a maddening experience. It is tedious and requires a great deal of concentration. There's no way that this type of programming could respond to the dynamics of a commercial application development environment. Even most scientists and mathematicians were not able to put up with the tedium and aggravation of machine language programming, and so assemblers, macro instructions, and compilers were introduced. One of the first compilers was FORTRAN, an acronym for *for*mula *tran*slation. It was used by scientists, mathemeticians, engineers, statisticians and even a few developers of commercial applications. COBOL, an acronym for *co*mmon *b*usiness *o*riented *l*anguage, followed a few years later and has since gained nearly universal acceptance as a commercial application development language. More about this later. Let's first take a look at assemblers and assembler languages.

Assembler Language

Two factors can be associated with the introduction of assemblers and assembler language programming, symbolic addressing, and the assembler process. Symbolic addressing was a major advance. It allowed programmers to specify constants and to give names to statements, to data work areas and to the data elements and fields contained within those work areas. Programmers no longer needed to lay out or map their programs. The assembler did it for them.

The assembly of a program is essentially a two-step process. A program, written in statement form by a programmer, is scanned in its entirety by the assembler. Incidentally, the statements written by programmers make up a program in what are frequently referred to as *source* statements. In this first pass, the assembler determines the start and end points of the program and determines the addresses of all statements and data work areas, fields, and data elements that contain names. The assembler then scans the program statements a second time and translates the instructions into machine executable form. A program in its executable form is sometimes referred to as an object program or as a load module, which Figure 5.3 illustrates.* In the first

*This figure is intended to illustrate the compiler process only. The assembler language used is purely hypothetical, grossly oversimplified, and would never work in a real situation. For those who must know, the program instructs the computer to read records into a work area, list the names and salaries of individuals making more than $25,000 and to total those salaries over $25,000.

Program as written:

Name	*Operation*	*Operand*
START	BLST	EOJ
	RR	WKAREA
	ZA1	WNAME
	ST1	PNAME
	ZA1	WSAL
	C1	''25000''
	BL	START
	A1	COUNT
	S1	PSAL
	P	PNAME, PSAL
	B	START
WKAREA	DA	1X32
WNAME		13, 24
WSAL		25, 32
EOJ	ZA1	COUNT
	S1	PCOUNT
	P	PCOUNT
END	H	END

First pass *Address*			*Second pass* *Machine execute*
001	<--START		@081
005			R049
009			R049
013			S005
017			1073
021			C099
025			L001
029			A125
033			S117
037			P105
041			117
045			B001
049			
053		W	
057		K	
061		A	
065	(WNAME)	R	
069		R	
073	(WSAL)	E	
077		A	
081	<--(EOJ)		1125
085			S133
089			P133
093	<--(END)		H137
099	<--(0002)		0002
101	<--(5000)		5000
105			
109	<--(PNAME)		
113			
117			
121	<--(PSAL)		
125			
129	<--(COUNT)		
133			
137	<--(PCOUNT)		

Figure 5.3 Results of a program passing through a compiler

scan, the assembler determines the beginning and ending points of the program and establishes addresses for constants like 25000, variables such as WNAME and PCOUNT, and labels such as EOJ and END. In the second pass, machine executable instructions are generated using the addresses established in the first pass.

With assemblers, it was no longer necessary for programmers to concern themselves with exact locations as they had had to do with programs written in machine language. The symbolic addressing capabilities of the assembler handle that. If instructions have to be added, deleted, or moved around within a program, if constants have to be added, or if work areas have to be expanded, programmers can change their source statements and have the program reassembled. During the reassembly, addresses are established anew and the instructions are generated with the new addresses.

Assembler languages are still in use today. Each assembler language is the exclusive domain of a single computer or line of computers. This can bring both a blessing and a curse. First the good. Since an assembler language is made for a particular machine or line of machines, it can be used to take full advantage of the capabilities of that machine or line of machines. Programmers familiar with the architecture of a machine are able to write programs that are economical and efficient in terms of computer resource utilization. In the realm of system software, this is very important. In the realm of application software, it is less critical. Now the bad. Assembler language programs developed for a machine or line of machines can be executed only on that type of machine. The programmers who develop the programs must be skilled on the equipment as well as in programming. The assembly process is illustrated in Figure 5.4.

Macros

A macro statement is one from which a number of machine executable instructions can be generated. Macro assemblers are a natural follow

Figure 5.4 The process of the assembly of a program.

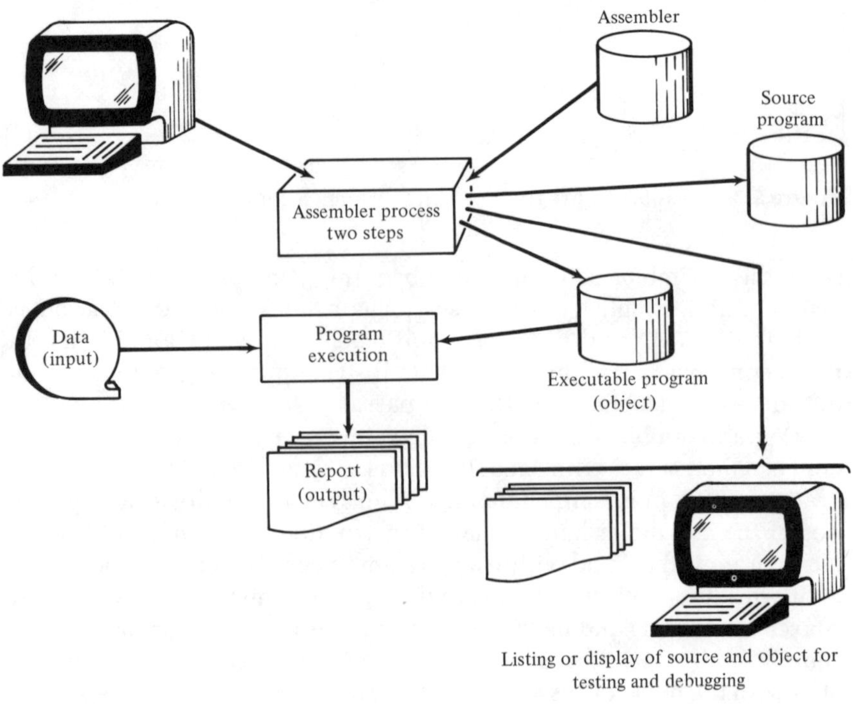

on to assemblers. Simple assemblers have the capability of generating one machine executable instruction for every programmer statement. The usefulness of macros is fairly obvious. In most computer installations, there are a number of programs. Usually, many of the programs perform tasks that are similar such as reading records from files on disk or writing records to files or disk. The actual machine instructions required to perform input/output operations such as this number in the hundreds. As we mentioned in Chapter 4, programs that perform these tasks are called access methods. Sets of instructions (modules) from these access methods are invoked by means of macro statements coded by programmers.

Let's say a programmer is coding a program and comes to a point in the program where it is necessary to read a record from a disk file. Rather than unite all the individual assembler language statements to accomplish the read task, the programmer can simply use a macro statement,* include some parameters and when the program is assembled (compiled)† the appropriate machine instructions are included. Figure 5.5 illustrates the compilation process. Macro statements represent a conceptual transition from one for one assemblers to many from one problem oriented languages like COBOL, BASIC, PASCAL, and PL/1.

Problem-Oriented Languages

A common characteristic of all problem-oriented languages is their orientation toward making more work for computer configurations and less work for programmers. As we have shown, assembler languages require that programmers code a statement for virtually every machine executable instruction in a program. Of course, macros alleviate that situation somewhat, but even the macros had to be coded one for one by programmers initially. The problem-oriented languages are oriented toward the language of the problem. The statements written by the programmers result in the generation of many machine executable instructions.

*This assumes that some other programmer, in this case employed by the vendor of the access method, had already developed the macro itself. Macros themselves are programs, they have to be written, tested, and debugged like any other programs. Once finished, they can then be used by all who wish to use them.

†Generally speaking, assemblers perform translations of programmer statements to machine instructions on a one for one basis. Compilers perform translations of programmer statement in problem oriented languages to machine instructions on a many for one basis. Macro assemblers (compilers) fall somewhere between the two.

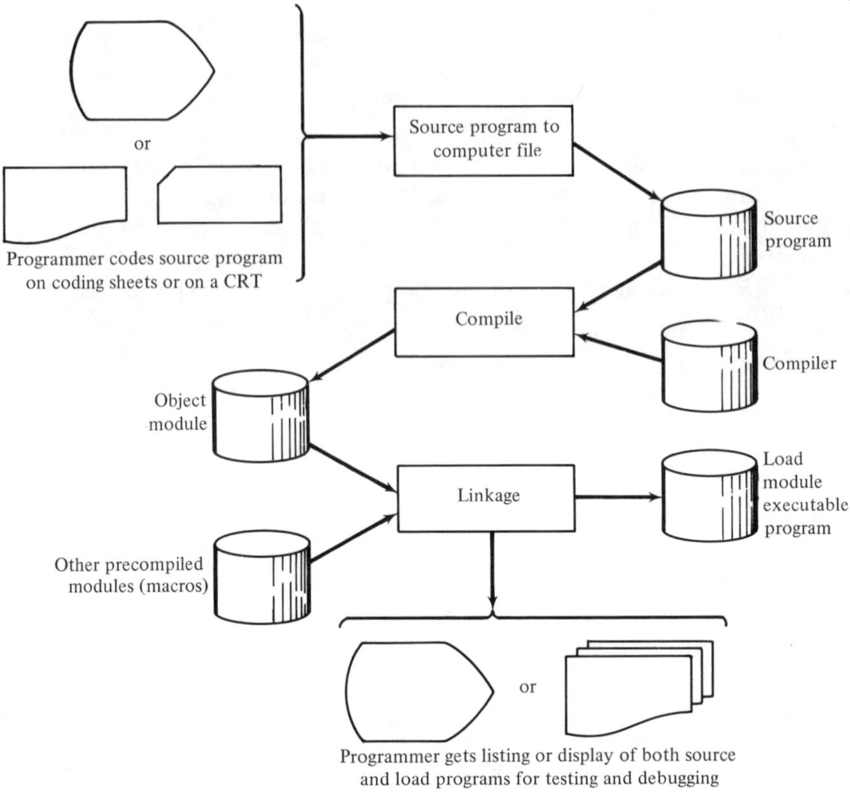

Figure 5.5 The process of the compilation of a program.

The simple BASIC* program shown in Figure 5.6 when compiled would generate hundreds of machine executable instructions.

While it is no doubt true that you are not now ready to begin programming because that little BASIC program just cleared everything up for you, it is also true that you can begin to appreciate that learning how to use BASIC would be easier than learning how to use an assembler language.

There has been and will continue to be a proliferation of problem-oriented languages. Listing them all would be superfluous, but a brief review of the most commonly known is in order.

- FORTRAN was one of the first problem-oriented languages to be developed. It is a language used by mathematicians, scientists, and engineers. FORTRAN facilitates program development for applications requiring the use of mathematical formulas.

*BASIC is one of a large number of problem-oriented languages. There are even many versions of BASIC. That used here is Microsoft BASIC, a version used on many microcomputers.

- COBOL is a problem-oriented language that has received nearly universal acceptance for use in business application programs.
- PL/1 (Programming Language 1) is business-application-oriented programming language that is supported on a wide range of IBM-manufactured computers.

There are other problem-oriented languages not so widely known, and with the rapid growth in the use of small personal computers new ones are quickly gaining acceptance. Many of these have interpretive capabilities, which leads to our next discussion.

Interactive Facilities

Interactive facilities make it possible to code programs by directly keying statements into a computer by means of a keyboard. The keyboard is either connected directly to the computer or to a CRT device or typewriter printer that itself is connected to the computer. In the latter cases, the typewriter printer or the CRT can be connected to either a locally located or remotely located computer. In all of these situations, the software facilities are similar in function. The difference is one of complexity based on the number of potential users of the facilities. The interactive facilities of small personal computers allow one individual at a time to develop one program at a time. The interactive facilities of a large-scale computer allow many individuals to develop many programs concurrently.

Figure 5.6 A problem-oriented language (BASIC) program

```
100 REM   THIS PROGRAM LISTS NAMES AND
110 REM   TELEPHONE NUMBERS FROM A FILE
          CALLED 'NUMIN'
120 REM
130 REM   TELEPHONE NUMBERS OUT
140 REM
150       OPEN ''I'', #2, ''B:NUMIN''
160 REM
170       PRINT ''NAME'', ''PHONE NUMBER''
180 REM
190       IF EOF (2) THEN 240
200       INPUT #2, AME$, TELNUM$
210       PRINT AME$, TELNUM$
220       GOTO 190
230 REM
240       CLOSE #2
250 REM
260       END
```

Interactive facilities are often integrated with improved compilers. These advanced compilers are able to perform other functions besides translating statements to machine executable instructions. Some of the functions of advanced compilers are:

- *Syntax checking*. As a statement is entered, syntax is reviewed by the compiler and if a syntax error exists, a message is returned immediately on the CRT screen or typewriter.
- *Optimizing*. Sophisticated compilers can translate statements into sets of machine language instructions that will execute efficiently.
- *Interpretive*. Statements are compiled and become ready for execution as they are entered. This allows the individual coding the program to test it as it is being written, as opposed to completely coding the program and then compiling and testing it.

USING SYSTEM SOFTWARE FACILITIES

Commercial computer applications depend upon and use the facilities of system software. As we saw in the preceding chapter, even in a small personal computer, an operating system or control program underlies everything else. At the very least, an operating system in a small personal computer includes the input/output facilities. In larger computers, the operating systems provide the facilities that make it possible for many jobs and many tasks (multiprogramming and multitasking) to be executed concurrently. Analysts and programmers who develop applications are required to familiarize themselves with a language that is used to control and coordinate multiprogramming and multitasking activity. The names of these languages vary somewhat from one machine configuration to another, but they're usually referred to by a name like job control language (JCL)* or operational control language (OCL). The larger systems also have facilities that perform the transfer of data between primary storage and devices, be they secondary storage or terminals. These facilities are sometimes known as access methods. Their entire function is the storing and retrieving of information from secondary storage or the receiving and sending of transactions to terminal devices.

Operating Systems: Job Control

Computers are able to execute one job or one task at a time when directed to do so by a program or a program module. To execute many

*JCL is the acronym for one of the most universally known job control languages, that one which is used with a number of IBM's operating systems.

jobs concurrently, they need further instructions. These instructions are provided by means of a special function macro-like language, JCL. The primary functions of JCL, job management, task management, and data management were explained in Chapter 4. In this chapter, we are looking at JCL from an application development and application execution perspective.

There are essentially three types of JCL statements, the job statement which identifies the job, the step statements which identify individual programs within the job, and the data statements which identify the files used by the jobs. Parameters must be specified in each of the JCL statements that accompany a job. The job statement is relatively simple, but the step and data statements can be quite complex. Included within the step and data statements are parameters which specify:

- Condition codes that indicate whether a series of job steps should continue or stop, depending on the outcome of a particular job step within the series
- What to do in the event of a failure of a particular job step in the series
- The entering and removing of file names from the system catalog
- The allocation of storage space for files and programs
- The sequence in which a series of jobs is to be executed

From an application development and support point of view, the skill and dexterity needed to navigate the intricacies of a job control language far exceed those of a programming language. In fact, the difficulty of working with JCL led one writer to define it as follows:

> **JCL** *n.* (**Job Control Language.**) A deliberate abstruse software barrier between the USER and the OPERATING SYSTEM, set up to prevent ordinary programmers from running their own programs.
> As the name partly implies, JCL was devised to create jobs for otherwise displaced intellectuals, to thwart the gloomy predictions of computer-induced employment made in the 1950s.
> (*The Devil's DP Dictionary*, Stan Kelly-Bootle, McGraw-Hill Book Company, 1981, p. 72.)

This humorous definition reflects some degree of truth. Veteran application programmers will bear this out. Individuals not versed in the fundamentals can be severely hampered by the requirements of JCL in their attempts to interact with a large-scale or medium-sized computer configuration. The rapid expansion in the use of small personal computers reflects this. This is no JCL to contend with when jobs are run one at a time.

All is not futile, however. An application programmer or even a user who possesses some literacy in EDP/MIS technology can interact successfully with a large-scale or medium-sized computer configuration. There are individuals who have acquired the skill and dexterity needed to work with JCL. These individuals have developed streams of JCL statements that can be used by application programmers and some users. These streams, called PROCs (short for procedures) are often stored in an operating system library and can be invoked by issuing a single JCL statement. The development of PROCs goes a long way toward overcoming the difficulties imposed by the complexities of JCL.

Access Methods

Access methods are programs that were written as generalized input/output mechanisms to transfer information. Specific access methods exist for the different types of file organizations and for the different types of data transmissions. There are access methods for:

- Sequential unblocked files
- Sequential blocked files
- Direct access files
- Indexed files
- Partitioned files
- Direct transmissions
- Queued transmissions

When an application program is being developed, a particular access method is used for the transfer of data between a device and primary storage. Figure 5.7 illustrates. When the individual coding the program comes to the point where an input/output operation is required, an input/output statement is written. This statement contains parameters indicating the file or terminal with which it is dealing. The specifications of the terminal on the file are contained within the program also. The compiler analyzes the statement and the definitions and translates the statement into machine instructions at the same time it is translating the rest of the program during the compilation and link process.

Utilities: Sort, Copy, Storage Dump

All operating systems, from the CP/Ms* of the small computers to the MVSs† of the large IBM computer configurations, have associated with

*CP/M is one of the more commonly known operating systems used on small microprocessor-based computers.

†MVS (Multiple Virtual Storage) is an advanced version of IBM's OS (Operating System) used on large-scale IBM computers.

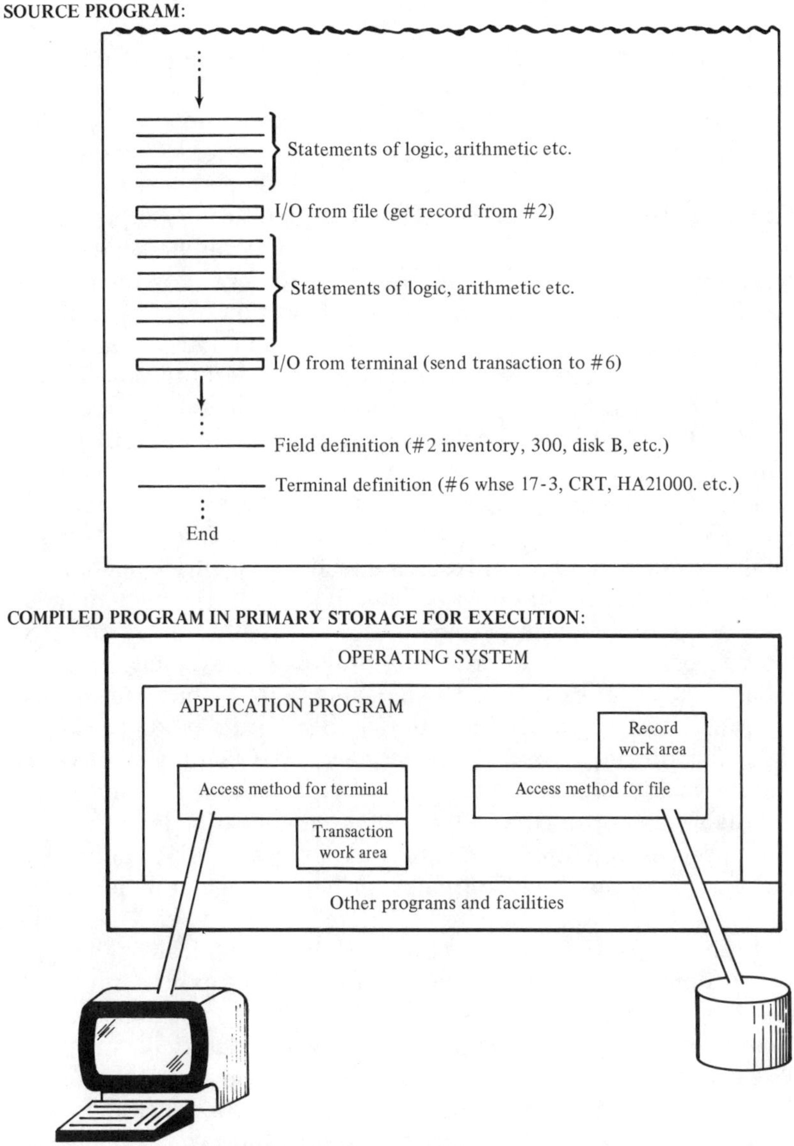

Figure 5.7 Access method facilities within a program.

them, a set of utility programs. These utilities, as they are called, provide two types of services, internal housekeeping and application support. An example of an internal housekeeping type is the dump/restore utility, used to periodically back up (dump) disk storage devices, so that in the event that damage occurs, they can be recovered (restore). In this chapter, however, we are concerned with applications. The most commonly known utilities are the sort, the copy, and the storage dump. When we get into database/data communications applications a little later on, we'll see reorganization, backup and recovery, load, and back-out utilities.

The sort utility is a generalized sorting program into which parameters defining the sequence and the key fields are entered. There are a number of sorting techniques that have been developed over the years. Some of them are quite sophisticated and can significantly expedite the sorting process. Application developers and programmers need not concern themselves with the techniques. They merely fill in the parameters, and the sort utility performs the sort. Selection of the sort utility program that is best suited for a particular installation is one of the tasks performed by systems software technicians. Sort utilities, by and large, are able to sort one file or several files, or to merge together two or more files that are in the same sequence. Many of them are also able to sort and summarize.

Copy utilities are simply what their name implies. They facilitate the copying of files, sections of files, or groups of files from one secondary storage device to another or from one section of a device to another. There are many reasons for copying data. In the area of application development, copying a subset of some files is frequently a quick and efficient way to create test data for testing programs or systems. Another area where a copy utility is useful is in a situation in which it is necessary to transfer a copy of a file from one location to another. Simply copying a disk file onto a reel of magnetic tape and sending by an overnight express service to another location can sometimes be more economical than transmitting the data across communication facilities.

The storage dump utility is used primarily by large-sized computer systems and medium-sized computer systems application programmers. Basically, a storage dump is a computer "throwing up." This utility can be invoked either by a programmer or automatically. The purpose of the dump is to provide a programmer with the exact contents of primary storage and certain registers* as they are at some point in time. The dump can be printed on paper, microfilm, or microfiche, or it can be written onto a disk data set from which it can be accessed through a CRT device by a programmer. In the development of applications that include large and complex programs, the dump utility is a virtual necessity for the testing and debugging of those programs.

DATABASE/DATA COMMUNICATIONS SYSTEMS

Hybrid Software

Database/data communication system products have characteristics of both system software and application software. In a sense, they are hy-

*Register. Computer components that hold information vital to the execution of a computer program. Accumulators and address pointers are examples.

brids. The more elaborate database/data communications systems found in data processing environments where large computers are used often require systems software support. They must be GENed and their performance is carefully monitored and measured. Periodic adjustments (known as system tuning) can be made to buffers, queues, and job mix to improve their performance or simply to adjust to a changing transaction mix. In that sense they are system software products. Yet, at the same time, database/data communications system facilities are used by application developers to define, store, retrieve, and manipulate information within databases by means of terminal devices in a communications network, and in doing so they interact with system software products, primarily access methods. The schematic in Figure 5.8 illustrates this idea. In this schematic, it is shown that the database/data communication system interfaces with the access methods to transfer data between both the devices on the network and the application programs and between the databases and the application programs. It is the data manipulation language (DML) facilities that initiate these tasks. Another facility, the data definition language (DDL) facility is used to define the database structures. The DML facilities can be thought of as input/output macros which make use of the database structure information specified in the DDL statements. As we men-

Figure 5.8 Hybrid software—a database/data communications system using operating system and access method facilities.

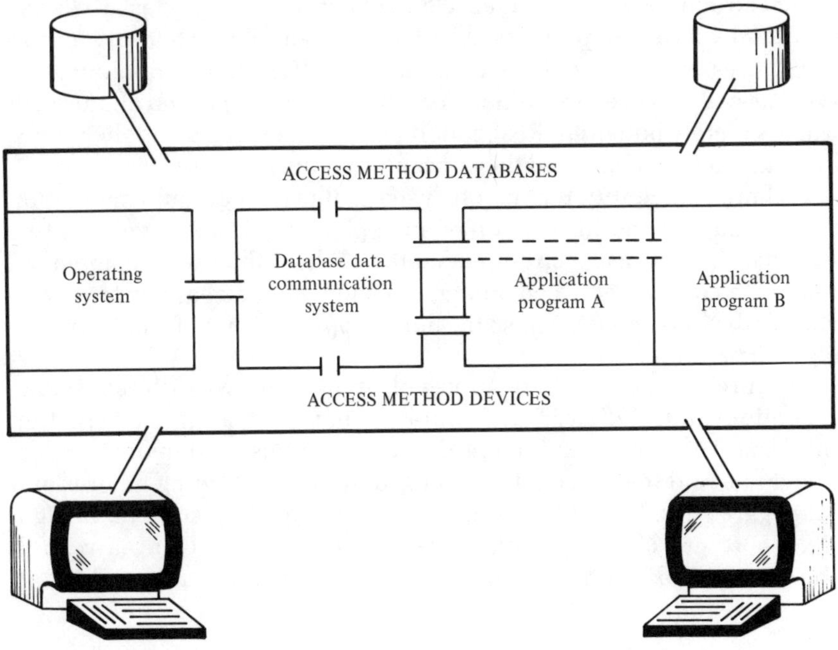

tioned in an earlier chapter, the DDL statements are compiled into machine executable form and are stored in internal data sets called libraries. The data manipulation statements are part of the application programs. The parameters within the statements reference the compiled DDL information in the libraries. During the compilation of the application programs, the necessary information from the libraries is "called" into and included within the programs in their executable form.

The data communication feature of a database/data communication product has similar facilities. There is a facility, in concept similar to the DDL through which terminal characteristics are specified, compiled, and stored in libraries. These compiled specifications are used by what can be thought of as data communication macros. These macros are the statements that effect the transmission of transactions and messages between a computer and the devices on a communications network. In a similar fashion when the application programs containing these statements are compiled, the parameters within the statements refer to previously specified and compiled information describing terminal devices. These compiled specifications are "called" into and included within the programs in their executable form.

Just What Is a Database?

In an earlier chapter, we discussed database in concept. We described logical structures and how their elements or data aggregates are linked together by means of pointers, which are in their physical form are storage addresses. The facility known as a database/data communication systems has also been explained. Yet, all these concepts and all this software is merely potential. Realization takes place when an application is implemented that has used the concepts and the software.

There is an entity that can be used to illustrate an implementation of a database. As an illustration of an application, it serves well for two reasons. First, it has been implemented without the use of computers. Second, a contrast between a database and a nondatabase implementation can be illustrated because the entity appears in both forms. This entity is the Bible.

Figures 5.9 and 5.10 are copies of pages from two different implementations of the Bible. Figure 5.9 is a copy from an implementation known as The American Standard Version. In this version of the Bible, it could be said that the data is arranged in files containing records and data aggregates. The Bible contains sixty-six books, each one being a file. There are chapters within the books, each one being a record. There are verses within the chapters, each one being a data element.

THE FIRST EPISTLE OF PAUL THE APOSTLE TO THE

CORINTHIANS

1 PAUL, called *to be* an apostle of Jesus Christ through the will of God, and Sos'the-nes *our* brother,

2 Unto the church of God which is at Corinth, to them that are sanctified in Christ Jesus, called *to be* saints, with all that in every place call upon the name of Jesus Christ our Lord, both theirs and ours:

3 Grace *be* unto you, and peace, from God our Father, and *from* the Lord Jesus Christ.

4 I thank my God always on your behalf, for the grace of God which is given you by Jesus Christ;

5 That in every thing ye are enriched by him, in all utterance, and *in* all knowledge;

6 Even as the testimony of Christ was confirmed in you:

7 So that ye come behind in no gift; waiting for the coming of our Lord Jesus Christ:

8 Who shall also confirm you unto the end, *that ye may be* blameless in the day of our Lord Jesus Christ.

9 God *is* faithful, by whom ye were called unto the fellowship of his Son Jesus Christ our Lord.

10 Now I beseech you, brethren, by the name of our Lord Jesus Christ, that ye all speak the same thing, and *that* there be no divisions among you; but *that* ye be perfectly joined together in the same mind and in the same judgment.

11 For it hath been declared unto me of you, my brethren, by them *which are of the house* of Chlo'e, that there are contentions among you.

12 Now this I say, that every one of you saith, I am of Paul; and I of Apollos; and I of Ce'phas; and I of Christ.

13 Is Christ divided? was Paul crucified for you? or were ye baptized in the name of Paul?

14 I thank God that I baptized none of you, but Crispus and Gaius;

15 Lest any should say that I had baptized in mine own name.

16 And I baptized also the household of Steph'a-nas: besides, I know not whether I baptized any other.

17 For Christ sent me not to baptize, but to preach the gospel: not with wisdom of words, lest the cross of Christ should be made of none effect.

18 For the preaching of the cross is to them that perish foolishness; but unto us which are saved it is the power of God.

19 For it is written, I will destroy the wisdom of the wise, and will bring to nothing the understanding of the prudent.

20 Where *is* the wise? where *is* the scribe? where *is* the disputer of this world? hath not God made foolish the wisdom of this world?

21 For after that in the wisdom of God the world by wisdom knew not God, it pleased God by the foolishness of preaching to save them that believe.

22 For the Jews require a sign, and the Greeks seek after wisdom:

23 But we preach Christ crucified, unto the Jews a stumblingblock, and unto the Greeks foolishness;

24 But unto them which are called, both Jews and Greeks, Christ the power of God, and the wisdom of God.

25 Because the foolishness of God is wiser than men; and the weakness of God is stronger than men.

26 For ye see your calling, brethren, how that not many wise men after the flesh, not many mighty, not many noble, *are called*:

27 But God hath chosen the foolish things of the world to confound the wise; and God hath chosen the weak things of the world to confound the things which are mighty;

28 And base things of the world, and things which are despised, hath God chosen, *yea*, and things which are not, to bring to nought things that are:

29 That no flesh should glory in his presence.

30 But of him are ye in Christ Jesus, who of God is made unto us wisdom, and righteousness, and sanctification, and redemption:

31 That, according as it is written, He that glorieth, let him glory in the Lord.

2 AND I, brethren, when I came to you, came not with excellency of speech or of wisdom, declaring unto you the testimony of God.

2 For I determined not to know any thing among you, save Jesus Christ, and him crucified.

3 And I was with you in weakness, and in fear, and in much trembling.

4 And my speech and my preaching *was* not with enticing words of man's wisdom, but in demonstration of the Spirit and of power:

5 That your faith should not stand in the wisdom of men, but in the power of God.

6 Howbeit we speak wisdom among them that are perfect: yet not the wisdom of this world, nor of the princes of this world, that come to nought:

7 But we speak the wisdom of God in a mystery, *even* the hidden *wisdom*, which God ordained before the world unto our glory:

8 Which none of the princes of this world knew: for had they known *it*, they would not have crucified the Lord of glory.

9 But as it is written, Eye hath not seen, nor ear heard, neither have entered into the heart of man, the things which God hath prepared for them that love him.

10 But God hath revealed *them* unto us by his Spirit: for the Spirit searcheth all things, yea, the deep things of God.

11 For what man knoweth the things of a man, save the spirit of man which is in him? even so the things of God knoweth no man, but the Spirit of God.

12 Now we have received, not the spirit of the world, but the spirit which is of God; that we might know the things that are freely given to us of God.

13 Which things also we speak, not in the words which man's wisdom teacheth, but which the Holy Ghost teacheth; comparing spiritual things with spiritual.

14 But the natural man receiveth not the things of the Spirit of God: for they are foolish-

110

Figure 5.9 A page from The American Standard Bible.

1 CORINTHIANS 1:11 1728 1 CORINTHIANS 1:27

you, but you be made complete in
[a]the same mind and in the same
judgment.
11 For I have been informed
concerning you, my brethren, by
[a]Chloe's *people,* that there are
quarrels among you.
12 Now I mean this, that
[a]each one of you is saying, "I am
of Paul," and "I of [b]Apollos," and
"I of [c]Cephas," and "I of Christ."
13 Has Christ been divided?
Paul was not crucified for you,
was he? Or were you [a]baptized in
the name of Paul?
14 I thank God that I [a]bap-
tized none of you except [a]Crispus
and [b]Gaius,
15 that no man snould say
you were baptized in my name.
16 Now I did baptize also the
[a]household of Stephanas; beyond
that, I do not know whether I
baptized any other.
17 [a]For Christ did not send
me to baptize, but to preach the
gospel, [b]not in cleverness of
speech, that the cross of Christ
should not be made void.

★11 [a]Rom. 16:10f.
★12 [a]Matt. 23:8-10; 1 Cor. 3:4 [b]Acts 18:24; 1 Cor. 3:22 [c]John 1:42; 1 Cor. 3:22; 9:5; 15:5
★13 [a]Matt. 28:19; Acts 2:38
14 [a]Acts 18:8 [b]Rom. 16:23
16 [a]1 Cor. 16:15, 17
★17 [a]John 4:2; Acts 10:48 [b]1 Cor. 2:1, 4, 13; 2 Cor. 10:10; 11:6

B The Causes of Divisions, 1:18–2:16

1 The misunderstanding of God's message of the cross, 1:18–2:5

18 For the word of the cross is
to [a]those who are perishing [b]fool-
ishness, but to us who are being
saved it is [c]the power of God.
19 For it is written,

"[a]I WILL DESTROY THE WISDOM
OF THE WISE,
AND THE CLEVERNESS OF THE
CLEVER I WILL SET ASIDE."

20 [a]Where is the wise man?
Where is the scribe? Where is the
debater of [b]this age? Has not God
[c]made foolish the wisdom of [d]the
world?
21 For since in the wisdom of
God [a]the world through its wis-
dom did not *come to* know God,
[b]God was well-pleased through
the [c]foolishness of the message
preached to [d]save those who be-
lieve.
22 For indeed [a]Jews ask for
signs, and Greeks search for wis-
dom;
23 but we preach [a]Christ cru-
cified, [b]to Jews a stumbling block,
and to Gentiles [c]foolishness,
24 but to those who are [a]the
called, both Jews and Greeks,
Christ [b]the power of God and
[c]the wisdom of God.
25 Because the [a]foolishness of
God is wiser than men, and [b]the
weakness of God is stronger than
men.
26 For consider your [a]calling,
brethren, that there were [b]not
many wise according to the flesh,
not many mighty, not many
noble;
27 but [a]God has chosen the
foolish things of [b]the world to
shame the wise, and God has cho-
sen the weak things of [b]the world
to shame the things which are
strong,

★18-25
18 [a]Acts 2:47; 2 Cor. 2:15; 4:3; 2 Thess. 2:10 [b]1 Cor. 1:21 23, 25; 2:14 4:10 [c]Rom. 1:16; 1 Cor. 1:24
19 [a]Is. 29:14
20 [a]Job 12:17; Is. 19:11f.; 33:18 [b]Matt. 13:22; 1 Cor. 2:6, 8; 3:18, 19 [c]Rom. 1:20ff. [d]John 12:31; 1 Cor. 1:27f.; 6:2; 11:32; James 4:4
21 [a]John 12:31; 1 Cor 1:27f.; 6:2; 11:32; James 4:4 [b]Luke 12:32; Gal. 1:15; Col. 1:19 [c]1 Cor. 1:18, 23, 25; 2:14; 4:10 [d]Rom. 11:14; 1 Tim. 4:16; 2 Tim. 2:10; 3:15; 4:18; Heb. 7:25; James 5:20
22 [a]Matt. 12:38
23 [a]1 Cor. 2:2; Gal. 3:1; 5:11 [b]Luke 2:34; 1 Pet. 2:8 [c]1 Cor. 1:18, 21, 25; 2:14; 4:10
24 [a]Rom. 8:28 [b]Rom. 1:16; 1 Cor. 1:18 [c]Luke 11:49; 1 Cor. 1:30
25 [a]1 Cor. 1:18, 21, 23; 2:14; 4:10 [b]2 Cor. 13:4
★26-31
26 [a]Rom. 11:29 [b]Matt. 11:25; 1 Cor. 1:20; 2:8
27 [a]James 2:5 [b]1 Cor. 1:20

1:11 *quarrels.* Or strife, which, according to Gal. 5:20, is a work of the flesh, or old nature.

1:12 The party of *Apollos* apparently preferred a polished style in preaching (Acts 18:24). The party of *Cephas* (Peter) appealed to the traditionalists, who wanted a leader who had walked with Christ. The party of *Christ* included those who disdained attachment to any group and flaunted their liberty in Christ (6:12).

1:13 The impossibility of these things being true demonstrates the fallacies of these factions.

1:17 *For Christ did not send me to baptize, but to preach the gospel.* Though Paul did baptize some (vv. 14, 16), it is clear from this statement that he did not consider baptism necessary for salvation.

1:18-25 In these verses Paul shows that worldly wisdom, which the Corinthians prized so highly, is the very antithesis of the wisdom of God.

1:26-31 Not only is the message of the cross foolishness to the perishing (v. 18), but God uses those who would commonly be considered foolish, weak, and of no consequence to convey that message. An illustration of this truth was their own church group, which did not include many *wise, mighty,* or *noble* (v. 26). God's purpose is to exclude all boasting in self (v. 29).

Figure 5.10 A page from The Ryrie Study Bible, The American Standard Version. Used by permission of Moody Press.

Even though all those files (books) are contained in a single volume, they do not constitute a database in the form as shown in Figure 5.9. However, in Figure 5.10, we have a copy of a page from a version of the Bible known as the Ryrie Study Bible. The text of the Bible is the same, that is, it is the American Standard Version translation. What is different about the Ryrie Study Bible is the notes in the right and left margins and at the bottom of the page. These notes establish relationships between verses (data aggregates) in one book (file) with verses (data elements) in other books (files). We therefore have relationships, not only among verses within a single book, but among verses in a number of different books. We have a database, according to the definition set down in a earlier chapter, a collection of data aggregates that are interrelated in such a way as to transcend record and file boundaries. The margin notes can be thought of as the pointers containing the addresses (book, chapter, and verse) of related data aggregates.

On-Line Access

The data communication feature of a database/data communication product is that which allows immediate access to information contained in the databases. There are two kinds of data communication features that can be used to access information from on-line databases: the single-thread, multipartitioned, and the multithread, single-partition. Figures 5.11 and 5.12 depict these two kinds.

In a single-thread, multipartitioned database/data communication system, there is separation of function. There is a separate processing region, sometimes called a control region, for the system software programs, and there are separate processing regions for each of the application programs that execute under the control of the system software programs in the control region. Interfacing between the application programs and the devices on the communication network is done in the control region. Buffers for the information being transferred between databases and the application programs are in the control region, as are the queues that hold the transactions and messages being transferred between the terminal devices on the network and the application programs.

In a multithread, single-partitioned database/data communication system, there is no separation of function. The system software programs, buffers, applications programs, and tables are stored in a single region. The tables found in this type of system, as opposed to the queues used in the other type, represent the main difference between the two. The multithread, single-partition system is designed with a primary objective of providing fast response to transactions. The single-thread, multipartitioned system is designed more for database integrity and

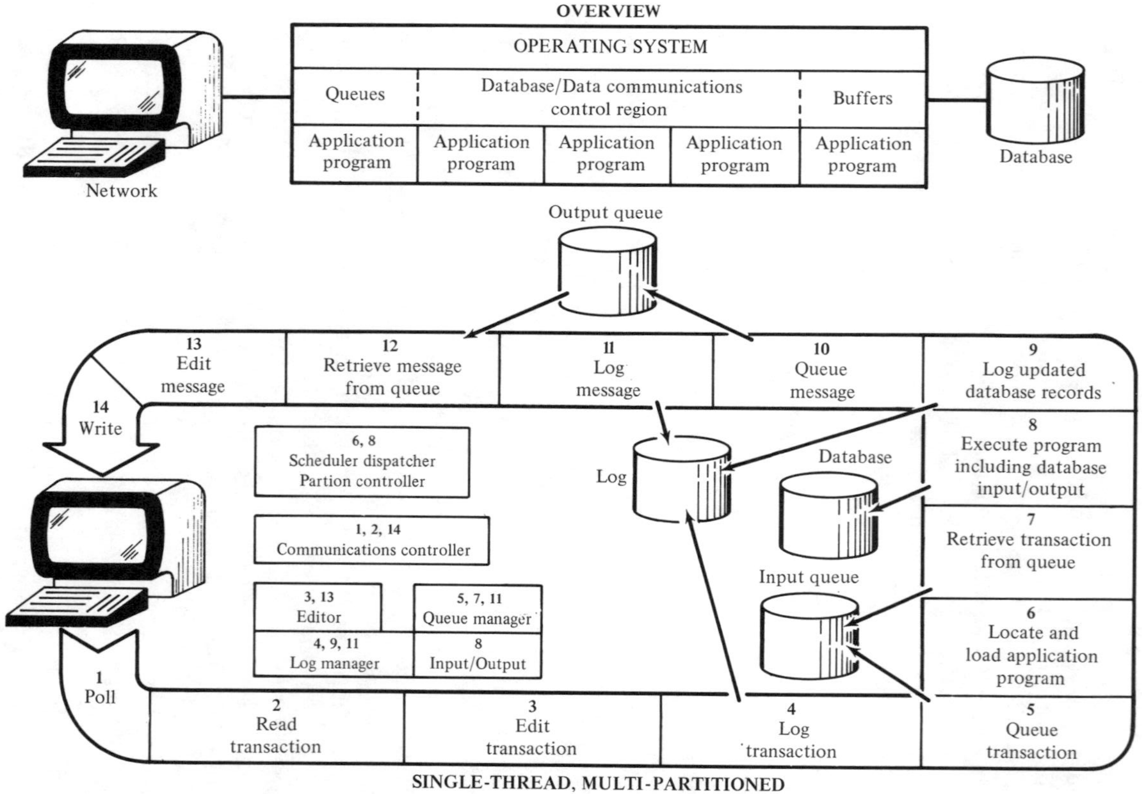

Figure 5.11 Single-thread, multi-partitioned database/data communications system.

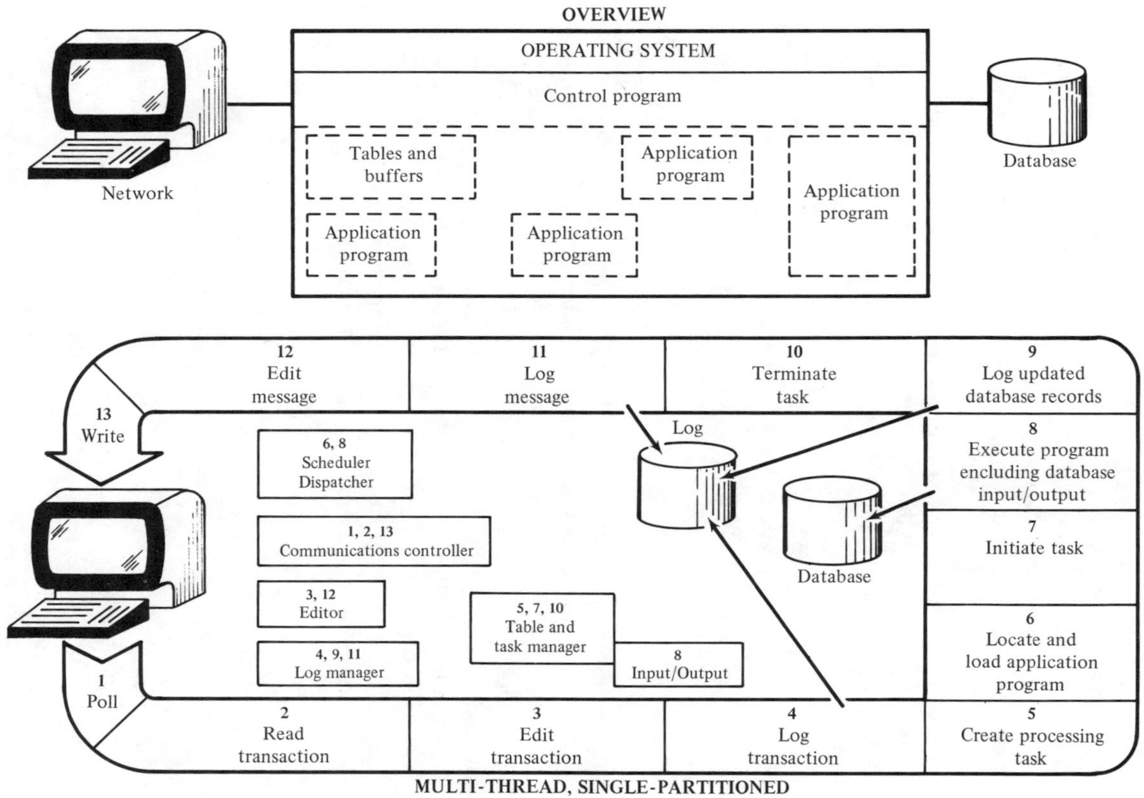

Figure 5.12 Multi-thread, single-partition database/data communications system.

system stability. In general terms, the multithread, single partition systems provide quick response to transactions on relatively low volume, relatively small database applications. Because of their single partition arrangement, it is possible for an error in a single application program to bring the entire system down. User-developed recovery and restart procedures can be relatively simple, but the responsibility for database integrity lies within each application using the system. In a multipartitioned arrangement, an error in an application program impacts only that program and the databases with which it is interacting. The remaining application programs continue processing. In those situations in which the entire system is halted, the recovery and restart procedures are relatively complex, but when executed they bring about complete restoration of the databases.

DEVELOPING APPLICATIONS WITH "CANNED" SOFTWARE

General Comments

Although application programming with assembler and problem-oriented languages is going to be with us for a while yet, there is a trend away from them. As computer components, primary storage, and processors become less costly, there is less of a need to be stringently economical in their use. Getting away from programming languages is facilitated in essentially three ways: through the use of generalized application software, often called packages, through the use of application development systems, and through the use of end user retrieval facilities. Let's look at these one at a time.

Packages

It's difficult to tell when software packages become a viable option, but it was probably somewhere in the early 1970s. Some of the first packages to appear were those relating to accounting and finance. There were general ledger packages, accounts receivable packages, budgeting packages, and so on. It has now gotten to the point where there are packages available for all but unique applications, such as a broadcasting networks election race estimating system. However, one might ask, if all these packages are available, how come application programs are still being written? To answer this question, it is necessary to take a closer look at what makes up packages.

First of all, an application package is nothing more than a collection of programs, file and record layouts, and procedures developed by an individual or a group of individuals possessing some knowledge about an application and electronic data processing. When a user agrees to purchase or lease a package, he or she is merely acquiring an application that has been developed by an outside organization rather than by an internal systems and programming department. There is, however, a simple way to install a package and there are other ways. Let's discuss the simple way first. Also, at this point, let's assume that we're dealing with large-scale and medium-sized computer installations. The use of small, microprocessor-based computers and packaged software is discussed later on.

A packaged application software product generally arrives at a user computer installation in source form on a reel of magnetic tape. A set of operating instructions for the computer operations functions should be included. There also ought to be a set of operating instructions for the users. Documentation is required on program functions, record layouts, report and screen formats, file or database specifications, transaction types, communications interfaces, and codes used by the system. Some of these requirements can be waived, but the consequences should be understood.

Once the product has been set up, that is, the programs have been compiled and space allocated for the files or databases, the user is then ready to load information and to begin processing in a test mode. In the best case, the tests are satisfactory, and the user is able to put the system into production. A shakedown period follows, and within a period of time the packaged software becomes an integrated part of the user's operations functions. That's the simple way.

In some situations, users determine that they like the application essentially, but wish to make a few modifications. Depending upon the complexity and quantity of these modifications, the simple installation process just described can be impacted to a greater or lesser degree. There is a trade off to be made here. Modifications to packaged software products are more difficult to implement than modifications to internally developed applications. In addition, not without reason, vendors of applications software products are reluctant to guarantee the performance of their products if they have been modified. The trade off is: if it seems that the modifications that are required are more than cosmetic, that is, minor changes to some report or screen formats, then it is advisable to either find another package or to develop the application internally. Modifying packaged software initially turns out to be a never ending project.

Application Development Systems

Application development systems are software products that are based on the assumption that there is commonality among most applications that are implemented on computer configurations. There is some truth here, and products of this type are going to be used increasingly as time goes on. These products are another example of the general thrust of making computer facilities available to application users, without requiring the skills of an application programmer.

An application development system is essentially a collection of skeletal programs which contain the basic input, processing logic and arithmetic, and output capabilities of most applications. They are based on sound reasoning. After all, virtually all computer applications take data in, manipulate it a bit, and then make it available as information output. The idea is that users can be given the facilities to define their input, processing, and output requirements by specifying parameters to the application development system. These systems are generally "menu driven," that is, once installed, they provide users with a list of items from which they choose. For example, a menu may present on a CRT screen a security option which the user may choose to exercise or to ignore. If exercised, another menu may give the user a choice of options such as terminal security, transaction security, password security, and user identification security. Generally, all the user has to do is enter a few characters or numbers through the CRT keyboard and the system takes care of the rest.

"WOW!" you say, "If it's that easy why isn't everybody doing it?" Well there are essentially two reasons. Both are economic. First of all, interfacing application development systems with existing technology can have significant impact. Eliminating the application programmer does not eliminate the work, it merely transfers it to the computer configuration. Since most organizations do not have a great deal of idle computer capacity, wholesale usage of a high-overhead application development system would have a severe degrading effect on existing computer configurations. The second reason why everyone isn't doing it is somewhat more subtle. The primary advantage of an application development system is it potentially can bring about a significant reduction in the amount of time needed to develop an application. If this potential is realized, then there is going to be an accelerated increase in the demand for computer configuration resources to accommodate the more quickly developed applications. While this seemingly gratifies hardware vendors, the organizations requiring the additional computer equipment have to evaluate the trade offs as far as their use of funds is concerned.

End User Retrieval Languages

There is a definite trend toward letting end users of applications store, manipulate, and retrieve information. It all started with the mnemonics that were developed for the earlier assembler languages. This development was followed by the introduction of macros and problem-oriented languages. Then came operating systems and job control languages, and the trend was interrupted. More about this later. Dealing with sophisticated operating systems and using job control languages are tasks for technically proficient individuals, not for end users. However, despite that, software vendors continued to develop and market products whose objective was the simplification of the tasks of storing, manipulating, and retrieving information from computers. Most of these products were concerned primarily with retrieving information. The developers of these products were attempting to meet a need, the need of end users to have a tool with which they could easily get at the information stored "in the computer." For a whole lot of reasons, this information either appeared to be or actually was inaccessible to end users. Whenever they asked for it, they were told it would take several weeks to design, code, and test an application program that would retrieve the information in the format they wanted.

The software products designed to meet these needs are called report writers and query languages. Report writers are less free form in that specifications, which are essentially nothing more than parameters, generally have to be written or keyed in a rather rigid format. Query languages are somewhat more free form, but they still must be learned. There is a wide range of products of both types. An example of the inputs and outputs of each appear in Figure 5.13.

Of the two types of products, the report writers are the easiest to implement, because most existing applications use the traditional, nondatabase file structures, sequential, direct, and indexed. Scanning a traditional file, sorting it if necessary, formatting the information for printing and specifying total and subtotal control breaks is one of the simplest of all EDP/MIS tasks. The individuals and organizations who developed report writer products merely made the task easier and removed some of the tediousness from it. There is a significant quantity of report writers available and all of them are adequate to the task of producing detailed and summary tabulations. Selecting a particular report writer for your own situation involves making sure that it can be installed in your environment and that it interfaces easily with your existing file structures and access methods.

Query languages, on the other hand, are relatively recent arrivals on the scene. While it is possible for query languages to be used to retrieve specific information from traditional direct and indexed files, the true potential of these languages is realized when they interact with databases. The query language example in Figure 5.13, for instance, involves a search of two interrelated files, a customer file, and an order file that have a boundary transcending relationship relating specific customers with specific orders. The response to the query results in

A REPORT WRITER PARAMETER SPECIFICATION

```
FILE   INVENTORY FB 320
COPY   PARTNAME
SORT   INVENTORY USING PARTNUM
LIST   PARTNUM, PARTNAME, PRICE, QTYONHAND, REORDQTY
TITLE  'PART STATUS', 'PAGE'
```

A REPORT WRITER LISTING

PART STATUS

PARTNUM	PARTNAME	PRICE	QTYONHAND	REORDQTY
74186	SCREW	.006	512	100
75311	FLANGE	3.270	17	19
76002	ANGLE	1.200	37	12
79853	ANCHOR	.190	103	46
80006	VALVE	19.200	4	3
81311	CAP	1.200	19	10
83966	UNION	1.470		
84012	NIPPLE	.970		

A QUERY LANGUAGE INPUT SPECIFICATION

```
QUANTITY, "LATE GREAT PLANET EARTH", ORDERS
JUN – SEP 1983, REGENCY BOOK STORE
ENGLEWOOD, NJ
```

A QUERY LANGUAGE RESPONSE

RESPONSE TO:

QUANTITY	ORDERS	DATE
2467	4	6-9-83

TITLE
LATE GREAT PLANET EARTH
STORE
REGENCY BOOK STORE
LOCATION
ENGLEWOOD, NJ

Figure 5.13 Report writer and query language specifications and outputs.

first locating the appropriate customer record (Regency Book Store in Englewood, New Jersey) and then the appropriate order records for that customer (all orders for June, July, August, and September of 1983) and then a scan of the line items on those orders to determine how many copies of *Late Great Planet Earth* were ordered and how many orders included that title. It is obviously a more elaborate task than the COPY, SORT, and LIST parameters specified for a report writer.

The actual installation of either a report writer or a query language facility is also a factor to be considered. Installations in which there are one or more large-scale or medium-sized computer configurations also have operating systems and job control languages. In such environments file and database specifications take the form of job control language statements required by the operating system. Therefore, in addition to the simple parameters or query specifications shown in Figure 5.13, it is frequently necessary for those who wish to use report writers and query language to become familiar with job control language or to find someone who is and then to depend on that individual to prepare the "technical" specifications necessary for interfacing the operating system and the report writer or query language.

More elaborate systems software is emerging that is reducing the need for that technical interface. Yet, the existing technology is in place in vast quantities. The migration from the current to the new is likely to take a number of years. This migration is already under way and is manifesting itself in a couple of ways. One way is through microcomputers, which we'll look at presently, and the other is through operating systems that use control languages that are less technical and more user oriented. These more advanced operating systems are making it possible for users to work with query languages and with interactive problem-oriented programming languages such as BASIC, APL, and PASCAL. But, their processing overhead is quite high. Consequently, discretion has to be exercised in their use. Unlimited use would adversely affect the performance of finely tuned existing computer configurations supporting current operational applications. Secondly, less technical operating systems are also found on computer configurations that are based on more advanced architecture. These configurations are making their presence felt, but the migration from existing technology to the new is restrained by the twin realities of logistics and economics. The phenomenon most likely to expedite this migration is the influence being exerted by the microcomputer-based small personal computers. Let's now have a closer look at this phenomenon.

DEVELOPING APPLICATIONS ON PERSONAL COMPUTERS

What Are Personal Computers?

As we have already shown, the term minicomputer has, for all practical purposes, become meaningless. During the late 1970s and early 1980s, the terms microcomputer and microprocessor came into vogue. Then, sometime in the 1980–1982 time frame, the term personal computer was coined. Many of the magazines for those who wished to apply small computers to business functions also made their debut in this time period. Slowly at first, and then much more rapidly, small computers were turning up all over the place. There were many manufacturers. Individuals who finally overcame the uncertainty about whether to buy were then confronted with so many makes and models that choosing a particular small computer become quite difficult. Change was also a factor, as newer models with faster processors and greater storage capacity were announced at a rate of one every month or two. Compounding the confusion of the situation even further was the veritable avalanche of books, articles, and "experts," creating a classic example of what has been affectionately referred to as information overload.

In spite of all this, there is a definition for some small computers that is reasonable in describing what could be called a personal computer. Basically a personal computer is with which a single individual can interact. It generally consists of a minimum configuration of a keyboard, a processor, primary storage, and an interface (a cable and some electronics) to a standard television or a monitor. There are makes and models that support additional components in varying sizes and quantities. Floppy disks, hard disks, tape cassettes, printers, and telecommunications interfaces are possible options for most personal computers. However, once a configuration permits concurrent interaction by more than a single user, it is no longer a personal computer, but rather it is a small business computer.

Personal computers are attractive for a couple of reasons. First, they are relatively inexpensive. Second, they are relatively easy to learn how to use. Prices of personal computers range from the hundreds to the thousands of dollars, but the computer (processor and primary storage) are the least expensive of the components. Prices escalate when peripheral equipment, especially disk and printers, are added. Ease of use stems from the facts that single user systems require no job control language and that there is a virtually unlimited amount of developed software (some of it free) available for use on most of the personal computers.

Off-the-Shelf Software

Software for application development with personal computers is available in every category imaginable. The biggest problem is finding exactly what you want. There are operating systems such as CP/M and UNIX, there are access methods for tape, for disk, from communications. There are database management systems. Application software abounds, accounts receivable, accounts payable, ledgers, checking accounts, budgets, inventory, taxation, and others are available.

There are, however, limitations—price, variety, equipment, and interfaces—to existing systems and applications. Let's examine these limitations one at a time.

- *Price.* Application software for personal computers ranges from a few dollars to several hundred dollars. For the most part "What you see is what you get." The caveat "let the buyer beware" is sound advice when purchasing application software for a personal computer. Check around, if possible, before buying.

- *Variety*. There are often many products of each application type. Some products have versions that run on several different personal computers. Specifications vary in quality and accuracy.
- *Equipment*. Personal computers currently have capabilities of including connections to disk storage devices capable of holding millions of characters of information. At some point, diminishing returns set in, and the amount of data available on-line will be sufficient to overwhelm a personal computer. While it is true that microcomputers will continue to get smaller and more powerful, there is a limit to that miniaturization. At some point, multiple processors or multiple users are required, and the transition from personal computer to small business system takes place.*
- *Interfaces*. Since personal computers can be used in a number of different situations, interface considerations are variable. An individual using a personal computer to teach or to write (word processing option) or a proprietor of a small business would have minimal concern about interfacing with existing applications. These individuals would probably use the personal computer as a stand-alone system to perform specific self-contained applications. However, an enterprise of some magnitude with an existing system of computer equipment and applications represents a different situation entirely. While personal computers would serve well in some capacities as stand-alone systems, there are two factors that ought to be considered. First, the uncontrolled acquisition of personal computers quickly leads to a number of individuals or departments each developing its own applications using its own input sources, resulting in an information base that is fragmented and uncoordinated. Considerable confusion would result when attempts were made to bring together the output information from these various applications. The second factor flows from first. To prevent the confusion, some sort of standards ought to be established, without creating a bureaucracy. At the very least, hardware should be restricted to one or two manufacturers, and those within the organization familiar with EDP/MIS functions should be used as consultants. These individuals can generally prevent an inexperienced user from making a gross error of commission or omission when acquiring a personal computer.

*The very dynamics of microprocessor and microcomputer technology make it impossible to be precise about all this; it varies from one situation to another. There's a trade-off to be made; at some point, large-volume applications become more economical on medium- or large-scale computers.

COMMENTARY ON SOFTWARE

Trade-Offs

Software can be thought of as the means by which we communicate with computers. As computer software continues to become more elaborate and sophisticated, making it easy for all of us to interact with computers, we have a tendency to forget that a computer equipment configuration is nothing but a machine that has the potential to add up numbers, move data around, display information, and manipulate things a bit based on comparisons. It is the software, that is, the data and the sets of instructions, that realize that potential. The idea of computers as giant electronic brains is somewhat naive.

A computer equipment configuration is an excellent vehicle for storing, manipulating, and retrieving information quickly and accurately. However, the computers have to be given very precise instructions on how, where, when, and under whose direction they are to perform these tasks. In general terms, the how issue is handled by application programs, the where issue is handled by database management systems and access methods, the when is handled by scheduling and data communications systems, and control of access is handled by security programs and procedures. The actual implementation of all this involves a number of trade-offs.

The first of these trade-offs is "efficiency of execution/programmer productivity" issue. Using simple file structures, pointer tables, customized input/output modules, and assembler language programming results in an application that uses a minimum of secondary storage for files and has programs that execute quickly using a minimum of primary storage, assuming a competent application design. In all probability it takes longer to design and program an application in this fashion, and the analysts and programmers needed to develop and maintain require more technical skills than those implementing applications using the facilities of problem-oriented languages and database management system products. With such facilities, some of the technical complexities are reduced, although basic design and analysis efforts are still required. Specifications for program logic is the same, yet the sophisticated technology of pointer tables and customized input/output modules are included within the database management system product. While analysts and programmers are required to understand them, they are not required to develop them. So, applications can be developed more quickly, but because of the more sophisticated software involved, they frequently require more storage and execute less efficiently—hence, the speed of execution/productivity trade-off. As software becomes more elaborate and sophisticated, the trend is toward using it rather than the skilled technicians. This offends the sensibilities of some EDP/MIS managers and technicians, but houses get built more quickly by carpenters who don't spend a lot of time counting nails and two-by-fours. The development of applications with assembly language, simple files, and customized input/output modules is becoming impractical. For centuries men have been inventing machines to do work for them. Computer software is an extension of that development.

Database/Data Communication Confusion

A significant manifestation of that development is database/data communications software. Database/data communication (DB/DC) software products, applied correctly, represent a tool that is absolutely vital if we are to realize the potential of MIS. And yet the entire discipline of database/data communications technology is engulfed in mumbo jumbo of incomprehensible jargon that creates an impression of near mysticism, which fosters confusion and intimidates all but the high priests of DB/DC. This confusion and intimidation is not caused intentionally or maliciously, but rather comes about as a result of naivete of some database/data communication "experts" and the credulity of some executives and managers. There is a gap between what executives and managers are led to expect by the experts and what can be delivered with database/data communication technology, between potential and realization. The technology is the potential. Realization is the job of EDP/MIS professionals and the responsibility of executives and managers.

Let's see how this gap has come about. In the conventional wisdom of database/data communication experts, something called *data independence* is seen as a key issue. To executives and senior managers data independence means nothing. Even when explained as a separation of data from programs, it is still somewhat irrelevant to executives and senior managers. Data independence as an issue to executives and senior managers is somewhat like an Eskimo finding a new way to make an igloo and then trying to make it a worldwide issue. And yet, not wishing to appear ignorant, many managers go along with database/data communication, understanding neither why have have done so nor their responsibilities. Projects fail, and database/data communication technology gets blamed.

Another reason for the gap involves a bit of terminology, specifically the word relational. In the early 1970s, an accomplished mathematician named Codd developed a theoretical methodology for creating databases that were simply structured and from which information could be quickly retrieved. It was apparent, however, that some time would pass and some additional technological advances would have to be made before Codd's theoretical model could become a practical reality. That consideration did not deter numerous vendors of database/data communication software products from claiming that their products had "relational" capabilities. Yet their definition of relational was somewhat different than Codd's. What followed was additional confusion because the term relational came to mean whatever the person or organization using it wanted it to mean.

Management Responsibility

Database/data communication software has the potential to facilitate the presentation of summary information to executive and senior managers. There are two ways in which this summarization can be done. One way takes time (minutes or hours) and is relatively inexpensive, the other takes less time (seconds) but is relatively expensive. In the latter, if the information is to be up to date, the expense is increased even further. It all depends on file structure and storage methodology. Let's look at three ways in which some summarized information can be requested, retrieved and presented.

(A) *The request:*
"What were my sales for videotapes and videodisks for September and October 1983, for Star Wars, E.T., and Raiders of the Lost Ark?"

File:
Sequential, sales by day for all videotape products, in sequence by product serial number, within invoice.

Retrieval:
Search entire file, one record at a time, if conditions (Sept, Oct; Star Wars, E.T., and Raiders) met, add sales to appropriate accumulators.

Presentation:

		Sept.		Oct.		Total	
		Units	$	Units	$	Units	$
Star Wars	Tape	xx	xxxx	xx	xxxx	xx	xxxx
E.T.	Tape	xx	xxxx	xx	xxxx	xx	xxxx
Raiders	Tape	xx	xxxx	xx	xxxx	xx	xxxx
	TOTALS	xx	xxxx	xx	xxxx	xx	xxxx
Star Wars	Disk	xx	xxxx	xx	xxxx	xx	xxxx
E.T.	Disk	xx	xxxx	xx	xxxx	xx	xxxx
Raiders	Disk	xx	xxxx	xx	xxxx	xx	xxxx
	TOTALS	xx	xxxx	xx	xxxx	xx	xxxx
	FINAL	xx	xxxx	xx	xxxx	xx	xxxx

In this situation, it would take at least several minutes to search the file. If the file contained sales data in detail (by invoice, for each day, for a year) it might take an hour or two.

(B) *The request:*
Same.

File:
A database containing fields that contain summary information on sales by title and product type for each month for the past twenty-four months. This database is updated weekly by the current week's sales activity.

Retrieval:
Using product type and title as keys, retrieve information directly from summary records within the database.

Presentation:
Same.

(C) *The request:*
Same.

File:
Same, but as each sales transaction is recorded, it is also posted to the appropriate summary record.

Retrieval:
Same.

Presentation:
Same.

In situation B, if the request for September and October information is going to be made only in November and beyond, there is no benefit gained by having sales posted to the summary immediately. In situation C, if the request for September and October information is going to be made in October and up-to-date information is required, then sales should be posted to the summary record as soon as they are recorded.

The point of the preceding discussion is to point out that there are factors other than technical which dictate how a database is to be structured. The choice among situation A, situation B, or situation C is a management responsibility. The technology contains the potential to support any of the three situations, but obviously the selection of one as opposed to the others is not a technical decision. Technicians can supply cost and response-time information to help managers and executives make informed choices, but the choices are management's responsibility. The trade-off to be made is whether to invest time and money for development of databases that include within their structures information relationships and summarizations that can quickly respond to anticipated management inquiries or to limit time and money investment in technology and to wait for information when it is needed.

User Friendly

There is a trend toward making computers more accessible. The term *user friendly* has been used to describe computer configurations containing software products that facilitate interaction between men (and women) and machines. Also, as part of this trend, are processes whereby functions that were once software are being fabricated as hardware. Repetitive functions that are executed over and over again are being manufactured. Six instructions here, four instructions there disappear and turn up as some microscopic circuitry on a semiconductor wafer.

User friendly involves trusting the vendor as opposed to dealing with a technician. Vendors advocating user friendly hardware or software are in essence asking us to trust them. The trend into problem-oriented software and semiconductor program modules take us further and further away from the "bits and bytes" of computers. The computer configuration becomes a collection of integrated components to us. When they work the way they're supposed to, everything is great. When they don't we have to get the vendor representative to fix things. If we choose to buck the trend, we can stay with "bits and bytes" and employ technicians to support us. Then if we have problems, we have our own technicians to fix things. Either way, we're dependent on someone.

CONCLUSION

The trend, from a management and user perspective, is definitely away from "bits and bytes" and toward "user friendly" hardware and software. Generally speaking, application development becomes simpler while systems software support becomes more complicated. Technicians will always be needed, it's just a matter of who they work for, users of computer hardware and software or vendors of computer hardware and software.

SUMMARY

In this chapter, the development of application programming was traced from the specifications of binary digits by scientists and engineers to the specifications of near English (or other) language statements by all kinds of users. Application programming was shown to involve more than just writing statements in a particular programming language. Application programmers need to be familiar with operating systems, access methods, job control language utilities, database/data communications systems, and interactive facilities. Also examined were application software package, application development systems and report writers and query facilities. Application development on personal computers with off-the-shelf software was discussed. Concluding the chapter, there was a commentary of software in general as it effects executives and managers. A general observation was offered and a conclusion was drawn.

CHAPTER 6

Computer-Based Technology in Office and Plants

INTRODUCTION

Computers are making an impact on business. You laugh. Perhaps, at this point in time, that is an understatement. However, it is only recently that executives and senior managers have consciously and outwardly acknowledged that computers are integral part of business and not just an optional appendage. It is difficult to imagine commerce without computers in today's world. The large quantities of data and the "horsepower" required to store, manipulate, and retrieve it make computer equipment an absolute necessity. This need has not come about overnight, although in relative terms it has come about quickly. In the late 1960s data communications, small computers, and database were embryonic technologies. All three caught on quickly though, and by the 1970s data communications was commonplace, and by the late 1970s, database was regarded by many as a viable technology and the ubiquitous CRT terminal device adorned many a desktop. With the 1980s underway, small business systems, personal computers, terminals, on-line databases, and data communications were as integral a part of business as accounts receivable, general ledger, manufacturing, inventory control, sales analysis, and business planning. As a matter of fact, EDP/MIS technology is involved with each of these business functions; it has permeated every aspect of business activity.

While these technologies, i.e., database/data communications, small business systems and personal computers, continue to grow and gain acceptance, a couple of other things also happen. The trade press creates a big hullabaloo about it all, creates buzz words and colorful phrases such as "DB/DC," "CAD/CAM" and "office of the future"; and "experts" in each of the technologies begin popping up all over the place.

Let's deal with the experts first. The newer the technology, the shallower the expertise of the expert. While there are indeed a number of truly knowledgeable individuals who are able to provide valuable insights into these various technologies, there are also a larger number of dissonant individuals whose acquaintance with the technologies involves nothing more than familiarity with the most current buzz words and colorful phrases. These latter individuals usually overwhelm and intimidate rather than edify and educate their audience. They are not too difficult to spot. They are generally opinionated and assertive and tend to favor one product over others and to ridicule what they don't understand. They use words and phrases with which others are unfamiliar, and when pressed for clarification, they unabashedly continue to speak, using obscure and mysterious but often apparently impressive terminology. They frequently "name drop," and the sentence "I don't know" never passes from their lips. In my opinion, an "expert" is an individual who knows a little bit more about something than you do, for a little while. Within a short period of time, say a few hours, or maybe a day or two, the "expert" through a series of lectures and some "question and answer" sessions ought to be able to convey to you what it is you want to know. The true "experts" may occasionally say "I don't know," or at least qualify their thoughts on some issues.

Hullabaloo and ballyhoo sell magazines and newspapers almost as well as gossip and innuendo. A number of trade journals and magazines run stories and articles that attempt to establish differences among things that are essentially the same. Of this generation it has been said: "When all is said (written) and done, much more will have been said (written) than done." Quite often, the fine points of EDP/MIS technology are emphasized at the expense of the essential. The reason that few individuals ever understand the essentials of technologies such as database/data communications and computer systems is that the essentials are rarely explained, while details are written about over and over again. Regarding database technology, for instance, hundreds of indepth articles describe *ad nauseam* the fine line distinctions between network, hierarchical, and relational database models. How many times must we copy notes from one set of notebooks to another?

Perhaps you are wondering what all this has to do with automated office and other technologies. Well, it is really something of a preface to my statement that automated office and other technologies are nothing more than an extension of the existing technologies of database/data communication, small business systems, and personal computers. There is the inevitable new terminology, some slightly different variations on the available technology, and a few new concepts. There is even some new technology, but it is merely a better, faster, and sometimes less expensive way of doing what is already being done.*

CONTEMPORARY TECHNOLOGY

There are a number of technologies available that have an impact on what we do in our offices and in our factories. Again, we're talking potential, with the realization of the potential coming from users. The potential is offered by two technologies, electronic data processing and telecommunications. We've already discussed electronic data processing in some detail. We've also discussed data communications. Let us now survey telecommunications.

Telecommunications is the technology which includes the equipment and facilities that establish communications among individuals and machines that are remotely located from one another. Figure 6.1 depicts potential telecommunications applications. Included are in-building wiring networks, across town communications arrangements and intercity and even international communications. These telecommunications arrangements are composed of equipment and facilities provided by a number of organizations. Beginning in the late 1960s, these organizations began offering services that until that time had been the exclusive domain of Western Union and AT&T in the domestic United States. International arrangements are also possible with current technology, although there are some political and legal restrictions.

Making all this possible are many kinds of new (since the late 1960s) technology such as satellite communications, microwave radio links, cellular telephones, cable television services, fiber optics, and digital communications. And yet despite all the breakthroughs and accomplishments made in technology, it still only represents potential. It still remains for the user to realize what is made possible by the potential. The sophistication of the technology, especially the computer and

*None of this is intended as a swipe at technology or technicians. Without them, none of this would happen. However, presentations of technology can sometimes be hampered when those describing it lose sight of the forest while describing the trees. We are attempting to describe the forest. The trees have been described elsewhere and often.

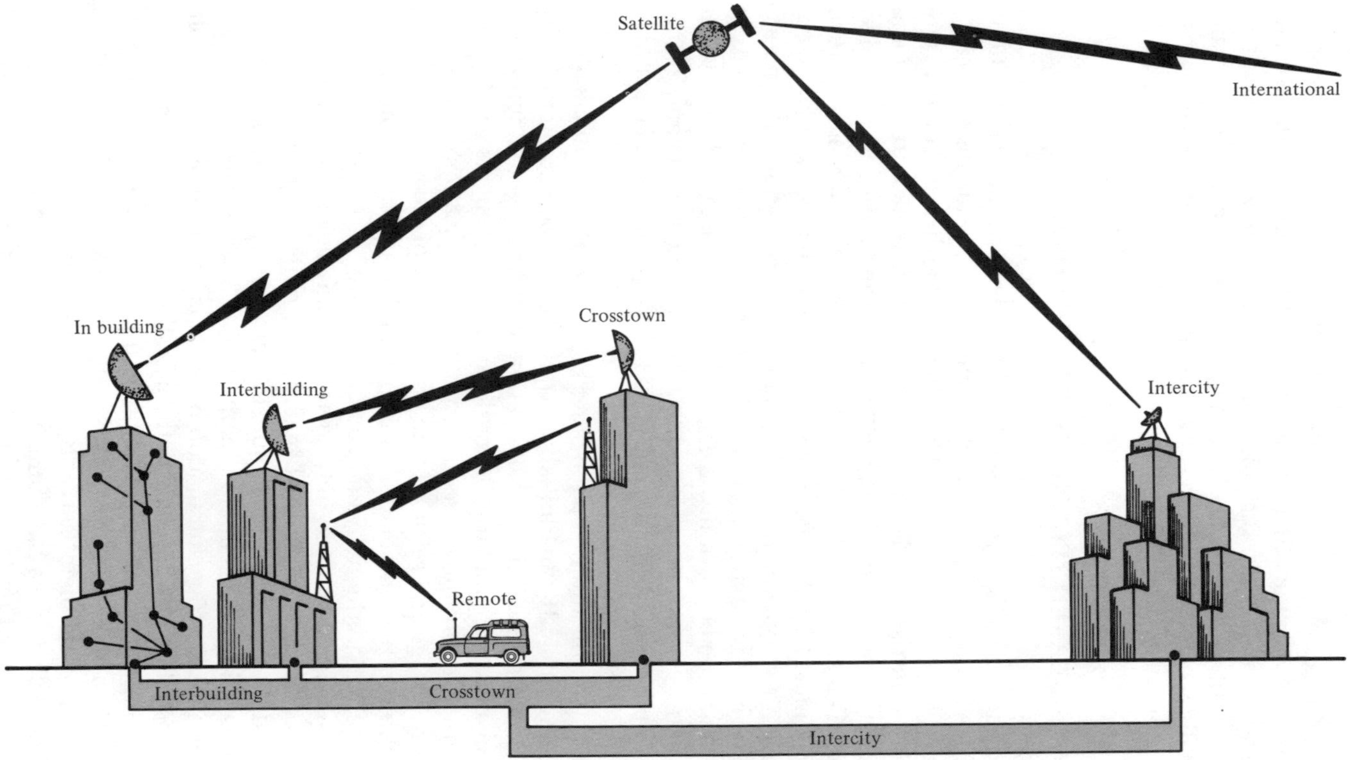

Figure 6.1 Potential telecommunications application.

telecommunications technology, provides the foundation for those applications found in the office, those found in the plant, and those found in the executive suite. In the pages immediately following, we will examine computer-based technology in both the office and the plant, and then finally we will attempt to show how management themselves can make use of this technology.

COMPUTER-BASED TECHNOLOGY IN THE OFFICE

By this time nearly everyone has heard the terms "office automation" and "office of the future." For quite a while, data processing managers, and systems consultants, especially computer hardware vendors, were using these terms quite loosely and trade journals had articles about them in every issue. Especially the "office of the future"; it sounded so exciting. Well as all the dust began to settle, a real difference between what was meant by the two terms began to crystallize. The "office of the future" is a concept, an ideal situation to be strived for. It is potential; the technology exists; again it is the users who must realize the potential. What the concept involves is: (1) rapid storage and retrieval of on-line data; (2) messages sent and received among many people; (3) decision support systems for managers and professionals; and (4) distribution of work to various locations.

"Office automation," on the other hand, is the reality of what's actually being done. It's the initial realization of the potential offered by "office of the future." It is the utilization of technology to improve the efficiency of office functions. Its basic functional elements are: (1) document preparation and reproduction; (2) communications; and (3) information storage and retrieval through a variety of media. The driving force behind office automation is economic because of its promise to improve office productivity and communication. As a result, office automation has gone and will only go as far in any business organization as is economically feasible and beneficial. It's quite pragmatic. Once we get beyond the hoopla and ballyhoo, the question must be asked: "Why spend money if no measurable benefit is going to be derived from it?"

What makes office automation possible is the technology available and the cost of this technology. In the past, the tendency has been to apply technology to office work by moving the work out of the regular office and into a technology center, not unlike a mysterious temple where "high priests" and their "servants" monitored and cared for the "electronic god." Today we have minicomputers and microcomputers that can be located within feet of our offices. Their size and cost make it possible to have more than one, with each dedicated to performing a specific office task. With this processing power available, very specific office tasks can be performed that were never before considered automatable.

Along with improvements in computer technology are advances in peripheral equipment with which we are able to communicate with computers. Office automation requires that secretaries, clerks, supervisors, managers, and even executives use computer equipment. The computer equipment components most frequently used in office environments are terminals, the most common being CRTs.

Terminals

The terminal technology available today falls into three main types. First there is the oldest of the three, now popularly called a *dumb* terminal. It is called dumb because it does not have a computer built into it. Its only capability is to act as a communications interface between an individual and a computer. As technology progressed some manufacturers put "intelligence" into their dumb terminals and created *smart* terminals. These terminals still do not have a computer built into them, but they do provide capabilities in addition to communication. They allow users to manipulate the data displayed on the screen. For example, a smart terminal allows users to insert and delete lines and characters. These capabilities are possible because additional circuits are built into the terminal devices. One of these circuits is a memory circuit which serves as a local storage area for the data displayed on the screen. The advantage of a smart terminal is that you can change anything displayed on the screen without communicating to the computer.

Besides dumb and smart terminals there are also available *intelligent* terminals. These terminals are equipped with a built-in computer. Actually, microprocessors that are user-programmable and support at least one programming language are built right into the terminal devices. They have the capability to process data on their own without communicating to a host computer. In addition, they usually possess more extensive communication capabilities than either dumb or smart terminal devices. Their main advantages are a reduction in the amount of communication that takes place between users and host computers, and they allow users to keep working even when a host computer is temporarily out of service.

Communications

No matter what type of terminal individuals have, there is a need to communicate with a computer. Whether it be a computer in the next room, across town, or across the country, some type of telecommunications arrangement is necessary. It is telecommunications that is really the basic underlying technology of office automation. It can be considered the glue that binds together all the other elements. Without telecommunications only limited office automation is possible.

The telecommunications arrangement that allows computers and terminals in physically different locations to communicate with one another is called a network. Networks come in many sizes and types. The size of a network depends both on the number of locations where interconnected terminal devices (called nodes) are installed and on the degree of redundancy (number of connections) necessary. A network can span one building, one geographic region, or the entire world. A network may include a simple coaxial cable connecting two offices or a satellite linking buildings in different cities or countries.

Though networks may physically be the same size and look the same, they may be of different types. The type classification is based on the kind of data that is transmitted over the network. These different kinds of data, voice, video and, digital (i.e., computer talk) all produce a different electronic signal and travel at different speeds along the network. This is one reason why you need a separate wire to hook up to cable television and cannot use your telephone wire. Some networks are designed to handle voice and digital, while others are only for digital, and still others for video.

When it comes to office automation, a network that can handle the difference types of data is the most desirable. Such networks tend to be expensive and relatively small. This is why current office automation plans usually start with only one or just a few physical locations, perhaps several floors in an office building. For this reason a special class of networks called local area networks (LANs) were developed.

LANs play a very important role in office automation simply because they can be tested locally, and if successful, they can be expanded easily. Basically, the technology applied to LANs falls into two categories. They are broadband LANs and baseband LANs. Each type has been developed and is in commercial use today. Two commonly known LANs are Ethernet made by Xerox (a baseband LAN) and Wangnet made by Wang Labs (a broadband LAN). The basic difference between the two types is how a message gets from one place to another and how many messages can be sent and received at any one time, i.e., simultaneously.

A baseband LAN is nothing more than a coaxial cable connecting computers, terminals, and other peripheral devices. At each end point where a device is attached is an interface between the device and the LAN cable. The LAN is a passive device; it does nothing until someone tries to send a message. A baseband LAN is not unlike a single-lane highway with entrances and exits wherever there is a town (a device), at each entrance a checkpoint (interface) checks to see if the highway is clear before allowing a vehicle (message) to proceed onto the highway. This single-lane highway (LAN) can handle traffic going in both directions, yet only one vehicle (message) can be moving on it at any one time. Occasionally multiple messages are sent, and there are collisions. One message going in one direction and another going in the opposite direction cannot pass through each other, so they collide. When this happens both originating checkpoints are notified, and each waits a random interval of time before retransmitting its message.

When each message is sent, it contains the address of the destination device. As it travels along the highway it stops at every checkpoint to compare addresses. When it finds a matching device address it stops, since it has arrived at the right place.

To minimize the number of collisions occuring when messages are sent simultaneously from two devices, a set of rules are used. These rules indicate that a device must check if the lane is clear before sending a message and must listen while the message is being sent. In other words, check if the highway is clear before sending a vehicle and then, once it is sent, watch out for collisions.

A broadband LAN is more complicated than a baseband LAN. In some ways it can be considered multiple baseband LANs tied together. To use the same analogy, a broadband LAN is a multilane superhighway, except that there is a traffic cop (computer) controlling the flow of vehicles (messages). This computer constantly monitors the network. All messages sent by a device on the network must first go to this controlling computer which then transmits the message to the proper destination. If the intended destination is not part of the network then the message is returned to the sender. Because a broadband LAN can be considered a multilane highway, it can handle many messages concurrently. Think of the messages as all waiting in line to pass through the control point and be directed to their destination. No collisions occur because every device has its own direct path to the computer. However, because all messages must pass through a central point in the network, it represents a potential bottleneck. It may take a message a relatively long time to be completed if it has to wait in line behind many others.

The other distinguishing feature of a broadband LAN and what really makes it a superhighway is the type of messages it can handle. Voice, digital, and video electrical signals can all be communicated with a broadband LAN. Broadband means there are multiple data channels available on the network to transmit messages. A data channel is like one lane of a multilane highway. Each data channel is used to transmit a particular kind of message. Just as a highway has a slow lane for trucks and buses, so a broadband LAN has separate data channels for different types of messages. A baseband LAN, on the other hand, has one data channel that can only transmit digital messages as described earlier.

Because of their differences, baseband and broadband LANs are applied differently. In situations where information traffic among many users is a requirement, a broadband LAN would be preferable, particularly in large facilities like a highrise office building, where voice, digital, and video messages need to be transmitted. A baseband LAN is more suitable where traffic among a few users is relatively light. The lower cost of installing and maintaining baseband LANs also make them attractive. A baseband LAN is particularly suited for transmitting messages when the devices on it are computers instead of terminals, since computers can check to see when a line is free before sending a message.

With the terminal and communications technology currently available the potential exists for almost any level of office automation. However, as with all computer and telecommunications hardware configurations, the potential is realized by the software. As we've shown earlier, the software enables computers and other hardware to perform specific tasks. One way to look at it is that the computers, terminals, and communications networks form the body and skeletal structure of the system, giving it some organization, but it is the software that brings it to life and allows it to perform office functions.

Word Processing

Not all office functions can be automated, but some can be. By viewing the office as a system, it can be broken down into its component parts, some of which can then be automated.

A first step into office automation taken by many organizations is word processing. Word processing is basically document preparation with automated facilities. Advanced word processing involves other functions such as the storage and selective retrieval of documents. Selective retrieval means being able to specify search criteria with keywords and conditionals such as "and," "or," "not." Some advanced systems also provide some data processing capabilities such as adding columns and rows of numbers. Primarily though, word processing deals with text rather than numbers, as opposed to data processing which concerns itself primarily with number crunching.

Although it has received more attention lately, word processing, as an application, has been around for sometime now. The first word processing equipment was introduced by IBM in 1964. However, it was not until the mid-1970s when display terminals became economical and available in quantity that word processing increased in popularity. Today there are four categories of word processing systems. They are (1) stand-alone, (2) text-editing typewriters, (3) shared resource, and (4) shared logic.

A stand-alone word processing system is one terminal, connected to a computer or perhaps with a built-in computer, a printer, and a storage device. It functions independently of any other system and does not have any telecommunications capability. It provides full-screen display and edit capability, storage of documents, and perhaps selective retrieval of documents.

A text-editing typewriter allows users to type documents and then review and edit them before printing. Some models may also be able to store the documents on diskettes for later use. Usually a one-line window display and edit capability is available. Like stand-alone systems, this type also does not have any telecommunications capability.

The first real step into office automation is with a shared logic or shared resource word processing system. These systems are equipped with telecommunications capability and usually data processing also. The principal difference between these two types is where the word processing software is located. In a shared logic system the software is stored in the main computer. Each terminal uses the same program in the computer to do its task. In a shared resource system each terminal has its own memory and processing power. This way each retains its own copy of the word processing software. The terminals do not share the main computer's logic in performing the word processing task. In both bases they share the storage devices and printers attached to the system.

What this means is that you can produce a document on one terminal and later edit it or print it from another terminal. Also if there are multiple printers any one of them can be selected to print the document. More advanced features of these systems include interfaces with photo composition equipment and computerized paper copiers for output, and with OCR equipment (Optical Character Recognition), for input.

With a shared logic or shared resource word processing system and a local area network it is possible to store on the computer all the documents a company produces. This simplifies filing and retrieval for the individuals who use the documents. In addition, by combining the capabilities of word processing, a local area network, and software, word processing documents can be distributed electronically, i.e., without printing and making copies first. This is one aspect of what is sometimes known as electronic mail.

Electronic Mail

Electronic mail is really a catch-all term that encompasses transmitting textual information. These methods include (1) facsimile, (2) Telex (TWX), (3) communicating word processing systems, and (4) CBMS (computer-based message switching). The first two have been available for a number of years, and the third is an advanced word processing application. However, it is CBMS which holds the most promise in the automated office.

CMBS operates the same way the postal service does. Let us say that everyone who uses the postal service has a post office box number. When you send someone a piece of mail it is addressed to the person's post office box number. The person will periodically check for mail in his or her box by opening it with a personal key.

The situation is very similar conceptually with electronic mail. The computer is like the post office. Attached to the computer is a storage device which contains a file (box) for every person who uses the system. When you want to send someone a message you type it into the system via a word processing terminal, address it with the file number of the person to whom it goes, and then send it by depressing a particular key on the terminal keyboard. The computer then stores the message in the specified file number. The next time that person scans his or her electronic mail file he or she will find your message. However, access to mail files required the use of unique codes that act like keys to permit entry to the files. The computer with its specialized electronic mail software performs the job of the postal service.

A primary benefit of using electronic mail is the reduction in the creation of paper documents. However, if it is necessary, documents can be printed. The ability of a computer system to keep track of the documents is another benefit of electronic mail. For example, a sender can check when a receiver has "opened" his or her mail, and if a receiver has passed the document along to someone else, the computer also keeps track. Some electronic mail systems also provide a tickler service to advise when certain documents are received or due.

Some potential advantages of electronic mail are: (1) all messages can be reviewed at one time; (2) paperwork can be "batched" and all handled during a single period of the day; and (3) it provides the speed of a telephone with the permanence of a letter.

An extension of electronic mail is the ability to send and receive voice messages. Known as voice mail, it is a catch-all term that encompasses several areas. First, there are voice messages which provide audio annotation in a way similar to that in a text-based system. Audio annotation allows users to add audio notes and comments to a document stored in a computer. (This is similar to writing in the margin of the text). This technology is available today and can be extremely helpful in reducing "telephone tag."*

*Telephone tag—you call, he's out; he calls back, you're out, you call again, he's on another line, and so on.

Second is the integration of dictation and word processing. To do this the computer needs to have automatic speech recognition capability. This involves correlating human speech sounds with stored machine recognizable information. This technology is progressing in stages. First there is the recognition of isolated words, second the recognition of continuous speech, i.e., two or more words, and finally, natural language recognition.

The third area of voice mail is computer-generated speech, that is, the ability to produce speech from prerecorded sounds that are stored separately and assembled to create words. This can be accomplished in two ways. The first uses a computer to "speak" a prerecorded response. This is being done now by telephone companies responding to certain types of calls. The second is computer synthesized speech. This involves recalling phonetic sounds in a specific sequence. It is much more difficult to do this successfully because of the subtleties of language.

Finally the capability to convert word processing text into speech is still in the future. Some researchers estimate it may be several years away. So for the present and near future most of our communication with the computer will be nonspoken, i.e., written and pictorial. The written involves numbers and words which we are all familiar with. The pictorial involves graphics and pictures usually in color and is better known as image processing or computer graphics.

Image Processing

Image processing includes facsimile, micrographics, CAD/CAM (computer aided design/computer-aided manufacturing) and business graphics. Facsimile, sometimes abbreviated FAX, involves the transmission and reproduction of images or words using telecommunications facilities. It's been in use for years. Historically, the quality of the reproduced material frequently left something to be desired. Although quality is improving, there are generally better ways to send printed or pictorial material over distances that while not as fast, certainly result in better quality. However, if it's "quick and dirty" that's needed, FAX can do it.

Micrographics is a process for storing information on either microfiche or microfilm directly by a computer. It saves paper, storage space, and printing time. Laser technology is used to print 700 pages of computer printout on a 4 inch by 6 inch piece of microfiche. This technology has progressed so far that a COM device is seen as just another printer by the computer. No special programming is required to use a COM device in place of an ordinary line printer. As more and more documents are handled by an office computer and less paper is generated, the need to store this information permanently and securely will arise. COM is an ideal choice to provide this archival storage of documents because of its low cost and high quality. Complete replacement of printed output by microfiche is hampered by the need to use microfiche viewers for reading the material on the fiche cards. It is a cumbersome process.

The other major area of image processing affecting office automation is computer business graphics. The expression "a picture is worth a thousand words" has taken on new meaning, as computer users, swamped in columns and rows of computer-generated output, are turning to computer graphics. Managers especially have found that by having computers draw charts and graphs they can comprehend the information more quickly and increase their productivity.

Actually, computer graphics involves nothing more than nonalphanumeric computer output, that is, displaying a ten-year sales trend as a graph on a CRT or printer/plotter, instead of as columns and rows of numbers. Computer graphics are nothing exotic or magical, but they are appealing because they make computer-generated output more aesthetically pleasing. The electronic technology necessary to produce color computer graphics is a complex and very much an equipment-oriented one. Until recently, the equipment needed to produce color graphics was quite expensive. There was little incentive to develop the software to support graphics, since most of the funds allocated for EDP/MIS technology was going into the more traditional technology that used columns and rows of numbers and textual information. More recently, however, graphics technology has become less expensive, and some funds are flowing in that direction. While the electronics and software are rather complex, the basic concepts used in graphics technology are relatively straightforward. The CRT is basically an electronic pencil and paper. It has an electronic gun (pencil) which shoots (writes) a beam of electrons (lead) across a phosphor-coated screen (paper) one line at a time. The ability to form symbols on the screen using an electron beam is the basis of computer graphics. From this basic arrangement various techniques are used to enhance the display and give it color, thus creating computer graphics. Color graphics are also possible with printers, or plotters as they are commonly known. The various colors are produced by a combination of hardware and software directing pens with inks of various colors to position themselves and draw curves or lines among coordinates. However it is CRT technology that is the most promising. Printers and plotters are electromechanical and more prone to failure and ink is potentially sloppy and pens run dry at inconvenient times. CRTs are electronic, less prone to failure, neater, and cleaner. Displays can be photographed or CRTs can be interfaced to photographic equipment, to product slides or prints.

Computer graphics has significant potential but again realizing the potential is the responsibility of the users. This is another situation where the tools are available. It is the arranging of the data and formulating of the requests for information that represent the formidable tasks to be addressed. There is no doubt that computer graphics can go a long way toward remedying situations where managers are provided with too much information in the form or printouts and reports. With terminals in their own offices, decision-makers can generate graphs themselves. As a result, better analysis and decision making can take place, but before it can, the data upon which these graphs depend must be in order, accurate, timely, and accessible.

In summary, office automation is an integration of several of the various computer technologies developed during the 1960s and 1970s. It is the culmination of years of research, experimentation, and practice by thousands of persons in the computer industry. Its aim is to automate as many of the mundane and mechanical office tasks as possible, thereby improving productivity and ultimately profits.

COMPUTER-BASED TECHNOLOGY IN THE PLANT

Terminals, Communications, and Networks

In addition to appearing on desks in offices, CRTs, and other terminals are also found on shop floors, in warehouses, and in quality control and production control facilities in plants. They employ the same basic type of technology that is used to support the commercial activities going on in offices. The CRTs and printers are essentially the same. The cases and keyboards are perhaps of a heavy-duty variety to withstand the punishment of shop and warehouse environments, but the insides, the electronics are the same. The telecommunications, if necessary, or the local networks software is essentially the same; it is only the application software that is different. And yet, even much of the application software is conceptually similar to that which is used to support office functions. Both use files, and information is entered on terminals to update the files. Queries made through the CRTs are responded to from information contained in the files and reports are produced periodically that reflect in tabular form the information contained in the files. In an office application, orders are entered, credit is checked, checks are produced, registers are printed. In a shop environment, finished goods are entered, on-hand and reorder points are checked, manufacturing order tickets are produced, and production schedules are printed. The general ideas are the same; the particulars differ. However, there is one area in which plant-related computer support activity is currently more sophisticated than that of the office. In the use of graphics, the plant uses three-dimensional CAD/CAM, while the office uses primarily two-dimensional bar charts, pie charts, and graphs.

Image Processing: CAD/CAM

As mentioned previously, the acronym CAD/CAM stands for computer-aided design/computer-aided manufacturing. In computer terms, it is a relatively old and established technology. It is used by engineers, designers, draftsmen, and architects as a tool for designing and manufacturing new machines, automobiles, airplanes, and buildings. With its three-dimensional and rotational capabilities, it allows users to develop detailed design schematics on a CRT device and to examine these schematics from every angle. Combinations of hardware and software make CAD/CAM an extremely versatile but expensive tool. Yet, because of the time saved, it is economically justifiable in many situations.

CAD/CAM is currently being employed in the design of semiconductor chips. Because of their increasing complexity and miniaturization, computer-aided design has become an absolute necessity.

COMPUTER-BASED TECHNOLOGY FOR MANAGEMENT

All Coming Together

The use of computers in manufacturing, warehousing, and other plant and operational business functions has proceeded in tandem with commercial data processing in business applications. Generally speaking, process control computers have been used in manufacturing for many years, but were never considered a part of the commercial data processing realm. The same could be said for computers that were designed and developed primarily for the scientific, mathematical, and engineering community. The high computational–low input/output requirements of these applications demands a different configuration of equipment than did the low computational–high input/output activity of commercial applications. As we explained earlier, all computers have the same basic functional components, the differences are in size, speed, and sophistication. Computers that were used for process control had little if any secondary storage, limited primary storage, and their input/output capabilities were limited to the manufacturing process they were monitoring and controlling. The scientific, mathematical, and engineering computers had extremely fast processors and primary storage components, limited secondary storage, and limited input/output capabilities. The commercial configurations had massive quantities of secondary storage and high performance printers for high volume output, and were connected to CRTs located throughout the organization, in the office, in the warehouse, in the plant, and in the laboratory. The separation of function between plant, laboratory, office, and commercial data processing is disappearing as interfaces, both technical and personal, are tying previously separate computerized areas together. Telecommunications also plays an important role as different types of computers that were once totally incompatible as far as communications with one another is concerned, can now interact. For example, it is currently possible for process control computers to pass exception information to another computer which can summarize it and produce an output report or display that manufacturing management can use to monitor, control, and possibly alter the manufacturing process. It is now commonplace for computer terminals to be found on shop floors, at the stations at which the steps in a manufacturing process are performed. As the steps are performed, information about the quantity and quality of the operations performed at those stations are entered into the terminal devices. This information from these CRTs is passed along to a computer that produces output reports and displays that can be used by production control managers to monitor, control, and coordinate production.

In addition, it is also quite likely that shop floor information is combined with inventory information that reflects shipments of finished goods and receipts of raw materials. This combined information is passed along to still another computer configuration, in all probability the same one that is performing the organization's commercial data processing activities such as order entry, accounts receivable, and forecasting. A further combination of data takes place, and at this juncture the potential exists to combine, evaluate according to some predetermined parameters, and present some truly strategic information to executives and senior managers. Combined information reflecting inventory, work in process, forecasts, orders, and aged accounts receivable, for instance, is exactly the kind of information that is required for strategic decision making. It is precisely this type of information that executives and senior managers historically have had difficulty obtaining. It continues to be difficult, but the reason for the difficulty has changed.

Historically, the software and the interfaces were not available. The promised MISs (management information systems) of the 1960s were beyond the capabilities of the technology available at the time. This is not the case currently. The current difficulty involves the state in which the data is found. It is not uncommon in a contemporary organization to find data from several applications that were developed and implemented over a ten-year period, stored in different file structures and file organizations. The table in Figure 6.2 illustrates this.

Customer File for the XYZ Company.*

Application	*File Structure*	*File Organization*
Accounts Receivable	Conventional	Sequential (blocked)
Accounts Receivable	Conventional	Indexed sequential (for on-line access)
Billing	Conventional	Sequential
Order Service	Conventional	Direct Access
Marketing	Database	Indexed

*A situation that existed in a real organization. Name of company changed for obvious reasons. Other files in the same organization reflected a situation where data redundancy and duplication of procession were commonplace. This type of situation is not unusual. Solutions are time consuming and expensive.

Figure 6.2 Example of mixed file organizations.

During that ten-year period, executives and senior managers did not pay a lot of attention to computer systems. Earlier promises of computer-based management information systems had not been fulfilled, senior managers and executives became skeptical and abdicated responsibility so that direction was set and technology was chosen by aggressive middle managers. These individuals, who spent about two years in a position before moving up or out, fostered an environment of fluctuating direction and technology. All of them, because of their aggressiveness, had to establish themselves. As each new individual came into a middle management position, a new direction was often set and a new technology was chosen. The result, after ten years, is reflected in the table.

Now, executives and senior managers are taking another look at management information systems. There are several reasons for this. First, some of the aggressive middle managers of the last ten years are now executives and senior managers and are aware of the potential if not the limitations of computer technology. Second, computer equipment, especially CRTs and small computers, are all over the place, and computer technology has permeated virtually every aspect of commerce. Finally, the current potential of computer and information systems technology is creating an irresistable force that is rapidly reducing the available options.

The Problem

Until recently, when data processing was being performed or when it was being explained, the emphasis was generally on the processing.

Well, that emphasis has now shifted. The emphasis is now on data. As far as processing is concerned, the tools are available, but the state of the data is such that storing it, processing it, and retrieving it has become extremely expensive. The situation reflected in Figure 6.2 is an example. Having five files, each carrying information that is between twenty- and eighty-percent redundant is not only wasteful of storage space, but also results in synchronization problems and extra processing. Five files have to be maintained, either by data entry processes or by copying information from one file to another. Depending upon the elapsed time between data entry processes and/or copying, the information in one file is out of synchronization with one or more of the others. In situations where accounts receivable, billing, order service, and marketing are running as independent applications, this lack of synchronization is only of minor consequence. This was indeed the situation, until recently. For instance, information about a new customer could be added to the order service file, for credit checking and order fulfillment. Getting the same information onto the billing file so that an invoice could be prepared and then onto the accounts receivable file could wait a few hours or even a day. Another day to get it to the marketing file was acceptable. Posting of sales could also take a day or so, and at various periods during that time, the billing, order service, accounts receivable, and marketing files would be out of synchronization as "batch" sequential processing updated one file after another over a twenty-four to thirty-six-hour period. Only at month-end, or in some cases week-end, were the files brought into synchronization for a short period of time. Once the week-end or month-end processing was completed, the cycle began again and files were again out of synchronization.

The advent of on-line systems and the potential they offered for individuals to interact with files and databases changed all that. Initially, the accounts receivable manager, the billing manager, and the order service manager could not understand why each of them had different figures for information such as open orders, and orders shipped. They were not familiar with separate files, scheduling of file maintenance processing, and other data processing functions. All they knew was what came up on their CRT screen, and when the accounts receivable display reported one number for open orders and the billing display showed another number, their reaction was usually to believe that the "stupid" computer was giving out confusing and conflicting information.

In addition to being organized differently (sequential, direct, indexed, and database) individual files that have been developed and implemented as part of specific applications over a period of time may be, for technical reasons, inaccessible to other applications. For instance, suppose the operations support application developed in 1974 and 1975 is a direct access file and was implemented using the file and data communication technology available at that time. Let's say that the operations support application and files were implemented using the "O" operating system, the "D" access method, and the "C" data communications monitor. This and other applications developed in this general time frame run in production region of a computer that we can call "ODC." See Figure 6.3A. In 1977–1978 new technology became available, and the billing application was developed and implemented. It used a "V" operating system, "I" access method for its indexed files, and a new version of the "C" data communications monitor, incompatible with the older version. The billing application and some others developed in this time period went into production on the computer in a region that we can call "VIC." See Figure 6.3B. In 1979–1980 the decision was made to try using database technology. A marketing application was developed and implemented using "H" file structures, "I" access methods, the "V" operating system, and the "Q" data communications monitor. The file structure component, either "H" or some other type, is required for database applications. It is an additional function required to support database technology, not required for traditional files. And so the marketing application was put into production in a region we'll call "VHIQ." Finally, in 1981 an accounts receivable program product was purchased. Thankfully, it was able to use the same operating system, access method, and data communications monitor as the billing application, and it was put into production in the "VIC" region.

In 1982, because of the obvious duplication of data (for example, each application mentioned above inlcuded a customer file) investiga-

Figure 6.3 Example of mixed implementation technologies.

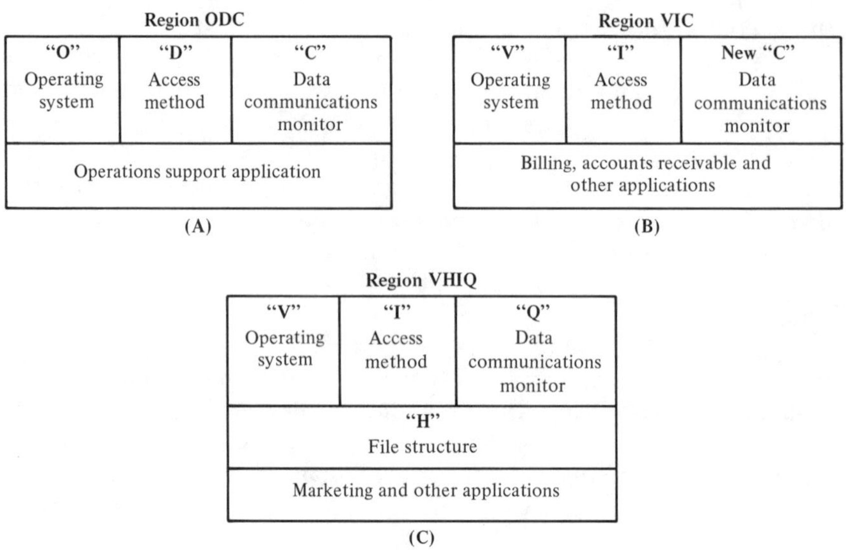

tions were undertaken to determine the magnitude of the task of consolidating the applications into a single integrated group. It quickly became obvious that such a task was quite a bit easier to conceptualize than it was to achieve. While the difficulties involved in specifying a single logical record format for a customer file, for example, were seen as surmountable, the amount of work to make changes mandated by physical and technical considerations was found to be significant. The task is not unlike trying to build an ideal truck using the parts from a Ford, a Mercedes, and a Mazda. Logically it's possible, but wait till implementation starts.

For example, if a single record layout could be agreed upon for the customer file, and if all customer data were put into a single physical file, into which region would that file be put? Which file organization would be used? Since the file was needed for both direct and sequential access, it would have to be "I." All the programs in the marketing and operations support applications would have to be modified to access the "I."

However, there was an even greater problem. Let's call it the interregion communication problem. There are two options. If there was to be a single customer file from which all application were to get their information, then all applications would have to run in the same region, or interregion coordination would have to be established.

Unless the applications were in the same region, or unless interregion coordination were established, the following scenario could easily occur. A long-running transaction comes into the "VIC" region that accesses a particular customer record for updating. Another short running transaction comes into the "ODC" region and accesses the same customer record for update. Since no interregion coordination exists between the regions, the "ODC" transaction retrieves, updates, and returns the customer records to the file before the longer-running "VIC" transaction completes. When the "VIC" transaction does finally complete, it returns the record to the file and completely overlays any changes that may have been made by the "ODC" transaction.

"Well," you ask, "when the modifications are made that make a common record layout, why not put all the applications into a single region?" That is definitely the best way to go, but there is a qualification. A detailed analysis must be performed to determine if a single region can handle the activity of all the applications, without its performance degrading to an unacceptable level.

If it is determined that a single region cannot handle all of the activity, then two or more regions may have to be used. This can be implemented in either of two ways. Two or more copies of a multithread single-partition data communication monitor can be used, or a single copy of a single-thread, multipartitioned data communication monitor can be used. These were described in Chapter 5. If the former is chosen, additional software is required to coordinate interregion communication. Further coordination is necessary if more than one computer equipment configuration is used.

Information systems depend on data that is available on-line. The data has to be accurate and consistent. The presence of multiple files residing in two or more regions, each maintained or updated at different intervals, is not the best environment in which to implement a management information system. And yet because of the complexity and expense of converting existing files and their associated application programs into more suitable structures and organizations, we may have to settle temporarily for something less than the full potential of MIS.

The most frequently offered solution for the disheveled data situation is database. Mountains of literature and untold numbers of seminars proclaim the virtues of database. With all the ballyhoo, hoopla, and fanfare, there must be something to it, you ask. Well, in many respects it's all true, especially in a conceptual or logical sense. It's only in the physical implementation of database technology where things can get troublesome. To begin with, let's try to crystallize a few things, and to straighten out some misconceptions. Following that we can show where the real problem is with database and can suggest a solution.

First, by and large, database technology is sound and works according to specifications. Although the apparently labyrinthine interconnected data elements that make up a database seem, from a human perspective, to be overwhelmingly complex and impossible to manage, it is this type of task for which computers are best suited. Database management is the kind of thing that computers do well. Database disasters, about which uninformed after-dinner speakers tell jokes, are often the result of human errors based on misunderstanding of the technology.

Second, database technology is invariably supported by other technologies. As we pointed out in an earlier chapter, database management system software depends upon an operating system, uses the facilities of access methods, and quite often is interfaced to a data communications monitor. This is true in large-scale computer equipment configurations as well as in smaller ones. Since there is probably no individual alive today who is technically proficient in all these technologies, there are likely to be some problems in implementing database software, some of which are purely technical, others due to misunderstandings and personality conflicts among highly skilled technicians.

Third, implementing a database management system software product and implementing a database/data communications application are two separate and distinct processes, each of which require different skills. The former is a system software support task and requires knowledge and experience in systems software, computer operations, and database/data communications concepts. The latter is an application analysis and file or database design and development task and requires knowledge and experience in those areas. It is also necessary that the system software support technicians have a general acquaintance with the applications being implemented. It is even more important that the applications analysts and file or database designers be familiar with the methodology* of the database/data communication system that is being used.

Fourth, installing a database/data communications software product does not result in an on-line database that is ready to be used; it results merely in the establishment of potential that can be realized. Installing a database/data communication application involves:

- Designing and implementing database structures using the facilities of the installed database/data communications system product.
- Specifying to the data communications facilities the characteristics and attributes of the terminal devices that are to be used.
- Loading limited application information into the established database structures for testing of the application.
- Analyzing and developing application transaction programs that are to store, manipulate, and retrieve information from the databases.
- Coding application programs and testing and debugging them on both a unit and integrated basis and preparing procedures for their use.
- Loading application information in total into database structures for using the application in a production environment.
- Interacting with system software technicians to monitor and adjust the application to changing conditions.

So much for the conceptual and what ought to be done, let's now have a look at the difficulties involved in getting it done and how to overcome them.

Database/data communications systems presentations and demonstrations are generally made in rather pristine environments on computer equipment configurations that are dedicated to that purpose. What these presentations and demonstrations show is that the database/data communications products do work and that they can perform

*Application analysts and file or database designers ought to be familiar with the file structure facilities (hierarchical, network or relational), the principles of the pointer mechanisms and the architecture (single partition, multithread or multipartition, single thread) of the database/data communications product being used.

to specifications. What they don't show is the difficulties encountered in installing a database/data communications system product and in implementing a database/data communications application in a real-world situation. Real-world situations include:

- An EDP/MIS landscape cluttered with technologies of the past two decades; incompatible files, awkward square peg/round hole interfaces for applications that when developed had not been designed to interface.
- Limited capacity, in terms of equipment.
- A dynamic environment in which both technology (hardware and system software products) and applications are constantly changing.
- A business organization where the main idea is making a profit and not installing the latest technological phenomenon.
- An organization that finds itself drowning in a sea of data out of which it is unable to extract any useful information.

The problem, then, faced by many contemporary organizations, is to find a way to get from where they are (the real-world situation just described) to where they ought to be (a database/data communications environment), where one set of detail files or databases can be used to support the operational functions of the organization and another set of summary files or databases can provide senior managers and executives with the information they need to operate the organization at the policy and decision-making level. The composition of the detail files is determined by the needs of the applications using them. The skill of the analysts and file designers is employed to determine which data elements are required on-line and which data elements are only needed for batch processing. The summary files need not contain up to the minute information, but they ought to be kept on-line. A senior manager or an executive may wish to know what the sales were for a given product six months earlier. When such individuals want that information, they want it right away, not twenty-four hours later.

The Solution

OK, what's the solution? Well, there is no single solution. However, there is one that definitely won't work, and there is another that probably will work, but it won't be easy and it's not cheap. Let's dispense with the one that won't work first. This is the approach advocated in a great deal of the database literature and the seminars that are offered. It involves a process where some individual or group of individuals interview key managers and executives of an organization to find out what their information requirements are. Having determined this, these individuals then proceed to design a database or databases that reflect these organizational information needs. The resultant database is what has been called a conceptual or logical model of the organization. The problem arises after the logical model is designed. What does one do with it?

It would be possible to acquire a database/data communication product and, using the data description language feature of the product, to specify database definitions. These could be compiled and loaded into a library and then the data from existing files could be loaded into them and new transaction programs could be developed and so on. Nonsense! Anyone who has worked in real-world situations knows that such scenarios never occur. It's just not that simple. It is totally impractical to convert to a new operational environment from an existing one in a single step. Jobs have been lost by those who have attempted it. Organizations have spent millions of dollars trying it, only to scrap the entire effort.

And yet, there is a way that may work. It is slow, it is costly, but the costs can be incurred incrementally, and over time they ought to be recovered as improvements in both processing and storage efficiency come about. It involves a gradual shift from contemporary technology to database/data communication technology. The gradual shift is necessary so that as the new technology is introduced in increments, in one or two application areas at a time, those involved are given an opportunity to get used to it, and the converted applications are given time to be shaken down. The problem with this type of approach is that there is a period of time where redundant processing (the existing version of the application and the converted version run concurrently) is necessary. This increases costs and frequently generates extra work for application users as they are required to maintain files and databases in both versions and are obliged to handle and correlate certain output information from both versions. In addition, interfaces to applications that are yet to be converted must be established and maintained. This also generates extra work and increases costs. And yet, what are the alternatives? Attempt a massive conversion? Everyone with any experience knows that will not work. Stay with existing technology and dedicate large percentages of EDP/MIS staffs to perform maintenance on applications that become more cumbersome and obsolete with each passing week? Some of those responsible for EDP/MIS departments choose that alternative. Perhaps they think "Sooner or later I'll get out of this job and someone else can worry about it."

Let's suppose that a responsible senior manager or executive decides to "bite the bullet" and take the steps necessary to make the conversion to database/data communications technology, which is the technology that undergirds the automated office. Assuming the interest and approval of senior management, what then occurs?

In many organizations, there are a number of functional application areas that are supported in varying degrees by the EDP/MIS function. The most heavily supported is generally finance and accounting, followed by operations support (order entry, inventory, shipping). The interface between operations support and finance and accounting, is generally in the billing and accounts receivable areas. When product is shipped, information is passed to billing and accounts receivable. Eventually cash is received and somewhere between the shipping of product and receipt of cash, sales are recorded. This information gets into the marketing and sales applications which are also supported in varying degrees by the EDP/MIS function. Depending upon the type of organization, there are other application areas such as manufacturing and warehousing.* The EDP/MIS support for these functional areas of business generally consists of combination of batch processing and on-line applications that have been developed, implemented and periodically modified over a period of fifteen years. These applications generally utilize a range of physical file organizations (sequential, indexed, direct, and database) and are interfaced with one another in a variety of ways. The most recently developed applications may be truly integrated, that is, they share common files or databases. Older systems share data by making copies of major files and passing them from one system to another, a costly and inefficient way of doing things. The oldest systems in the organization probably have several independent file maintenance procedures by means of which several files are updated with the same information, a very wasteful way of doing things, in terms of both money and time.

Making the transition to a database/data communication environment, involves determining the organization's major files, major keys, and data aggregates. Many organizations have three major files, a customer file, an order file, and a product file, and some secondary files such as general ledger and a series of tables used to supply policy and indicative information to applications. Pricing tables and location tables are examples. A suggested approach involves zeroing in on one major file and performing the analysis necessary to reduce all copies of that file to one and having all applications requiring information from

*EDP/MIS supported applications vary from industry to industry. Banking, airlines, trucking, mail order, brokerage, media, publishing, communications, retail, wholesale, and even farming all have some unique application. Nearly all industries have interfaces between their unique applications and the fundamental applications of finance, accounting, and operations support. Most industries have marketing applications also.

that file to access that file. Once that task is completed, then begin working on another file.

As we stated earlier, the task is neither easy nor inexpensive. A significant amount of effort is required, and some of the technical obstacles may appear to be virtually insurmountable. For instance, in a given organization, it might be found that there are five distinct customer files. The accounts receivable application has two, one indexed on-line, and one sequential. The billing application has a customer file that is a sequential version copied from the operations support's directly accessible customer file. The marketing application has another copy, and since it is a recently developed application, its customer file is a hierarchically structured file, only accessible through a database management system. There are three independent file maintenance operations, one for the operations support file, one for the accounts receivable file, and another for the marketing file. It can also be assumed that the same kind of situation exists for the product file, i.e., there are numerous copies, each record type able to contain some redundant information and some unique information, several separate file maintenance operations are performed, and somewhere between three and six different file organizations are employed.

Following a review of the inventory of the data elements of one of the major files by managers of the departments using the data elements, a choice has to be made. What technology is to be used for the future? Is one of the existing file structures to be used, is the existing database management system to be used, or is a new database/data communications product to be employed? Regardless of the choice made, two things are certain, a common file or database methodology must be used for all applications, and some kind of a data dictionary* product is required to automate file and record, or database and data element documentation.

After the choice is made, specifications for the file or database are made by analysts, who are known as database administrators. They are compiled and stored in an internal library. An input/output module for accessing the file can also be developed concurrently. Over time, the programs accessing the current versions of the customer file can be modified to access the new version. Since some applications access it directly and others access it sequentially, it is immediately obvious that if there is to be a single copy, it requires an index so that it can be used for both sequential and direct access processing. Otherwise, two copies, a direct version, and a sequential version are needed. This is a trade-off that can be made by analysts working on the project.

*The next chapter deals with the data dictionary product in some detail.

There are additional tasks to be performed by the analysts. One of these is the determination of the appropriate source of input for the file. Duplicate file maintenance functions are to be eliminated. Getting rid of such redundant work may partially offset the increased cost of maintaining the new file or database during the transition period while the old files are being phased out.

Even this type of a transition process is easier to write about and describe than it is to put into practice. To be sure, there are difficulties. In addition to increasing costs, there are the political considerations. Consolidations invariably appear threatening. Reducing or eliminating redundant work may be or at least appear to be a reduction in jobs. Those who perceive such threats are sure to resist somewhat. Sandbagging, inability to attend meetings, and other such techniques of passive resistance are certain to be somewhat less than helpful as the transition is made. Yet, consider the alternatives. Change nothing and continue into obsolescence or attempt a massive conversion to new technology and provide another entry to the list of the uninformed after-dinner speaker's "database disasters" stories.

One final task the analysts ought to perform while they implement a new detail database or file is the establishment of a summary file or summary database. Let's use customer file or customer database as an example. The detail file or database is used by the operational functions of the organization. Senior managers and executives generally work with gross numbers, that is, with summarized information. It is up to the analysts to determine what format the summary information takes. This is accomplished through a combination of skill, experience, and interviews with executives and senior managers. In brief, at this point in time, it is an art, not a science.

CONCLUSION

Word processing and text editing are but two aspects of automated offices. Currently, they are the most visible. Electronic mail and facsimile transmission are a couple of other applications that are frequently discussed as features of an automated office. Yet they are merely applications that rest upon the technology of telecommunications. Complete office automation is going to come about as commercial applications are implemented using the combined technologies of database/data communications. Software products that facilitate the setting up of file structures in which data elements can be related in a file and record boundary transcending fashion provide the potential for office automation that is of value to senior managers and executives. The realization of that potential depends upon the applications to which it is put. Once implemented, as vendor demonstrations clearly show, the technology is sound and information can be retrieved quickly. The difficulty lies in the implementation. Database/data communication technology is not a quick fix, applying it is a long-range (at least a few and perhaps several years) project. It requires a sustained commitment of senior managers and executives. Middle managers are seldom in their positions long enough to see such efforts through to completion.

SUMMARY

In this chapter, we have taken a look at what has become known as office automation. We discussed how executives and senior managers are finally beginning to notice computer and telecommunications technology. These two technologies are providing the foundation for all office automation functions, including word processing, electronic mail, facsimile transmission, and communications across cities, across countries, and around the world. It is possible to transmit voice data and video signals on the same physical cable.

Different types of terminal devices, dumb, smart, and intelligent were discussed. The two types of local networks, baseband and broadband were given treatment. Word processing, electronic mail, and graphics were surveyed. The use of computers and communications in plants was also examined.

The latter part of the chapter explained how database/data communications technology forms the foundation for office automation in the fullest sense of the term. Explanations were given as to why implementations of true office automation are difficult and an approach was suggested.

CHAPTER 7

Data Dictionaries and Software Security

INTRODUCTION

Realizing the potential of information systems and at the same time limiting that potential are two objectives that seem at times to be working at cross purposes. Database/data communication systems have as their objective making as much information as possible available to as many people as possible in the shortest period of time as is possible. And yet, we are aware that providing unrestricted access to information in databases is unnecessary and possibly hazardous. Database/data communication productions are developed primarily to facilitate the development and definition of structures to hold data in such a way that it can be quickly accessed and to provide the mechanisms with which to perform the accesses. Installing a database/data communication system product and allowing unrestricted use of its facilities makes it possible for any and all individuals who are willing to take the time to learn how it works to access and update information in the systems' databases. In an organizational (business, governmental, or other), such a situation is just not feasible. Therefore, some measures have to be taken within organizations to limit the use of database/data communication system facilities and to limit access to information in databases. Two types of product are available to enforce the necessary restrictions, data dictionaries, and software security products. Data dictionaries can be used to limit the use of database/data communication system facilities, and software security products can be used to limit access to information in databases. Let's look first at data dictionaries and their functions.

Contemporary commercial and governmental organizations are, among other things, guardians of certain assets. In accounting and financial terms these assets commonly include buildings, equipment, and property. The specific assets and their value vary from one organization to another. Lately, another organizational entity is being discussed in some circles as also being an asset. That entity is information. The dramatic growth in the use of computer equipment for storing, manipulating, and retrieving information has led to a significant increase in the amount of information that is kept "on the computer." The sheer volume of the information that is stored on computer equipment has fostered an atmosphere that encourages technological experimentation to bring about ways of storing and retrieving that information more efficiently. Contemporary results of this experimentation, specializations in their own right, are the technologies known as database or database management and data communications or computer networking. These particular branches of computer technology have introduced certain efficiencies in the processes of storing and retrieving information and in the transmitting of information over distances. As with everything, however, there is a price. In these cases, the price is complexity. To permit efficient information storage and retrieval, complex structures that relate basic groupings of data and information to one another are required. In addition to the complex data structures, elaborate computer networks are being put into place that facilitate the transfer of information among locations a few yards, several floors, a few city blocks, or many miles distant from one another. This complexity has led to the development of an auxiliary component to database/data communication software. This component has become known as data dictionary.

CONCEPT AND DEFINITION OF DATA DICTIONARY

Most of us are familiar with the term dictionary. When we hear the term used, we immediately think of a book that resides on desks in our homes and offices. It is basically a book containing an alphabetically ordered list of words, in our case English language words, making up the vocabulary that we use to communicate with one another. The words in the list are defined, pronunciations are explained, synonyms are given, parts of speech (noun, pronoun, etc.) are indicated, and so on. In sum, the characteristics and attributes of the words in the English language are found in an alphabetically ordered list in an English language dictionary. For example, let's look at how *Webster's New World Dictionary of the American Language* describes the word dictionary:

> **dic-tion-ar-y** (dik'she ner'e) n., pl. **-ar'ies** [ML. *dictionarium* LL. *dictio*: see DICTION] **1**. a book of alphabetically listed words in a language, with definitions, etymologies, pronunciations, and other information; lexicon **2**. a book of alphabetically listed words in a language with their equivalents in another language [a Spanish-English dictionary] **3**. any alphabetically arranged list of words or articles relating to a special subject [a medical dictionary]

A data dictionary, in concept, is somewhat like a dictionary. Within a data dictionary reside the terms used to identify the data elements used in computer applications as well as the terms that define the components found in computer networks. Data and information are defined in terms of fields, records, files, databases, and data elements. Network components include terminals, computers, peripheral devices, and communication lines. Each field, record, file, database, data element, terminal, computer, peripheral device, and communication line can appear in a data dictionary along with its attributes and characteristics. So much for concepts; let's now take a closer look.

DATA DICTIONARY: A SET OF FILES (A DATABASE) AND AN APPLICATION

When the term *data dictionary* is used, it can imply either of two things: (1) a set of files or a database containing the kind of information mentioned above, or (2) a software product consisting of some programs and having the potential for creating the set of files or database containing the kind of information described above. Webster's dictionary is a fine book and an indispensable tool, but it had to be written originally, and it requires periodic maintenance and modification. The same is true for a data dictionary. The schematic in Figure 7.1 illustrates a data dictionary, both files or database and an application.

One way to look at a data dictionary is to visualize it as an automated documentation tool. The files or database of a data dictionary can constitute a central repository of an organization's computer application and network documentation. It has been stated that a data dictionary contains data about data. The table in Figure 7.2 illustrates this idea. There is an essential difference between the kind of data stored in a data dictionary file and the kind of data that is stored in an organization's other files.

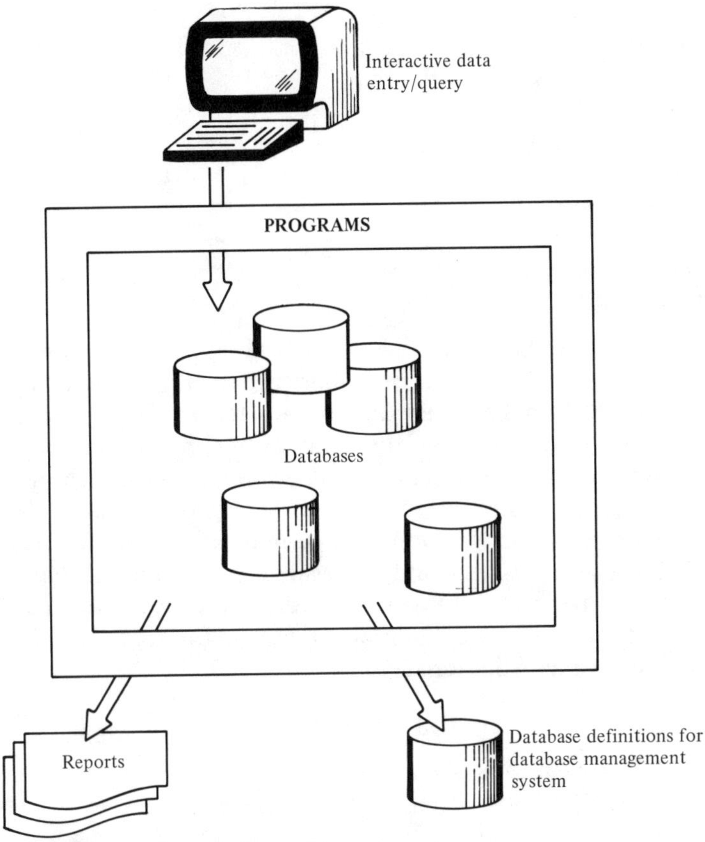

Figure 7.1 A data dictionary system.

For instance, an organization is likely to have files or a database containing data or information about the products it produces, the personnel that it employs and its financial condition. The data values found in those files would look like the values in the second column of Figure 7.2. The data values found in the files or database of the data dictionary would be values like those in column one of Figure 7.2.

It is not only data about data that is carried in the files or database of a contemporary data dictionary, but also data about network components. Therefore, in the configuration of files or in the database of a data dictionary, there might be a file for each of the following:

- Files
- Records
- Data elements
- Fields

- Narratives
- Terminals
- Computers
- Peripheral equipment
- Vendors
- Software products
- Network nodes
- Application descriptions
- Program descriptions

Going down the list, two things become patently obvious: first, more entities can be added to the list, and second, there are relationships among the entities in the list. Contemporary data dictionary products are constructed to handle growth and to use the facilities of database/data communication system software to support the necessary relationships that exist among entities. Data dictionary products, like database/data communication system products, provide the *potential* to support the relationships. It's the users' responsibility to realize the potential. Figure 7.3 illustrates in record format the kind of information stored in a conventional application. Figure 7.4 illustrates in record format the kind of information found in a data dictionary.

Figure 7.2 Data about data.

Types of Data	*Data*
Product description	ENGINE, TRANSMISSION, CLUTCH, BOLT
Product number	V84367-113, T37-16002, JHL19847, 7963CTH, 9411B
Plant location	604, 706, 1141, 333
Office location	753, 914, 11, 17C
Employee name	BARWINSKI, SMITH, JONES, CHUNG, GRECO
Social Security number	052-13-9962, 078-22-3065, 091-12-4813
Sales tax rate	.025, .034, .10, .004
Income tax rate	.22, .25, .33, .48
Order number	11637, 111780, 9432

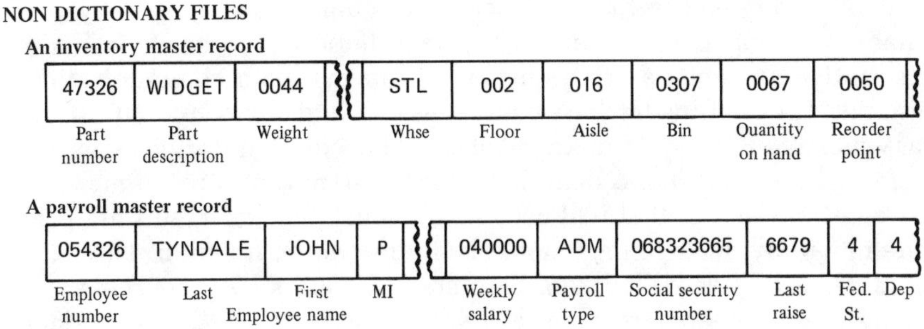

Figure 7.3 Nondictionary file and contents.

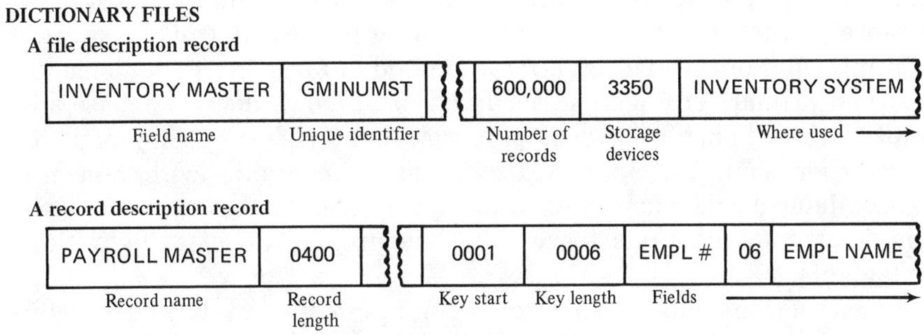

Figure 7.4 Dictionary file and contents.

HOW A DATA DICTIONARY SYSTEM WORKS

Data dictionary software, like any other software product, arrives at a computer installation on a reel of magnetic tape. Performing the GEN* is basically the same process as that performed to install other software products. However, the GEN is only a single step in a series that need to be accomplished to implement a data dictionary.

When database/data communication systems and data dictionaries came into common usage in the mid-1970s, a function called database administration came into existence. It took quite a while for the dust to settle, but when it did, the function of database administration turned out to be a function staffed by technically skilled individuals who translated database requirements as stated by application development ana-

*GEN is an abbreviation for generation or system generation. Sometimes referred to as a SYSGEN, it involves a process of selecting from a list of options those facilities of a product to be used in an installation. The facilities are stored in system libraries and are used when needed.

lysts into the semi-technical descriptive statements required by the database management system or the data dictionary system. Database descriptive statements are required by database/data communication systems. They define database characteristics and attributes to the database management system. In database/data communication environments where there is no data dictionary system (not a recommended practice for reasons that will become obvious), the statements are prepared by individuals in the database administration function. These individuals are often called data base administrators (DBAs). The statements they prepare are compiled by facilities of the database/data communication system. In their compiled form, these descriptions are sometimes called control blocks. In this form, they contain the information used by other facilities of the database/data communication system to store and retrieve data elements. In other words, control blocks contain information needed by access methods to transfer data elements between primary storage and secondary storage devices. Database administrators, then, need to possess a combination of skills. They ought to have expertise in file and database design, to be familiar with the work ings of database/data communication systems, and to have some knowledge of the applications for which they prepare database definition statements.

Installations with database/data communication systems generally have a data dictionary system. In those environments with conventional systems, that is, nondatabase, a data dictionary system can also be a useful tool. It can be used as a documentation aid. In a database environment, a data dictionary system is virtually indispensable. When it is installed, it is an aid to the database administrators, but it also introduces further responsibilities. The DBAs become guardians of the dictionary, and they must become familiar with the workings of the data dictionary system and also with the content of the data dictionary's files or databases.

Installations where a data dictionary is used may require additional work to get applications implemented. The trade-off is additional work for the sake of control and documentation. In an environment where there is a data dictionary, the statements prepared by the DBAs are entered into the data dictionary, rather than directly into a database/data communication system. The descriptive information in the statements going into the data dictionary includes that which must ultimately reach the database/data communication system for compilation into control blocks. However, more information is required if the full potential of the data dictionary is to be realized. For instance, data dictionaries have the ability to hold alternate names for entities such as fields and data elements. The alternate names, known as aliases, are useful for references to fields and data elements in application programs written in different programming languages. Data dictionaries also have the ability to hold "where used" information, that is, a given data element definition in a data dictionary may be referenced by several application programs. This information can be stored with the data element definition. Relationships between entities, such as those that may exist in a database environment, can be stored in the data dictionary. A given data element may be related to other data elements in several other files. This information can be stored in the data dictionary. For example, sales order information in a data element may be related to customer number and customer descriptive information in a data element of another file. This last type of information may be kept in the data dictionary and is also passed to the database/data communication system for inclusion in the control blocks. In addition, as mentioned earlier, there is capacity in a data dictionary for all kinds of other information, not necessarily needed by the database/data communication system.

A data dictionary system should not require double work. If statements containing database, data element, or other information are entered into a data dictionary, they should not have to be reentered manually into a database/data communication system.

If the two systems are incompatible, then double work may be required, or an interface can be developed. In situations where compatibility exists, the data dictionary system has a feature that can create the statements of descriptive information required by the database/data communication system. Through manipulations made possible by job control language (JCL) procedures, these statements can be passed from the data dictionary to the database management system with no manual intervention required. Many data dictionary systems have additional manual work-saving abilities, for example, the creation of programming language file descriptions or database structures that are used by application programs. By making these available, application programmers are freed from the task of coding these definitions and structures when writing their programs; they need merely write a statement that can "call" in from the data dictionary the definition or structure required. As the program is being compiled, that statement retrieves the file definition or database structure from the data dictionary for inclusion in the compilation process. Figure 7.5 shows schematically the flow of information in a typical data dictionary/database management environment.

A data dictionary system has an output facility by which the contents of the dictionaries files or databases can be displayed. The displays can be in the form of reports that are printed on continuous form paper or in the form of formatted displays on CRT devices. Security procedures, discussed later in this chapter, are required to assure that

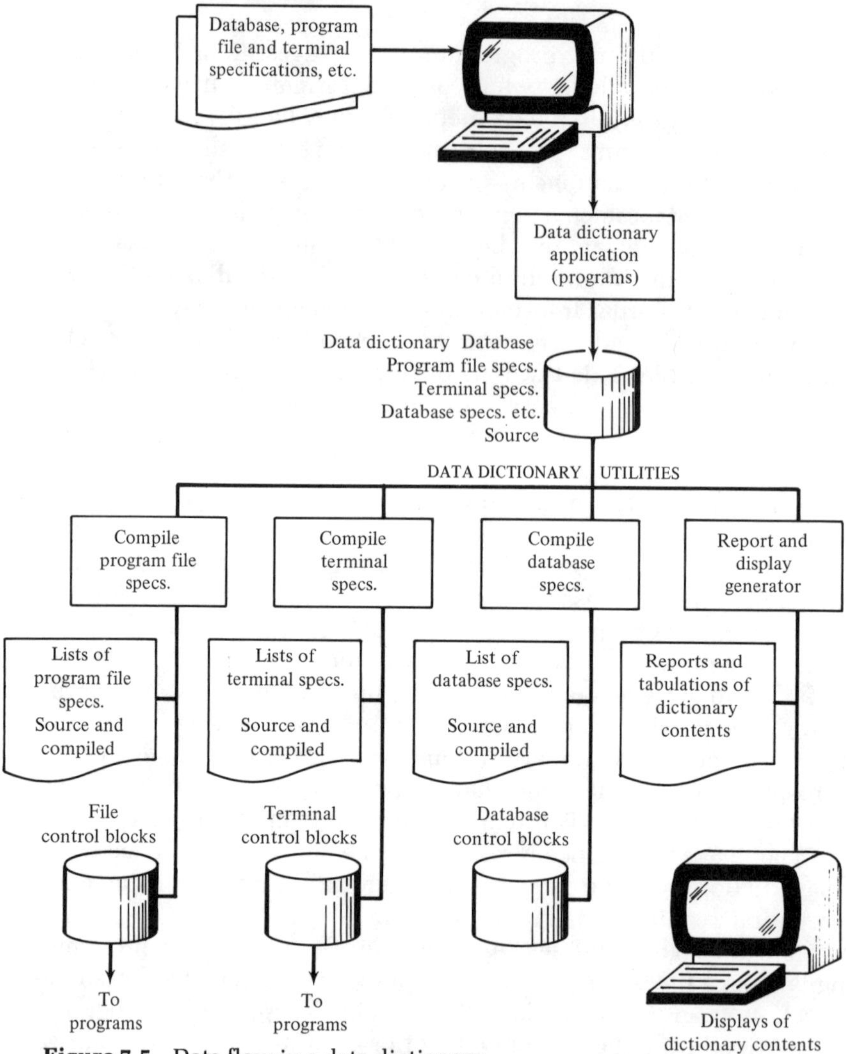

Figure 7.5 Data flow in a data dictionary.

updating privileges are limited to authorized database administrators. The information in a data dictionary should be available for all to see, but unrestricted updating would soon reduce it to a chaotic collection of random data.

Making good use of a data dictionary requires some additional steps, the development of standards, and forms or screen formats. In a typical situation involving a data dictionary product, it is quite probable that a database/data communication system is also present. Since the two generally interface with one another, it is frequently necessary for database administrators and system software technicians who support the two to work together. There are several tasks that have to be performed in such an environment. These tasks include:

- Recovery and restart procedures must be defined.
- Backup procedures must be established and frequencies scheduled. Database reorganizations are required periodically.
- Compilations of database descriptions must be performed from time to time.
- Productivity aids (other software products) need to be evaluated. If selected for use they need to be installed.
- Compilations of network configurations are required.

Compilations and backup operations can be scheduled. Recovery and restart operations are required to respond to unexpected malfunctions. The point is this; schedules ought to be set up and responsibilities ought to be defined. There is no set way to do this. Each installation has its own unique organizational and political makeup. What is important, however, is that discussions and negotiations be held between the DBA group, systems software support group, and applications development group to determine "who does what."

While these negotiations and discussions are going on, it is also necessary to begin to establish standards and to design forms or displays for specifying inputs. Some of these forms or displays house the input to the data dictionary. Others contain input to the periodic compilations of the database/data communication system.

DATA DICTIONARY DEVELOPMENTS

As data dictionary capabilities are expanding, some titles may change. Database administrator, as a term, is restrictive. It connotes the administration of databases. However, contemporary DBAs perform other functions. Data communications administration is another function that is being performed in many places, but it often goes unacknowledged and unrecognized because it is quite often performed by a systems software programmer or an applications programmer analyst. Network configurations require the same type of administration as do databases. There is virtually no end to the administration of data or information used by MIS organizations. Documentation about MIS resources are found in various locations around an organization. For example, database definitions are found in the dictionary, computer room configurations are found on wall charts in managers' offices, network configurations are found in books in other managers' offices, procedures are found in libraries. There is something to be said for consolidating all this information into a central information inventory. The facilities of contemporary data dictionaries lend themselves to such an inventory. For instance, within a data dictionary it is possible to set up databases or files for several classes or categories of information, as we showed in an earlier list. With dictionary databases it is possible to set up connections to show relationships between categories. For example, the information inventory might include computers as a category. To further describe a particular computer, attributes such as model and serial number, feature codes, installation date, and type of computer might also be stored. Relationships could be stored in data dictionary databases which would show that the computer had relationships to primary storage and channel categories. The address of the particular channel to which the computer had access could also be stored. These concepts are illustrated in Figure 7.6.

As is the case with any software product, the data dictionary or information inventory is potential. Realization of that potential comes through effort. Individual entities have to be identified and classified. The attributes of the entities need to be specified. Relationships have to be identified. The magnitude of these tasks ought not be underrated. Once the identification and specification tasks are completed, then the data must be entered into the data dictionary databases. This usually involves a keying process where CRT devices are used by individuals entering the identifying information and attribute specifications. Data dictionary or information inventory systems generally have preformatted screen displays that aid individuals in entering the information.

Another development is that of integration, that is the interfacing of data dictionaries with database/data communication systems and other software products. This was partially explained earlier. It is possible for a data dictionary system to develop database descriptions for a database/data communication system and file descriptions for traditional/nondatabase applications programs. In additional to that, data dictionary databases generally have the capacity to hold several versions of database descriptions, one version for day-to-day production databases and the other database descriptions being used for development work. Several versions of a database are useful in helping database administrators evaluate the relative merits of different database structures. Other software products are also used by DBAs to perform such tasks. They can usually be recognized by descriptive terms in their names, such as database design aids or database prototype developers.

Most of the information kept in a data dictionary is kept there so that it can be accessed quickly and easily by those needing it. And yet, it is also true that not all of the information stored should be available for everyone to see. Some information must be protected by restricting ac-

LOCATION	COMPUTER FILE				Pointers		
6538	IBM 3033	PD1463	8	0678	14928	15062	
6742	IBM 3033	PD2781	12	0279			
6984	IBM 3033	RD7169	12	1179			
	IBM 4300	GD2166	4	0878			
	IBM 4300	GD2748	4	0479			
	IBM 4300	GD7103	6	1179			
⋮	⋮	⋮	⋮	⋮	⋮	⋮	⋮
	PDP 11/40	RFQ903					
	VAX 11/70	ZHL177					
	VAX 11/70	NPL428					
⋮	⋮	⋮	⋮	⋮	⋮	⋮	⋮

LOCATION	DEVICE FILE					Pointers	
14804	IBM 3350						
14928	IBM 3350					6538	
15062	IBM 3350					6538	
	IBM 3350						
	IBM 3350						
⋮	⋮	⋮	⋮	⋮	⋮	⋮	⋮
	DEC 7423						
	DEC 7423						
⋮	⋮	⋮	⋮	⋮	⋮	⋮	⋮

Figure 7.6 Data dictionary capabilities.

cess to it. This can be done by permitting access by specific devices, specific transactions, or specific individuals. Even more important, however, in terms of security is the protection against both accidental or intentional alterations of data in the data dictionary. A data dictionary's database or files should be dumped to a backup medium on a periodic basis, and logs should be kept of all data entered. The backup copy and the logs can be used to reconstruct the database or files if they are damaged.

SOFTWARE SECURITY

As the spread of EDP/MIS technology continues, bringing under its control increasing amounts of software and data, there is a corresponding growth in the vulnerability of this software and data. As with anything else, the more you accumulate, the more you have to worry about protecting. Computer software and data are not different.

Software security often comes under criticism as being inadequate. The feeling seems to be that some smart programmers can always get around anything written by other programmers. That sentiment correctly reflects the situation. However, the same can be said for lawyers: some smart lawyers can always get around anything in a contract written by other lawyers. Yet contracts continue to be written, and for the most part, they are effective. Computer software security routines can also be effective most of the time. Just because a security procedure is not 100 percent foolproof is no reason for not using it. In addition, while waiting for better security procedures to be developed, some security is certainly better than no security at all. The basic consideration is one of degree: i.e., how important are specific databases, files, data elements, and proprietory software and how important are their security. Some data require very little security. For example, a software library containing some programs that are similar to those found in nearly all computer installations does not require elaborate security procedures to guard it. Other data requires extensive security. For example, a database containing the financial data for the marketing strategy of a large corporation requires some rather stringent security procedures to maintain its confidentiality. The decision, on the amount and type of security to be applied to specific elements of data lies with the individuals responsible for them.

BASIC COMPUTER INSTALLATION SECURITY

Underlying any system of software security is a minimum amount of overall security of an installation. Normal safeguards ought to be put in place to exclude unauthorized personnel from computer installations. Stationing a security guard at the main entrance to an installation is basic. Keeping delivery entrances locked when not in use is another fundamental precaution. Fire prevention procedures, for example, strategically located fire extinguishers and smoke detectors, are too basic to even mention, but they are sometimes overlooked. Some kind of pass key or card entry into a computer room is advisable. These few items, mentioned in passing, represent rudamentary security provisions.

Without these, the most elaborate and sophisticated software security measures can be neutralized and rendered ineffective.

Assuming these basic overall security precautions are in place, there are three types of software security to be examined:

- Protection of software products
- Protection of data in on-line systems
- Protection of data in conventional "batch" processing systems

Security by means of software is provided by computer programs designed to protect data and to protect themselves. Both data and software require varying degrees of protection, based on their sensitivity and confidentially. Some data and software must be kept strictly confidential and made available only to selected individuals. Other data and software must be restricted as far as modification is concerned. Substantial amounts of on-line data require periodic copying in the event that the original data is damaged or destroyed.

Data protection can be looked at in a couple of ways: data integrity and data accuracy. Data integrity involves the protection of or recovery of data from damage due to equipment or software malfunction. Data accuracy involves protection of or recovery of data from errors caused by sources external to equipment or software. Data integrity is maintained by means of recovery and restart software and procedures, backup procedures, logging, and back out software. Data accuracy is assured by means of editing, control totals, hash counts, reasonableness checks, and balancing procedures. These are treated in more detail later.

Let's first review systems software and examine overall software security practices and methods.

AN OVERVIEW OF THE LAYERS OF SOFTWARE

The complexity in software security stems from the fact that there are several levels of computer software. The schematic in Figure 7.7 illustrates that even a superficial examination of the layers of software of an information system reveals its complexity. The schematic shows seven general layers. In actual practice it is not uncommon for over a hundred program modules to be invoked from the time a single transaction is keyed into a terminal device until a response is returned to the device. The seven general layers are named. The numbers in the schematic indicate the general function points at which each of the general levels is invoked. The number 1 indicates that a security system is able to vali-

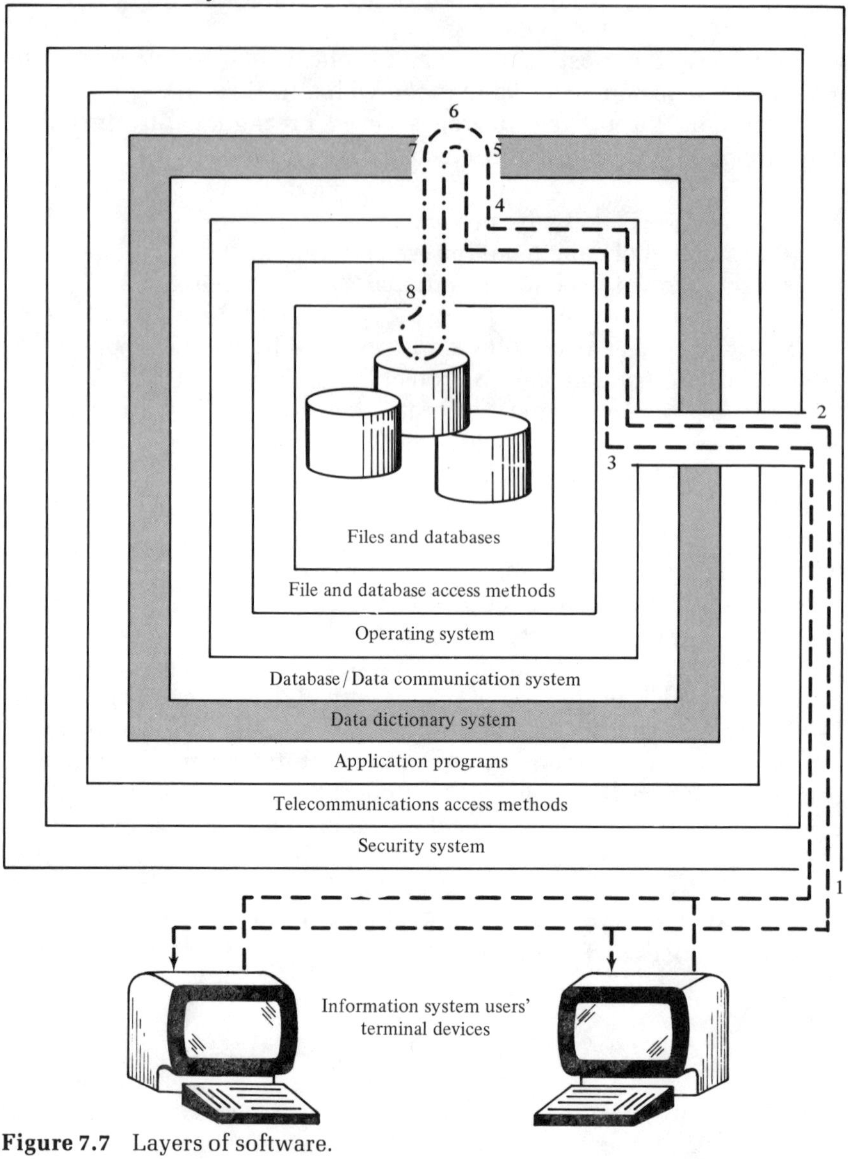

Figure 7.7 Layers of software.

date terminals, operators and transactions. Any or all of these functions may be validated, depending upon the comprehensiveness of the security system. The number 2 shows that a telecommunications access method handles transactions as they come into the computer configuration from the communications network. When transactions are received, the telecommunications access method alerts other modules within the operating system. This is shown by the number 3. The operating system signals the database/data communication system, number 4 in the schematic, and collectively they locate and load the appropriate application programs, indicated by number 5 in the schematic. The application program issues CALLS or READS to the databases or files. Number 6 indicates this. These CALLS or READS use some modules within the database/data communication system, number 7 in the schematic, and file and database access methods (different than the telecommunications access methods) to retrieve and update databases and files. Number 8 in the schematic shows this activity. Responses back to the terminal devices are shown in the sequence 5, 4, 3, 2, 1 in the schematic. Basically, the responses follow the same path out as the transactions did coming in, although they use different program modules. Also shown in the schematic, but not actually involved in the interactive handling of transactions, is the data dictionary system. And yet, the data dictionary system can also provide some of the security for the system. A dictionary serves as an administrative tool and a centralized source of documentation. All file, field, element, and database definitions can be kept in data dictionary databases. As we have seen, the dictionary system itself has facilities producing the definitions that the database/data communication system uses in generating control information needed for retrieving data from and updating data in databases. It is possible to restrict to database administration the entering into the computer of database specifications. For the price of creating something of a minor bureaucracy, an additional safeguard is introduced, and indiscriminate entry of database specifications into a system is eliminated.

In contemplating security, some caution should be exercised so that in making data and software secure, they are not at the same time made inaccessible. As stated earlier, technically oriented individuals are inclined, because of their own knowledge and capabilities, to develop security procedures so encompassing that only very clever individuals are able to breach them. This can sometimes be counterproductive in emergency situations where it becomes necessary to bypass some security and some "mere mortals" are unable to do so because the procedures are so cleverly designed. Contrary to the belief of many technically oriented individuals, there is a degree of security in the technology of software itself. Outside of the technicians within a computer facility, there are not many individuals possessing the capabilities of getting into that facility's files. However, there are some who can, and security procedures need be implemented to protect against them. Realistically speaking, there is no formula for establishing security procedures. Trade-offs need to be made in all situations.

ELEMENTARY PROTECTION BY MEANS OF SOFTWARE

Whether trying to provide security for either software or for data, there are some rather elementary practices that can be put into effect. Those practices include the use of data dictionaries, the use of passwords, restriction of functions by means of terminal and/or transaction security, and the use of the database management concept of segmentation of data records.

A data dictionary system has several ways in which it can be instrumental as a security instrument. For example, the files or databases of a data dictionary system can be set up as a centralized repository of the documentation describing an organization's databases, files, records, data elements, and fields. Procedures can be established and enforced making it impossible to use database definitions or control blocks that have not been specified in the dictionary. A data dictionary system can be an important stabilizing and controlling factor in an environment where there are several users of a single data processing installation. Without one, a chaotic environment, with a proliferation of redundant file and database definitions, duplicated data elements, and unrelated applications may result.

Another rudimentary but reasonably effective method of security is the issuance of passwords. Individuals who have access to the various data files or software modules of the computer system can be issued passwords. Passwords may be several characters in length, and specific passwords may allow certain individuals to access specific files or modules. Various computer facilities, such as time-sharing systems and interactive compilers, are set up so that an individual attempting access must key in an appropriate password before access is permitted. To keep passwords confidential, they can be changed periodically. It is also advisable for passwords not to appear on a CRT screen as they are keyed in. This makes it somewhat difficult for one individual to "steal" another's password. A long way from being totally effective, passwords do provide at least a minimum of security.

Another way to provide some security to data is to set up within various software products such as database/data communications systems or applications monitors a table of values that correlate transactions with terminals or transactions with passwords or even terminals with passwords. These correlations might specify for instance that terminal device ABC can only be used for transactions PDQ, XYZ, QXR, and RRD. Any attempt to enter other transactions through this device would fail. This kind of arrangement assures that no access is possible to data files other than those used by the transactions specified and the only activity against the databases is that which is performed by the authorized transactions. This kind of security is quite common in major on-line systems where there is a great deal of activity of a limited and repetitive nature. These security measures that have just been examined are rather fundamental and can be applied economically to the protection of both data and software.

PROTECTION OF SOFTWARE

Two areas of software protection are discussed here: protection of software as it is stored in secondary storage in a computer configuration and protection of software as it is being executed by a computer. Some of that which immediately follows is familiar, because we surveyed it in an earlier chapter. A feature of most computer operating systems is a facility called a library. Actually, there can be several libraries in which both programs and procedures are stored. There are libraries for programs in source form and for programs in object form (machine language). There are also libraries for procedures, operating instructions, and other software components. Access to the elements stored in libraries is made through another operating system facility called a catalog. The catalog contains the name of the elements that are stored in the library and their addresses. Some libraries are stored in secondary storage. The address of the elements is either a primary storage location or a secondary storage location. Catalogs and libraries are not intended as security facilities per se. However, they do lend a degree of security that is not found in software contained in a deck of IBM cards stored in a file cabinet or in the desk drawer of some programmer.

The use of libraries in a large data-processing installation is a common practice. In the case of programming, for example, there may be several data sets within a library used to contain programs. One particular data set is used to hold production status programs, that is, programs used in day-to-day operations, as opposed to those same programs in development status. Development status programs become production programs eventually, but an orderly procedure for moving them from test to production status is recommended. Since verbal communications sometimes break down or result in misunderstandings, a simple form, often called a transmittal, either on paper or on the computer itself can be used to facilitate transfers of programs from test to production status. Figure 7.8 (courtesy of CBS, Inc.) is an example of a paper version of this concept.

Another feature of an operating system is the facility that permits multiprogramming, that is, concurrent execution of several application programs giving the overall impression of simultaneous execution. In actuality, the operating system allocates computer resources to different job steps (application programs) according to a priority scheduling

CBS DATA CENTER COMPUTER SYSTEM TRANSMITTAL

STANDARDS & DOCUMENTATION	1) FROM	2) DIVISION	3) DATE
4) APPLICATION NUMBER/NAME	5) PROGRAM NUMBER/NAME	6) LOCATION	7) TELEPHONE EXT.

8) CHECK THE APPROPRIATE BOXES AND ENTER THE REQUIRED INFORMATION

A ☐ This is a new application tobe installed before ________________.

B ☐ This is a change to be applied before ________________.

The change is: ☐ An insertion ☐ A removal.

The change involves: ☐ A complete deck ☐ Individual cards.

The number of cards involved is ________.

C ☐ Move modules From (Library) ________________ To (Library) ________________

(List modules to be moved under "Programmer/Analyst Remarks" below)

D ☐ Other:

9) CHECK THE APPROPRIATE BOX FOR DOCUMENTATION OF THE ABOVE NEW APPLICATION OR CHANGE.

☐ New documentation attached ☐ Modified documentation attached ☐ No documentation required.

10) Programmer/Analyst Remarks

11) AUTHORIZED BY DIVISION DIRECTOR		12) DATE CHANGE TESTED
13) PROGRAMMER/ANALYST NAME		14) HOME PHONE NUMBER *(Include Area Code)*
ACKNOWLEDGED RECEIPT	15) SIGNATURE	16) DATE APPLIED

CBS 1037 REV 6/80

SYSTEMS DIVISION COPY

Figure 7.8 A transmittal form. Courtesy of CBS, Inc.

and dispatching scheme. One of the resources that is allocated is primary storage. In a typical large-scale computer, several application programs reside in primary storage at a given instant of time, although only one of them is being executed. A feature in most operating systems, called *storage protect*, assures that each program is restricted to its own section of primary storage. With storage protect, it is impossible for an error in one program to cause a problem for another program. Without this feature there would be nothing to protect one program from being damaged by an error in another program.

Although damage to software is always a possibility, the more serious threat is the damage to or theft of information from an organization's files. Let's now turn our attention to that subject.

PROTECTION OF DATA IN ON-LINE FILES

Increasing numbers of computer systems contain data that is on-line, that is, data that is directly accessible through the use of a terminal device. In addition to being accessible, there are also many environments in which this on-line data can be updated. In an on-line environment, when updating takes place, the data in a location prior to the update is overlaid. In practical terms, it disappears without a trace. Since it is an imperfect world, there are occasions when data is changed when it shouldn't be. Changes may be made incorrectly, inadvertently, or maliciously. Since the data that was in place before the change disappears, steps need to be taken to recover that data in the event that errors, mistakes, or mischief are subsequently discovered.

To guard against the destruction of data in an on-line file or database, several practices can be instituted. One of the most basic of these practices is copying or backing up the file or database on a periodic basis. This involves nothing more than copying the file or database onto another device at some point in time. Files stored on magnetic disk can be copied to another disk or onto magnetic tape and recopied in the event of destruction.

In its primitive form, this method could involve copying a database at 9:00 A.M. If damage were discovered at 11:00 A.M., work would be suspended, the copy made at 9:00 A.M. would be copied again (to back it up again in the event of another failure), and the first copy would represent the restored database; then the work done between the time the original backup copy was done (9:00 A.M.) and the time the damage was discovered (11:00 A.M.) would have to be redone. That would result in a loss of two hours work plus whatever time was used to make the second copy and get the first copy set up for use.

In many installations, the loss of two or more hours of work in the event of a failure is intolerable. In such cases, it is possible to post to a log file each transaction that updates the file or database. It is also possible to post to the log file the updated record both before and after it is updated. In the event of failure, the process of using the copy of the file taken at 9:00 A.M. and recopying it would also be used. However, rather than redoing the work, the log file could be used to apply the updated records to the backup file, bringing it up to date in less time than the two hours required to redo all the work. The value of the log file increases in importance as the time between backup copying and failure increases. Processing from a log file is significantly faster that reentering data from terminals. This type of processing is sometimes known as "recovery and restart" processing.

Log files have an even more important function to perform. Failures of systems that process data in computers often take place at very awkward times. For instance, a program may malfunction right in the middle of a transaction that consists of four database updates, having completed only two. The two completed updates must be deleted (backed out) from the database so that when the program that processes that transaction is corrected and rerun, it does not perform the two completed updates twice. A combination of programming technique and the log file makes this type of backup possible.

The practices of logging, backup, recovery/restart, and backout are forms of security used to maintain data integrity. As measures, they are applied to the databases and files to recover them after damage has been done. There are other forms of security that attempt to prevent damage. Included are the practices examined earlier, such as password, transaction, and terminal security. Also there are some other things that can be done to prevent erroneous updating of files and databases. For instance, reasonableness checks can be made on data being used for updating purposes. An example might be a table of valid product codes against which an entry to update might be checked. If the entry contains a product code not on the table, it would be rejected as an error. This is a relatively simple kind of security measure to implement, although it does add the additional task of maintaining the product code table.

In addition to the log described above, another log can be used. This log file would constitute an audit trail of the transactions and updates made to the files or databases. It would contain the information required to audit the activity against the files and databases. It would contain similar information to the original log but also other information not carried on that log. The original log is intended for use as a backup, recovery, and restart vehicle. The information contained on it is used by the computer to recover and restart applications. The speed with which this log can be processed is an important factor. Therefore, the amount of data contained on it is kept to a minimum. The audit log, on the other hand, should contain sufficient information so that it is meaningful to the auditors. The audit log should contain, for instance, an operator identifier on each transaction, either update or inquiry. Again, although not perfect, the idea that an audit log records such information may be intimidating enough to deter some unauthorized individuals from tampering with databases. The auditors for their part should not be overly demanding as far as information on the audit log is concerned, since increments of processing overhead are added for each data element put on the log.

Within database/data communication systems, there is a concept that could be called segmentation that is able to provide another level of data security. Essentially, in segmentation, data records are subdivided into components. Each of the components is in itself a retrievable entity. In a simple form, a record might contain two segments. Application A might have need of one segment, and application B might have need of the other. A set of specifications is made up by the database administrator (DBA) describing each segment as a separate entity as well as the two segments as a complete record. Two application programs are written, with each requiring a different segment. Because of the specifications made by the DBA, each of the application programs only accesses that segment of the entire record that it needs. The other segment is not accessible to it. The segmentation process introduces a potential level of security that is not possible in nondatabase systems, where each program would have access to the entire data record.

PROTECTION OF DATA IN BATCH PROCESSING APPLICATIONS

The practices just discussed are most often used with on-line or real time systems, although they can also be used in batch systems. However, there are other more well-known security or control practices commonly found in batch systems. In on-line systems, files or databases have to be periodically copied or dumped onto another device, because updating is done in place. In batch processing, this is generally not the case. In most batch systems, processing is sequential, and when updating is done, the entire file is recopied as part of the update process. To provide backup, a copy of the file before updating must be kept together with the activity file that updated it. In this way, if a file is damaged and cannot be processed, a rerun of the job that created the file can create it again. It is generally assumed to be safe if two generations of the updated file are kept. This technical is known as the "father, grandfather file" or as generation data sets.

Another type of security in batch systems is the use of batch control totals. In most batch systems, a batch of information is submitted to be processed. The most commonly known example is a batch of employee time cards submitted for processing in a payroll system. When submitted, they are accompanied with an adding machine tape containing a total of all the hours worked for all the employee time cards in the batch. Often, there is also a count of the number of time cards in the batch. When the data is entered into a computer system, one of the first jobs run produces control totals. The totals include the number of time cards and total hours. The total from the computer run should be equal to the totals on the adding machine tape. If so, processing continues on the remainder of the payroll. If not, steps are taken to determine where the error was made. Once corrected, the total balancing job is rerun to make sure it has been corrected properly. Once it is correct, the rest of the payroll processing commences.

Within a batch processing job stream, control totals can be kept from step to step so that if there is a malfunction as the system progresses, it is highlighted by an inconsistency in the control totals. When an inconsistency occurs, processing is suspended until the problem is resolved. For instance in a payroll system, the difference between the total year-to-date earnings for the completed payroll and the year-to-date earnings before the payroll was run should be equal to the total gross payroll for the pay period being processed. If a discrepancy is discovered, payroll checks are not to be produced until the discrepancy is found and corrected. There are other types of control totals that can be used to check at the completion of various steps within a job stream to determine whether the steps have completed successfully. There are also controls at the end of a system that can be used to be sure that it has run successfully. For example, a completed general ledger should balance to zero; in a payroll system, the dollar total in the check reconciliation file sent to the bank should equal the dollar total of all the checks run.

ENCRYPTION

One of the more sophisticated methods of security is encryption. It is currently being practiced on a somewhat limited scale. Basically, encryption involves the coding of data, but coding it in a sophisticated fashion. Encryption of data is an outgrowth of cryptology which had its beginnings hundreds of years ago. Modern cryptology makes use of transposition and substitution methods for transforming messages into coded or cipher form. Transposition is the simplest of the methods. It is nothing more than a jumble of the letters of the text. Substitution has the letters of the text replaced by other letters, numbers, or symbols. Substitution systems are more complex and diverse than transposition systems.

Codes and ciphers are two methods used for encryption. Codes represent a more elaborate substitution transformation method. Codes generally consist of thousands of words, phrases, letters, and syllables that are used as replacements for plaintext elements. Code books are required, both to encode and to decode messages. One book, in sequence by plaintext element, enables the user to encode messages. The other book, in sequence by code elements, enables the recipient of the message to decode it. On the other hand, most ciphers employ keys that specify things like the arrangement of letters within a cipher alphabet. In elaborate cipher systems, key numbers, key phrases, or key words are used.

The words encipher or encode describe the process of transforming text to cipher or code. Decipher and decode are the words used to describe the process of legitimately reversing the encoding or enciphering. Cryptoanalysis is the process of breaking the code or ciphers.

In the interest of controlling the collection, transmission, use, and storage of data about individuals, the National Bureau of Standards has adopted an IBM developed algorithm for data encryption. Known as the Data Encryption Standard, it is still the subject of debate.

SECURITY PRODUCTS

Computer software security products that have been developed for the sole purpose of protecting either data or other software are available in the marketplace. Some products can be used to protect certain types of data sets and program libraries from unauthorized access and have features permitting reports to be produced that show all authorized as well as unauthorized attempts to access data in protected data sets and libraries. Other packages have security features as part of a repertoire of functions. For instance, they might have control over program libraries and restrict access to those libraries. Reports can be produced by these products that facilitate auditing of program usage, permit evaluation of operational effectiveness of programs, and allow predictions of future resource requirements to be made.

More comprehensive software products devoted to security are known as access control facilities. There are basically two types, and they are fundamentally different. One type enables the protection of data sets by exception, that is, the user of the product picks the data sets to be protected; while with the other type, protection is by default, that is, all data sets are automatically protected, and the user makes up "rules" so that the restricted data sets can be accessed.

Users contemplating the use of security software are well advised to determine their security requirements first and then to select the software that meets those requirements. Selecting software first and defining security requirements afterward leads to confusion and may dictate that modifications be made to the selected product.

CONCLUSION

Difficulties arise in determining the proper security for data elements in large organizations. When the responsibility for safeguarding data elements is divided among several functions within an organization, disputes sometimes arise. The disputes generally center around who is responsible for which data elements and how much security is required for different data elements. The more technically inclined individuals, those closest to the computer generally are in favor of tight security. It is these individuals who have the technical capabilities to bridge virtually any type of security system. Knowing this, they favor a security methodology that can prevent individuals with technical capabilities from having access to or tampering with data. On the other hand, there are the systems-oriented individuals who attempt to develop information systems that can make available as much information as possible with as little difficulty as possible. While they do not ignore security altogether, these information systems developers are somewhat more cavalier in their approach to security than are the technicians. In addition, in those organizations using large databases and files there are several other individuals who would have some ideas on data security. Those individuals might include: users of the data in the databases and files, managers, directors, application programmers, and in some cases even senior managers and executives. Reaching a consensus among so many individuals can be a trying experience. One of the major reasons for the difficulty is the lack of clear understanding of the types of software security that can be applied. This chapter has attempted to crystallize some of the factors involved so as to help in clarifying that understanding.

Data security as a subject is getting a great deal of coverage in data-processing journals, trade papers, and the general media. Stories of thievery, fraud, and accidental and malicious damage appear frequently. There is no doubt that there is a need for some level of security. And yet, it also should be pointed out that the introduction of security procedures is going to be costly in terms of time. It adds to the amount of time to process a transaction and it adds to the amount of time required to implement an application. The potential for all kinds of security exists within current software technology. What may be overlooked is the trade-off. The trade-off is in time and in aggravation. Most software systems today, either home-grown or purchased packages, are sold on the basis that they make more information available to more people more quickly. Security systems or practices by their very nature mitigate against this. Security attempts to restrict information accessibility to selected individuals. Time is the element to be traded. Security procedures, since they must be thought out, discussed, and included in specifications, add to the development and implementation time of a system.

SUMMARY

In this chapter, we examined some of the administrative information systems resources that can be employed in managing information within an organization. A data dictionary is an example of one of these resources. The concept and function of a data dictionary was explained. It was shown how a data dictionary is both a set of files (or a database) and an application. The workings of data dictionaries were examined, and developments taking place in related technology were discussed.

Then we took a look at the subject of security. Basic computer installation security was surveyed, and then software security was shown to be integrated into several layers of systems software found in most large-scale computer environments. The kinds of protection offered by software security, namely, elementary protection, protection of software, protection of on-line data, and protection of batch data, were reviewed. The highlights of encryption, a more sophisticated security methodology, were surveyed. Software products containing security-oriented components and products whose sole function is security were explained. The conclusion was drawn that security, while necessary in varying degrees depending upon circumstances, requires an investment of time in both application implementation and execution.

SECTION THREE

M Is for Management

In the past, the initials MIS were used to denote management information systems and to connote systems that produced information that could be used by management in evaluating alternatives and making choices. Each section of the book is headed up with one of those initials, but in rearranged order, ISM. The two preceding sections treated information and systems respectively. In this section, we deal with management. We are quite convinced that management is an art, and so this section, especially the two last chapters, takes something of an editorial, some might say, opinionated form. Up to this point what we've presented has been, in essence, factual; we've described the concepts of information and the tools used to store, manipulate, and retrieve that information. In this section we are going to deal with those factors that need to be considered to make the transition from potential MIS to real MIS. To do so requires an understanding of information, a general familiarity with the tools, that is, systems, and the execution of the prerogatives of management. The first two are behind us; let's proceed with the third.

CHAPTER 8

Operating Environments

DEPOTS, WAREHOUSES, AND STORES

A depot is a central location where large quantities of merchandise are stored. There are periodic shipments of merchandise to the depot and periodic shipments of merchandise out of the depot. Many of the shipments are scheduled, and if one were to observe the operations of a depot over time, certain patterns would begin to take shape. For instance, most shipments coming into the depot would be in greater bulk than those going out. Chances are that much of the incoming shipments would come in by rail or perhaps by ship if the depot was located at a seaport.

Shipments out of the depot would generally be in tractor trailers. These trucks would deliver material to warehouses located within a few hundred miles of the depot or perhaps to airports for airfreight deliveries to warehouses located thousands of miles from the depot. Such shipments would generally be in less bulk than those coming into the depot. Shipments out of warehouses to retail stores in the immediate neighborhood would be made in smaller trucks. Within the depot, the warehouses, and the stores, there is a need to store the merchandise in such a way as to make it accessible. Some merchandise moves in and out more quickly; some merchandise is small, some is large; some is light, some is heavy. Demand fluctuates. The equipment and manpower needed to perform storage, manipulation, and retrieval tasks in a depot is greater than that needed in an individual warehouse or a store. However, in some merchandising situations, a depot might not even be needed; product can be sent directly from factories to warehouses. The number of variables to be considered when describing the storage, manipulation, and retrieval of merchandise is virtually limitless.

The same can be said for the storage, manipulation, and retrieval of information. Just as there are large-, medium-, and small-scale storage and distribution facilities for merchandise, there are also large-, medium-, and small-scale computers for the storage and distribution of information. In an earlier chapter we indicated that the functional components of all computers were the same. Well, the functional components in the distribution of merchandise are also the same. Whether in a depot, a warehouse, or a retail outlet, the basic idea is to get many types of merchandise in, store them in such a way as to make them accessible, periodically combine them with one another to make up shipments, and get the shipments out the door as quickly and inexpensively as possible. At the same time, we know that despite the similarity of the functional operational components, the tasks performed and the type of management required differ from depot to warehouse to store. The same is true of data-processing facilities. In this chapter we'll examine the considerations of running a data center with several large-scale computers and the uses and limitations of medium-scale and of small personal computers. The bulk of the material in this chapter relates to the data center. In addition to its being more involved than the other two situations, it also includes many of their functions, so that when we describe a data center we also describe some of the other two. Therefore, when describing the other two environments, we'll deal with only that which is different.

LARGE-SCALE EDP/MIS

What Is a Data Center?

A data center is an organization whose function is the providing of service to its customers. The customers of a data center are organizations and individuals who have data storage, processing, and retrieval requirements. These requirements are most readily accommodated through the use of electronic data processing technology. This technology consists of computer equipment (hardware) and programs and techniques (software) that facilitate the storing, processing, and retrieving data electronically. Several types of computer technicians are required to support this technology. Quite often, a data center is a centralized facility used by several organizations. It is not uncommon, for instance, to find a corporate data center facility supporting the electronic data processing applications of several divisions in a divisionalized corporation.

Equipment

Within a typical data center, we usually find more than one large-scale computer equipment configuration and/or several medium-scale configurations. Anything less than that does not constitute a data center in the sense we are talking about here. In addition to the computers themselves, we are also talking about an installation that supports direct access storage devices in sufficient quantity to contain tens or even hundreds of billions of characters of information on-line, that is magnetic disk packs in quantities or tens or hundreds. Magnetic tape, used for logs, journals, and other sequential information not required on-line, on reels numbering in thousands or tens or hundreds. Magnetic tape, used for logs, journals, and other sequential information not required on-line, on reels numbering in thousands or tens of thousands, is also found in contemporary data centers. There are also usually a number of high-speed printers and perhaps a microfiche output device dedicated to producing high-volume listings and tabulations. Checks and invoices are also frequently produced on high-speed printers. Communications lines, numbering in the tens or hundreds, with their related equipment components, connect terminal devices at remote sites with the data center's computer equipment. It is through these devices that customers gain access to the data center facilities.

Software

Medium- and large-scale computer equipment configurations require elaborate software to function efficiently and effectively. This software, which is over and above that which performs actual application tasks such as writing checks, preparing invoices, and updating inventory, includes the following:

- Operating systems or control programs that allow a computer equipment configuration to process several jobs concurrently by allocating available resources within the configuration to those jobs as they are needed.

- Database management systems that facilitate the creation of databases and then handle the storage and retrieval of information from those databases.
- Telecommunications monitors that handle transactions that come into the configuration, calling the correct application program to accommodate a specific transaction and then routing the response to the transaction back to the communications network.
- Communications network managers that handle traffic on the communications lines, the transactions sent from terminal devices to the data center's computers and the messages sent from the computers to the devices.
- A host of other software including compilers, performance measurement and tuning tools, billing algorithms, input/output modules (access methods), and utilities such as sorts, dumps, reorganizations, recovery and restart programs, and security transaction handlers.

People

It is not uncommon to find a few hundred people working in a data center. A small percentage of them are management personnel. The remaining individuals are a mixture of skilled technicians, semiskilled clerks, and first line supervisors. There are several classes of operator, ranging from the most experienced computer console operators and the system master terminal operators to the least experienced magnetic tape hangers and printer operators. The most highly skilled individuals in data center environments are the systems software technicians who are responsible for "the care and feeding" of the software mentioned above. There is also a staff of communications technicians responsible for the support and maintenance of the equipment and communications lines making up the network.

Primary Concern: Service

As we shall see below, data center managers have many concerns. A number of things will vie for their attention on a day-to-day or hour-to-hour basis. However, the primary concern of data center managers is service to the data center's customers. All the other concerns, e.g., keeping up with new technology, maintaining a high-quality support staff, or reducing expenses, are subordinate to the providing of service to the users of data center facilities.

In day-to-day situations, this primary concern of providing service proves to be easier said than done. Make no mistake about it, a data center is "where the rubber meets the road." The shortcuts in application programming, the incomplete operating instructions, and the unclear procedures are all highlighted when an application "goes live" in the data center. Not that all data center problems are someone else's fault; data center personnel also make mistakes, but whatever the source of the error, its manifestation takes place in the data center. Something gets messed up; a report is late, response time to users degrades beyond an acceptable level, a database is destroyed and requires recovery or an operator misses a warning message and a four-hour rerun is required. In addition, there can be equipment malfunctions, system software ambiguities, communication line failures, and other problems that can distract a data center manager. Anyone who has ever worked in a data center can testify that it sometimes seems that surviving the day is the primary concern of a data center manager. And yet, that same individual, when not preoccupied with day-to-day operational difficulties, will say that service is the primary concern of the data center manager. The way to provide good service most of the time is through the proper management of the data center functions. These functions are described below.

Data Center Functions

Within a data center, there are two basic functions: operations and system software. Within those two basic functions there are several subfunctions. The operations function is equipment intensive, the bulk of the work being done by and the bulk of the budget going for equipment. Depending upon the size of the data center, it is possible to spend tens of millions of dollars each year in leasing fees and rentals, and in depreciation of purchased equipment. System software products' costs are rising to the point where millions can be spent each year on leases, rentals, and purchases, but in relative terms, a higher percentage of the expenditures in system software departments is for personnel.

Operations

The operations functions could be broken down into three subfunctions: computer operations, communications, and scheduling, control, and customer service.

Computer operations has the responsibility for allocating the available equipment resources among the jobs that are scheduled for processing on a day-to-day, hour-to-hour basis. This may include both interactive on-line and serially processed (batch) applications. In contemporary settings, there is an emphasis on interactive processing especially on the "prime shift," from say 8:00 A.M. to 7:00 P.M.* Computer operations is frequently charged with dedicating a significant percentage of its equipment to on-line interactive processing, including both database/data communications production systems and interactive facilities used for development work by application designers and programmers. Loss of one of the production computer configurations for any protracted period of time can have a noticable impact on the business of data center customers. Therefore, concern for the stability of equipment used for on-line interactive processing is high up on a data center manager's priority list.

During the remaining hours, from 7:00 P.M. to 8:00 A.M., computer operations concerns itself primarily with serial processing (batch) activities and the backing up of on-line databases that were updated during the 8:00 A.M. to 7:00 P.M. time frame. While not completely halted, on-line interactive processing is appreciably diminished during the 7:00 P.M. to 8:00 A.M. period. While backups and batch processing are critical, there is generally less immediate impact on the business during serial processing. However, severe disruptions can occur, if for example an on-line system cannot be started up at 8:00 A.M. because of batch processing work not being completed. So while the serial processing is not as high on the data center manager's priority list, it is on the list nonetheless.

In a contemporary data center, it makes both operational and economic sense to pool peripheral equipment such as printers, disk drives, and tape drives. If multiple computers are involved, it is possible to have the equipment wired to one or more of the computers through switches. In this way, single devices or groups of devices can be allocated to one computer or another, through operator control, as conditions dictate. As a result, as work loads vary in type and quantity, an operations supervisor may allocate magnetic tape drives, magnetic disk drives, or printers among several computers. In a similar fashion, clusters of terminal devices can also be shifted as major software support systems and applications are adjusted to meet situations such as peak load demands or emergencies.

Control of computer resources is exercised through CRT terminal devices, by operators, under the guidance of supervisors. Several ar-

*For a data center located in the United States serving domestic sites, the beginning and ending times may vary, depending upon the location of the data center. This is due to the time zones. With 9:00 A.M. to 5:00 P.M. as prime shift, a Midwestern data center could service four time zones in prime shift with 8:00 A.M. to 7:00 P.M. as beginning and ending times.

rangements of these CRTs, both physically and logically, are possible. Each computer requires a main console, as do database/data communication products, so that operators and supervisors can monitor performance and initiate corrective action in certain circumstances. The data center manager who avoids making the investment in the equipment and staff to handle these operational tasks is being "penny wise and pound foolish."

Communications are the "eyes and ears" of the data center. Communications have the responsibility for assuring that the communications facilities (lines, modems and front-end controllers) that carry transactions and messages between the data center and terminal devices located at remote sites serviced by the data center are kept in service. It is during the 8:00 A.M. to 7:00 P.M. time period that these facilities are most active. Most of the queries against on-line databases are made during this time.

A well-equipped communications function is equipped with a console and monitors, with which it is possible to take a reading of the traffic on any line. The schematic in Figure 8.1 illustrates this. The console includes a patch panel and display devices that are similar in nature to television monitors. Using patch cords, communications technicians are able to display on the monitor screen images of the traffic going across a communications line. Under normal operating conditions, with the patch cord out, there is a direct connection through the patch

Figure 8.1 A data center communications function patch panel arrangement.

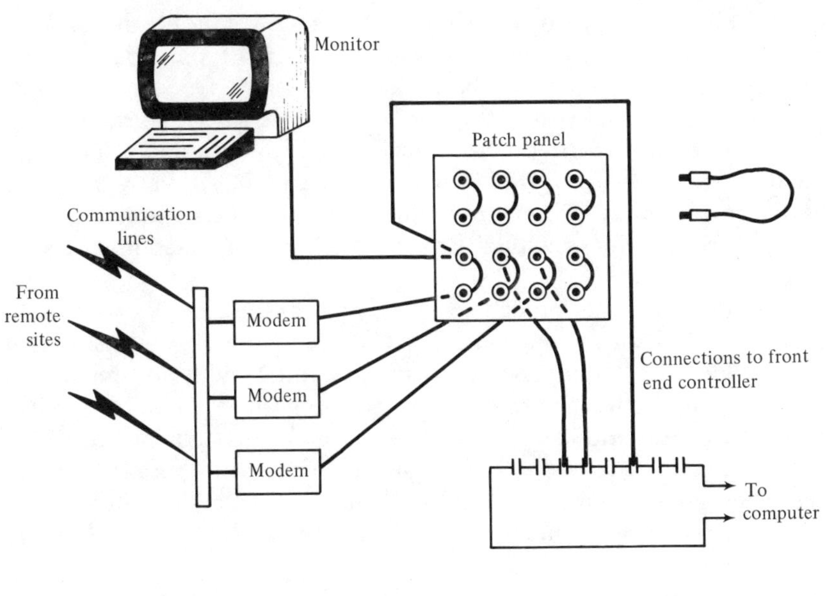

panel between the front end controller and the modem. When the patch cord is put into the panel, the direct connection remains, but the data is also displayed on the monitor. The arrangement is an indispensible trouble-shooting aid for the communications technicians, for without it, they must attempt to visualize and diagnose problems blindly. Data center managers have a choice. They can invest several thousand dollars in this equipment, or they can plan on longer outages when communications facilities fail.

Scheduling, control, and customer service are the remaining component groups making up the operations function. These, unlike computer operations and communications, are not equipment intensive.

Scheduling and control are made up of tasks that facilitate batch processing operations. Batch operations and on-line operations are handled differently in a data center. On-line applications, of course, are made up of randomly arriving inquiry and update transactions that are processed under the control of a database/data communications system. Transactions coming in from terminal devices enter the computer, processing takes place, and if things are normal, response messages are generated within a few seconds and returned to those devices. The scheduling task is minor; the database/data communications systems are started at one time and closed down at another. There are no control (as defined below) tasks to be performed. Batch operations, on the other hand, involve a significant amount of scheduling and control. Batch applications consist of series of jobs that frequently must be run serially. For example, paychecks can only be printed after tax calculations have been performed. In other situations, batch jobs can be run in tandem. For example, it is possible to update an inventory file with a series of "finished goods to warehouse" transactions, while at the same time printing a monthly sales analysis report. In a typical data center, there may be a few thousand batch jobs run each day. Some are daily jobs; others are weekly, monthly, or "on request." It is the scheduler's responsibility to perform the tasks necessary to determine the jobs to be run, their relationships (serial or in tandem), and the time at which they should be run. In addition, in conjunction with the computer operations supervisor, the scheduler lays out a schedule by machine by shift of the jobs to be run.

The control tasks precede, compliment and follow those of both computer operations and scheduling. Control personnel make sure that input needed for batch processing applications arrives on time and is balanced. Quite often the first one or two programs in a batch application perform edit and balance tasks. Control clerks make log entries either in manually maintained log books or in computer maintained log files. These logs are used to establish the basis of an audit trail of transactions through the application and to assure, when the last job of the application has been processed, that what comes out is in synchronization with what went in. For example, if 1273 employees had time cards going into a payroll application, then 1273 (minus any controlled exceptions) checks ought to be produced.

Customer service handles extraordinary situations. The establishment of this department rests on the assumption that there are going to be problems. The number of individuals assigned to the department varies depending upon the size and complexity of the data center itself and upon the number of customers that have to be served.

There are essentially two types of jobs in the customer service area: expediters and customer contacts. It is the former's responsibility to track down the causes of difficulties and to apply or recommend remedies. The customer contacts' responsibility is to deal directly with customers to precisely define problems, to initiate activity to address the problem, and to get back to the customer with solutions. Qualifications for the jobs include a general understanding of the data center's technology and application mix and persistence and patience. For instance, expeditors have to ferret out problem causes. This requires familiarity with both data center hardware and software in addition to some acquaintance with the various applications. It does not necessarily require the ability to solve the problem, but it does require the ability to discern by whom it can be solved and to bring it to the attention of that individual or department. The customer contact has to know enough about applications to be able to deal with programmers, analysts, and users in the customer organizations.

The data center manager has to develop and maintain the scheduling, control, and customer service departments by staffing them with individuals who possess a blend of operational, technical support and political skills. There is a tendency, sometimes, to be distracted by the "bells, lights, and whistles" of computer technology and to ignore or neglect these basic operational support functions. Improperly managed, these functions can be the causes of waste, inefficiency, and reruns, and they can also be a drain on productivity.

Software Support

This function can be broken down into four subfunctions, operating system and input/output (I/O) support, data communications or teleprocessing support, database management and interactive systems support, and performance measurement and tuning. All these functions are staffed with highly trained, technically oriented individuals who are responsible for the installation, support, and enhancement of the most comprehensive and complex computer program products in existence.

While their skills are similar, there is not automatic shifting of these technicians from one function to another. Cross-training is possible, but the dynamics of each discipline is such that keeping abreast in one of them is tough enough; keeping abreast in more than one is a virtual impossibility.

There are administrative similarities among most systems software products. Nearly all of them arrive at an installation of a reel of magnetic tape, generally accompanied by a set of manuals that can be literally one to three feet thick. Since these products are generalized, they need to be tailored to the requirements of the environment in which they are being installed. As we mentioned in an earlier chapter, the process of doing this is called a system generation, known in the trade as a SYSGEN (sis-gen) or more simply a GEN. Since these products are dynamic, new versions are released periodically, and each time a new version is installed, a GEN is required. Life cycles of these versions vary between one and three years. Since they are elaborate and complex (each one may contain hundreds of programmed routines), new versions require significant amounts of testing before they can be put into production. Also as a result of their complexity, they always contain a few latent errors (bugs). These bugs have a tendency to manifest themselves in ways that can be infuriating and frustrating. The effect of a bug often appears at some interval of time after the cause, and bugs feel no obligation to leave audit trails. Isolating bugs is a time-consuming task, and since, initially at least, there may be no apparent connection between its effect and its cause, there is a tendency for technicians to lay the cause off onto some other function. The persuasive skills of data center managers are tested when such situations arise.

In any event, bugs need to be isolated and fixed as they are uncovered. It is the task of the supplier of the product to provide the "fixes." It is the task of the individuals within the data centers' software support functions to apply the "fixes."

Operating systems and input/output software are found in every data center. An operating system is the "owner" of a given set of resources. It is a collection of programs that allocates resources (i.e., computer processor, primary storage, secondary storage, and display and print devices) among the transactions, tasks, messages, and tabular lists requiring those resources. As we explained earlier, operating systems, known also as control programs, are an integral software component in any contemporary computer configuration.

A basic task performed by an operating system or control program is the transferring of data between primary storage and secondary storage devices such as magnetic tapes and disks. In small personal computers, having the limitation of being able to execute one job (program) at a time, these data transfers or I/O operations represent the most significant operating system task. In larger computer equipment configurations, where that limitation does not apply, operating systems perform other tasks. In large-scale computer configurations such as those found in data centers, it is not uncommon for a computer aided by its operating system to execute several programs concurrently. The process, known as multiprogramming, makes it possible for very fast processor and primary storage components to attend to the computing activities of several jobs while the not-so-fast data transfers between secondary storage and primary storage are being carried out. Keeping track of all these jobs, allocating storage for them, suspending them and starting them up again, and performing the I/O operations are some of the tasks of an operating system of a large-scale computer configuration.

Data communications or teleprocessing software performs the tasks of initiating, controlling, and transferring data between the devices on a communications network and primary storage. The performance of these tasks takes place for each device on the network. In large-scale configurations there are many devices and there are many different jobs (programs) executed. In these large-scale configurations the telecommunications software gets transactions in from the devices and puts responses or messages out to the devices. In addition, it monitors and controls the transaction and message traffic involving hundreds of devices. Telecommunications software also provides interfaces among transactions, application programs, messages, and database or file management software (described below). Incoming transactions are interrogated by the teleprocessing software to determine the application program that is needed to handle them; the teleprocessing software then invokes that program that is needed to handle them; the teleprocessing software then invokes that program with some assistance from an operating system, and, upon completion of the program's execution (which includes the fabrication of responses), returns those response messages to the devices from which the transactions were sent originally or to some other devices specified by the transactions.

Computer configurations vary somewhat, but in most contemporary situations, the transaction program interface software resides in a main computer, sometimes called a host, and the data transfer software resides in a smaller computer sometimes called a front-end that is situated between the host and the network. The traffic monitoring and control software, sometimes called the network manager, is partially in the front-end and partially in the host. In addition to all these functions, data communications software also consists of some comprehensive error recovery routines, which are able to detect and correct "automatically" a high percentage of transmission errors that take place on the network.

Database software performs the tasks that facilitate the creation of the structures that hold elements of data that can be interrelated in relationships that transcend record and file boundaries. This same software also includes routines that make it possible to store data elements in and retrieve data elements from those structures.

Database software, frequently referred to as database management systems, contains interfaces (common connections) to other software. For instance, the storage and retrieval mechanisms of database management system use the input/output facilities of an operating system to transfer individual elements of data between primary and secondary storage. In addition, data communications capability can also be given to a database management system by integrating it with a data communications software product. Furthermore, when applied on a grand scale, database technology requires additional support from other software products such as data dictionaries, design aids, and database prototype products.

A data dictionary, as we have already shown, is a software product that consists of a set of programs that facilitate the creation of files that can contain descriptive information about databases, data elements, data sets, relationships among data elements, fields, programs, and systems—in short, an automated documentation tool. Some data dictionaries simplify the tasks of database administrators by making it possible to both document and enter structure parameters in a single input operation. Database design aids are products that produce alternative database structures from variable input, output, and processing requirements specified by database designers. Database prototype products are essentially analyzers that assist designers in determining the best design for a database from a series of simulation runs.

Other software support activities in a data center include: (1) performance measurement and tuning, (2) interactive personal computing support, (3) distributed systems support, and (4) security. Performance measurement and tuning is a resources "balancing act," in which an individual or a team of system software technicians monitor and control critical data center variables. Performance measurement includes the monitoring of: (1) response time (how long it takes for a transaction entered from a terminal device to get a response), (2) turnaround time (how long it takes for a batch job to get to its requestor), (3) length of queues (number of transactions or jobs lined up awaiting resources for processing), and (4) traffic on channels, i.e., the data on the paths between secondary storage devices and primary storage. Tuning is the process of making adjustments to relieve bottlenecks, to temporarily reassign priorities, to reallocate resources, or to inhibit certain types of processing for a time, so that overall data center performance is improved.

Interactive personal computing support involves the installation and maintenance of the so-called problem-oriented or high-level programming languages that are end user oriented. The data center staff of software technicians who support the interactive personal computing products are also required to provide technical advice and assistance to end users, who frequently have little or no EDP/MIS training. While there is a definite trend toward making computers and computing more user friendly, there is still a significant gap, and the interactive personal computing support technicians have to fill it.

Distributed systems make use of all the technology just described. Instead of its being concentrated in one site, it is distributed geographically. Supporting a distributed environment often involves GENing and maintaining several copies of an operating system, several copies of some data communications software, and possibly several copies of a database management system product, in addition to the support of the central data center. The technology, both the equipment and the software necessary to a distributed processing environment, is available and proven. Applying it represents a logistics and a management problem. With this particular type of processing, the data center manager's concern is seeing to it that applications that are using distributed technology have addressed the issues. What is to be distributed: files or processing or both? How is file distribution to be accomplished? How often are distributed files to be refreshed? How is this accomplished? How often are central files to be refreshed? How is this accomplished? Backup procedures and recovery and restart procedures are vital. Procedures for actions to be taken when the host computer is inoperative or when one or more of the satellite computers is inoperative must be in place. These are not technical considerations from a data center perspective, but they are issues that ought to be addressed. If they are overlooked, the support technicians will end up spending a great deal of their time involved with application teams, answering these questions and developing these procedures after the distributed applications have gone into production.

Software security, as we saw in the previous chapter, is another software support activity that needs to be attended to. In recent years, there have been dramatic increases in the quantity and sensitivity of data that is stored on-line and, without safeguards, is readily accessible to anyone having access to a computer terminal. A couple of well-publicized incidents involving fraud and theft have highlighted the vulnerability of organizations that have significant quantities of sensitive information stored on data center computer equipment.

At the outset, it can safely be stated that most organizations cannot afford the cost of total software security. While it is possible, at a reasonable cost, to provide reasonable security, it is virtually impossible, without the expenditure of a great deal of money, to inhibit the activities of an accomplished system software programmer bent on malevolence. However, apart from that, there are four relatively simple and inexpensive ways of securing on-line data from accidental or unauthorized access.

- First, creation of the position of data center security officer who has the responsibility for the protection of the data in the data center.
- Second, creation of a scheme of user identifications (IDs—pronounced *eye-deez*) and passwords by which users are "known" first to the data center and then to the particular data center facility they are authorized to use.
- Third, in production applications, establishment of a correlation table can be set up which relates transactions and files or databases and limits activity against specific files or databases to those transactions related to them in the table.
- Fourth, again in production applications, establishment of a correlation table between the application and specific terminals whereby access to a specific application is restricted to those terminals related to it in the table.

It is possible to create variations of the basic security options listed above, depending upon the specific operating environment. These options represent the fundamentals. No installation of any significant size should be without them. If the magnitude and sensitivity of data increases, then more elaborate security procedures can be put in place.

What Else Is There to Providing Service?

There are several other factors that a data center manager has to consider in providing effective and economical service to customers. Each of the eight factors that are presented below involve trade-offs that the data center manager has to make.

1. Electronic data processing equipment is constantly being improved upon. It becomes less expensive per unit of processing speed or per unit of storage. However, the number of units that can be acquired by an organization, because of vendor policies, are generally in quantities that require outlays of more money, not less. It goes something like this: the computer currently installed as a capacity of 4,000,000 positions of primary storage, can process 1,000,000 instructions in a second, and when purchased, it cost $1,000,000. A new computer is announced. It has a capacity of 16,000,000 positions of primary storage, can process 8,000,000 instructions in a second, and costs $2,000,000.

The current computer still has three years to go before it's fully depreciated, and to get a new one would result in a loss of investment tax credit. Projections indicate that the data center will be running at 100% capacity within six months. What should the data center manager recommend? This short scenario represents the kind of difficulties encountered by data center managers. The specifics are grossly oversimplified. There are usually a greater number of variables involved. Staying current in equipment over the long run is obviously necessary to avoid obsolescence, the difficulty is in knowing the right time to make a change.

2. Keeping system software current is another concern of the data center manager. System software products like any other technology have to be kept somewhat up-to-date. If they are not, the best technicians resign and go to where they are being used, and the data center's performance begins to slip. Most system software products are also vendor-supported, that is, vendors assume responsibility for their performance and will provide assistance if they malfunction. However, as an incentive for data centers to stay current, vendors generally withdraw this support for products not up to the two or three most current versions or releases. In a typical data center there may be several major system software products of considerable complexity (operating system, database management system, data communications monitor, etc.) and dozens of others (report writers, database design aids, performance measurement tools, etc.) of more moderate complexity. Quite often a number of these products operate interactively (interface) with one another so that a change made to one of these products can potentially impact the others. Because of this interfacing, the GENs for new versions and their testing require a significant investment of time on the part of the software technicians. The data center manager can minimize this investment of technicians time by encouraging them to participate in professional and user organizations through which they can both obtain and impart technical information about the most current versions of system software products. This information sharing is done by means of meetings held periodically in major cities and also by means of an interpersonal communications network established among the members of these organizations.

3. Large on-line files and databases require periodic copying, as a precautionary measure. There are occasions when an on-line file or database (let's call it the primary database) is damaged and cannot be processed. If a copy (let's call it the secondary database) had been taken at some point, the effects of the damage can be lessened somewhat. The secondary copy is sometimes known as a backup copy. The backup copy can be used to restore the primary copy to its form as it was when the secondary copy was made. Any activity that had updated the pri-

mary between the time the secondary copy was taken and the time the primary was damaged has to be done over. Operational procedures have been established to do this. The data center manager is ultimately responsible and, therefore, is concerned that these procedures be set up.

In data centers where the rapid and complete restoration of on-line files or databases is necessary, backup procedures alone are inadequate. In those situations, recovery and restart procedures are also needed. These can be somewhat more elaborate. To accommodate rapid and complete restoration, a log or journal record has to be kept in a file for each transaction that results in an update to the on-line file or database. Also kept on the log file are copies of the updated record from the on-line file or database. On those occasions where the on-line file or database is destroyed or damaged, the backup copy is used to initially restore it and then the entries on the log file are used to bring it up to the point in time when the damage or destruction occurred. Since on-line files and databases are frequently the most critical in a data center environment, a data center manager is concerned that procedures for recovering them are adequate.

4. A data center can be a department within an organization, an internal data center or it can be an organization in and of itself. Data centers within organizations are there to service the organization. Data centers that are organizations in and of themselves are sometimes called service bureaus, and they exist to make a profit. Data centers charge for their services, and the charges are based on rates for the different facilities within the data center. The following hypothetical schedule of rates conveys the idea.

Disk storage access	.00016
Tape storage access	.00072
Write to printer	.00098
Processor second	.02
Primary storage 1K for 1 hour	.0088
One reel of tape 1 day	.18
Disk storage 1 track 1 month	.051

Schedules of rates for service bureaus are more elaborate than those shown above, which are intended merely as a sample. Service bureaus' rates are more flexible, they charge based on volumes and the actual amounts of time contracted. Internal data center rates are generally less flexible than those of a service bureau. Actual charges are made by multiplying the usage and the rates.

To facilitate the planning for and acquiring of the necessary equipment, a data center manager can request that users submit estimates of what their requirements for a coming year will be. These estimates can be used to project cost estimates for the users also. For example, disk storage accesses, tape storage accesses, processor seconds, and storage increments can be estimated by users for each application. The data center can extend these unit estimates by multiplying them by the rates to come up with charges. This aspect of running a data center has little appeal to technicians but the negotiating between users and data centers managers can be rather stimulating.

5. Data center users are entitled, first and foremost, to service. For example, a data center may commit to a specific performance level, e.g., 95% of on-line transactions responded to within three seconds, or four turnarounds a day on batch development work. There are going to be times when that performance level is not met. When such situations arise, it is the data center manager's job to see to it that users are notified. The users should be provided with an explanation of the situation and also with an estimate (if possible) of when service can be expected to return to normal. Emergencies such as an unexpected outage of a large-scale computer or damage to a major database can cause a degradation in service that cannot be anticipated. When this occurs, a rapid and accurate communication to the users is helpful. Many current software products have the capability of broadcasting information to the terminal devices on a network. This is an extremely effective way of informing users about what's going on in an emergency situation.

On other occasions, a degradation or curtailment of services is known ahead of time. Reasons for such curtailments include cleaning of water towers that supply water for air conditioners or installation of new equipment where recabling and perhaps relocating requires that machines be shut down for a period of time. Information about such activities should be communicated to users well ahead of time so that they can adjust their schedules accordingly.

As we mentioned earlier, a data center is constantly bringing in new equipment and new system software products. Data center managers should set up periodic review sessions for users to familiarize them with current data center facilities and services. Perhaps every six months, a half-day seminar would be a suitable format to provide user management with an explanation of the features of the equipment and software products in the data center. On a more frequent basis, the system software managers and operations managers can present tutorials on the specifics of the most current products to user analysts and application programmers.

6. A data center, like any other large organizational function, is made up of a number of smaller subfunctions, formed along the lines of the major operations groups and the system software product support groups. While individuals in these groups talk to each other when necessary on a day-to-day basis, each group is primarily concerned with

achieving its own operational priorities. This is as it should be, with the data center manager and his or her immediate subordinates keeping it all tied together.

However, it is advisable to conduct a yearly planning meeting where the managers of individual operations groups and system software product support groups get together to set goals, objectives, and operational priorities for the coming twelve to fifteen months. This meeting ought to be held at a site away from the data center and should be between two and three days duration. Out of this meeting should come a plan within which the activities for all of the groups are integrated with one another so that the groups are aware of the impact that their activities have on each other. Data center managers who ignore such meetings should not be too surprised when internal bickering and "us 'n' them" situations arise among the groups.

7. Data centers are often at the leading edge of technology. Capitalizing fully on the technology requires that technicians be trained and that managers be educated. Training involves a series of courses that range in length from one day to two weeks. The systems software technicians require the most training. Console operators and communications technicians also require some. Data center managers generally see to it that their technicians receive the training that they need. What they often fail to realize is that they and their immediate subordinates require education to keep up with technological advances.

It is generally accepted that for individuals to manage well they have to divorce themselves from technical specialization. The higher in management they go, the further away they get from technology. However, data center managers require a general familiarity with the technology that is under their control. Since there is a significant amount of it, data center managers and their subordinates ought to attend seminars that cover topics such as database, data communications, interactive systems, operating systems, small computers, and automated office systems. Data center managers who do not attend such seminars have in their heads concepts and ideas of the technology they knew earlier, many of which are no longer accurate. This can result in bad judgment and may also be the cause of tension between technicians trained in the latest methods and managers who are somewhat out of date.

8. In addition to the basic software security mentioned earlier, there are also some basic physical security precautions that ought to be taken within a data center. While they could not prevent a gang of terrorists armed with machine guns and hand grenades from wreaking havoc, they can at least be a detriment to the smaller type of violations. For instance, having a uniformed guard at the main entrance to a data center and keeping other entrances and exits locked inhibit the entry of unauthorized individuals. The use of electronically controlled access

keys or identification cards goes a long way toward keeping unauthorized people out of certain areas. Schemes such as this can be simple, for example, restricting access to the computer room, or elaborate, where accesses to increasingly secured areas is made possible by electronically controlled mechanisms.

Internal television camera and receiver systems are a relatively simple and inexpensive investment in security. Cameras can be set up near entrances and exits and in other sensitive areas. Receivers can be set up near the guard's desk and at other areas where they can be watched or glanced at periodically.

Security precautions such as these, while not considered comprehensive, are certainly better than none at all. Even if some people snicker at their simplicity, they do serve a purpose. No security at all invites trouble, simple security procedures at least take steps to eliminate or reduce the most flagrant violations.

OBSERVATIONS ON DATA CENTER MANAGEMENT

While it is true that the primary concern of data center managers should be service to users, we have seen that they must also be in control of a host of activities in order to provide that service on a sustained basis. The job is a difficult one, because the best one can do in it is to break even. On a good day in a data center, when all the equipment is working and all the software products perform well, nobody notices; the data center manager is doing what's expected. On a bad day, when equipment malfunctions or software behaves inconsistently, the data center manager and the subordinates "take the heat."

The managers of data centers and their subordinates should be rotated into different jobs periodically. First-line supervisors should be moved laterally, or if possible, promoted every couple of years. In organizations where it is practical, first-line supervisors ought to be given job opportunities in user areas, and user personnel ought to be given opportunities in the data center. An individual should spend a maximum of four to five years as a data center manager. That is sufficient time for individuals to both plan and implement data center activities. It is also sufficient time for those individuals to be evaluated by their management in the performance of their duties.

There are some negative factors that accrue if both managers and supervisors are not given opportunities to change positions. The first of these is that inbreeding takes place. In such a situation, there is a tendency to always go with the tried and true and to suppress new ideas without giving them proper consideration. Second, in a data center, there is constant, unrelenting pressure to get the work out. As stated earlier, the best that can be done is to break even, and that doesn't occur often enough. Even if bad days don't outnumber the good days, the bad days are the ones that everybody remembers. Third, data centers, like any operations function, never seem to have enough resources (equipment, software, and people). They operate with sufficient resources to handle average workloads. That's great when the workload is average or under, but when it's over average, there's a scramble and pressure builds and performance slips. Constant exposure to these pressures fosters a "fortress or seige mentality." Individuals who work in a data center for a long time and who are not given an opportunity to work in another environment where the pressures are different begin to develop such a mentality. Attitudes become defensive, and when problems occur, they tend to cover up causes rather than to expose and correct them. Giving individuals opportunities to work at jobs both within the data center and in user areas offset these negatives by providing insights into the "other guy's problems." Individuals who transfer back and forth between user areas and data centers and who understand both sides of problem situations are more inclined to assist one another in solving problems rather than just being concerned with avoiding blame. Environments providing opportunity for transfer and advancement result in better service overall.

COMPUTER ROOMS

Computer equipment is used in some form in very nearly all commercial organizations. Large corporations often use data centers to support a major portion of their EDP/MIS activity. Smaller organizations use computer facilities also, but on a smaller scale. These smaller organizations may be individual companies or divisions or subsidiaries of large companies. In those situations involving individual companies, the small-scale computer configurations are generally "stand-alone" facilities that work independently of any other configuration. In situations involving divisions or subsidiaries, the computer configuration may be a "stand-alone" facility or it may be part of a distributed processing arrangement.

Contemporary computer configurations generally consist of a processor, primary storage, disk secondary storage, perhaps tape secondary storage, CRTs, and printers. Software frequently includes an operating system, a file management or database management system, a data communications monitor, and support for interactive programming for a couple of problem-oriented languages. These contemporary hardware/software configurations are somewhat more "user friendly" than the configurations of the 1960s and 1970s.

Stand-alone

A stand-alone contemporary computer configuration can be either a single computer-based or a dual computer-based system. There is a cost/availability trade-off that can be made here. If you are able to operate your business without your computer for several hours or maybe a day or so, then you can get by with a single computer-based system. Sometimes referred to as "plain vanilla," such a system is essentially a batch-oriented configuration. If you need a computer for things like keeping track of inventory, producing weekly and monthly reports for sales analysis, and accounting functions, a "plain vanilla" computer configuration can do the job. If, on the other hand, you want a computer system that will allow you to directly enter orders through CRT devices, relieving inventory as the orders are confirmed, allow you to make direct interactive inquiries for sales or other information, or allow you to do interactive financial modeling, a "plain vanilla" system just won't do. The configuration required for that kind of environment consists of at least two computer processors, one prime and one backup, and the software facilities to perform periodic backup and recovery/restart activities. Make no mistake about it, contemporary computers are quite reliable, but they do fail every now and then, and when they do, backup and recovery/restart is necessary.

There is a definite trend toward the latter of the two configurations described above. Interactive processing realizes the potential of computers to a much greater extent than does batch processing. There are however, some considerations that one ought to be aware of when contemplating the purchase or lease of medium sized computer configurations to be used as either stand-alone or dual computer-based systems.

- One of the most difficult problems to overcome in going to contemporary computer technology is the conversion from earlier technology.
- Interactive processing, backup and recovery/restart capabilities represent a significant investment of funds, invariably greater than initially anticipated.
- Medium-sized computer rooms have a tendency to grow, and with growth, they begin to resemble small data centers. While they don't service a number of different organizations the same way a large data center might, they do service a number of different functions with the same organization. This gives rise to the need for some kind of centralized function to coordinate the development efforts so as to minimize duplication of function and redundancy of data.

Distributed

Distributed processing is a term that can be legitimately used to describe an arrangement in which two or more computers interact with one another and each computer has the potential to have an impact on the processing of one or more of the others.

A distributed processing arrangement involving medium-sized computer configurations in a medium-sized organization would generally involve two or more, up to perhaps six, configurations interacting with one another. In a large organization, there could be several such configurations in each division or subsidiary interacting with one another on a intradivision or intrasubsidiary basis and interacting with a centralized data center configuration and maybe even with other configurations on a interdivision or intersubsidiary basis. The complications involved in doing this are twofold. First of all, the technology to support distributed processing is extremely sophisticated, especially the software. The system software technicians supporting the software must be constantly kept up-to-date, as the software in this area is continually being enhanced to support additional protocols and devices. Second, the operational and managerial tasks far exceed in complexity those of managing a computer room with one or two computer equipment configurations. In addition to the more elaborate backup and recovery/restart procedures that must be developed, there are the additional questions. To be addressed are questions like what is to be distributed (data and programs), how often are files or databases to be refreshed, how much of a file or database is to be distributed, are the system software (operating system, data communications monitor and database) to be maintained centrally or locally?

Observation on Computer Room Environments

A computer room consisting of one or two medium-sized computer configurations is much like a data center with several large-scale computer configurations. The concerns and complexities are similar in nature. In the data center with the large-scale computers, the workings and the problems are somewhat more complex in their details simply because there are more variables to deal with. In the computer room with the medium-sized computers, the situation is less complicated because there are fewer variables. In organizations with computer rooms containing one, two, or perhaps three medium-sized computer configurations, the technical skills are spread over fewer individuals. The loss of an individual with technical skill can have a greater impact in the medium-sized organization with a computer room than it would in an organization with a data center where there is more technical depth.

A computer room that consists of one or two medium-sized computers that are part of a distributed processing arrangement is a much more complex environment. Such a facility cannot be controlled or managed as a stand-alone entity. To be sure, all the stand-alone environment considerations and problems must be taken into account, but added to these are the additional requirements of data communications and the coordination of the division of data and of processing function among several computer configurations.

SMALL PERSONAL OR BUSINESS COMPUTERS

What They Are

Small personal computers started out as a product of semiconductor/microelectronics technology. In the early 1970s, the first 4-bit and 8-bit* semiconductor microprocessors were introduced. Each of these processors were made up of microelectronic circuits that were fabricated onto a small semiconductor wafer and given the nickname "computer on a chip." These 4-bit and 8-bit processors were followed by 16-bit and 32-bit versions, as small personal computers began to acquire the processing capabilities of what ten years earlier had been considered large-scale computers.

The sketch in Figure 8.2 depicts a typical small personal or business computer. These machines are microprocessor based and as such are quite small. However, a computer without secondary storage and input/output equipment is really quite useless. While it is true that computers equipped with thousands of positions of primary storage can be carried around in a pocket or purse, there is little to be gained by doing so. At the very least, some kind of CRT device or typewriter terminal device is required to perform even the most primitive of tasks with a computer. If saving what has been done is necessary, some form of secondary storage is required also, since turning off a computer results in the loss of all information in primary storage. Therefore, while it is true that microprocessors and primary storage continue to get smaller and less expensive, peripheral device size and prices are somewhat less dynamic. After all, you can make display screens, keyboards, and printers just so small, and after that they become novelties rather than pieces of functional equipment. Prices of these devices also can come down just so far, and then they begin to stabilize. So, while the prices and sizes of

*The number of bits on which a computer is based determines the amount of information (bits) that the processor can work with per unit of time, and the number of bits also determines the highest primary storage address that the computer can directly access without the aid of an indexing mechanism. To state it simply, the larger the bit base of the machine, the better (faster) its performance.

Figure 8.2 A small personal/business computer.

microprocessors and primary storage continue to be reduced, the size and cost of peripheral devices remains relatively constant. Also, software and supplies, taken in context are an additional expense that can easily be underestimated by uninitiated individuals.

The ballyhoo and fanfare surrounding small personal and business computers is a marketing phenomenon. It comes about as a result of the fact that many organizations are trying to market products (computers, peripherals, software, and supplies) that are essentially quite similar. Each organization claims its product to be the best. Small, relatively insignificant technological changes are hyped as being great significant advances. Senior managers and executives and even individuals who know something about computers find themselves "shorting-out" mentally because of information overload. There's just too much hardware and software; too many prices, too many options; it's changing too quickly, and rational selection is impossible. The way to buy a small personal computer is first to determine what it is you want to do with it (learning how to interact with computers is a valid reason for buying one, even if it can't be justified immediately on the basis of economics), and then to find out what kind of configuration of equipment and software will meet your objectives. Then make an informed estimate of whether the maker of the equipment that you like is going to remain in business and then buy it. If that approach to buying a small personal or business computer seems too simple and arbitrary, then it is possible to complicate the decision-making process by adding other variables. Some additional factors that you may want to consider are as follows:

- Is the configuration you want compatible with other configurations to which you have access?

- If the equipment breaks down, where and how quickly can it be repaired?
- How much and what type of software is available for the configuration you want?
- What are the expectations for the configuration in terms of expandability for the future?
- Is it user friendly?
- Does the configuration have the capability of producing graphic displays?
- If not totally compatible with other configurations, what interfaces exist that can make it compatible?

The list is virtually endless.* There are also numerous books in circulation that tell you a lot of things about computers that are nice to know and a lot of other things that you don't need to know. A number of these books are quite a bit like catalogs; that is, they contain quite a bit of information about specific computers, their peripherals, and specific software. These books can be helpful to the novice, but they should be used discriminately, because, like catalogs, the information they contain obsoletes quickly. When purchasing such a book, check its copyright date. If it's more than a year old, its contents are made up of information that is probably about two or more years old.

Uses and Limitations

As computers, that is, processors, controllers, and primary storage components, continue to decrease in size and price, the potential for their use is going to continue to expand. As it becomes increasingly common for small personal and business computers to interface and communicate with large-scale secondary storage devices, the potential is going to expand even further. This should take place during the decade of the 1980s. So much for potential. Let's take a look at practical reality.

The first microprocessors were used for pocket calculators, process controllers, and other special-purpose functions. However, it wasn't long before they were being used in the manufacture of small computers. There may be some debate on this, but software in the form of computerized spread sheets may have done more than any other single factor to push microprocessor-based small personal/business com-

*I purchased my own personal computer equipment based on three criteria: (1) price, (2) software, (3) an expectation that the maker would stay in business. It has its limitations, but basically it adequately performs the functions I require. It failed criteria (3), but I can still use it.

puters into prominence. Hundreds of financial analysts responded to the VISICALC software product and the APPLE II. Soon there were copies, and variations and small computers of all shapes and sizes were finding their way into homes and offices. Word processing applications software is also quite popular on small personal/business computers, as are programming languages such as BASIC and PASCAL, two problem-oriented languages that take quite a bit of the technological sting out of computer programming. User-friendly database/data communication (DB/DC) products are becoming more viable as larger (16-bit) microprocessors serve as a basic building block for small personal/business computers. DB/DC products are characteristically high overhead performers, but the more powerful microprocessors make them feasible for moderately sized database/data communications applications, or for larger applications where parts of a substantial database that reside in a large scale host can be distributed to several smaller microprocessor-based configurations. Microprocessor-based computers are also found in the local area networks (LANs) that were described in an earlier chapter. These networks combine data processing applications, word processing applications, and electronic mail.

Their Limitations

The limitations of small personal/business computers is not really a shortcoming of the computers themselves, but rather limitations imposed by the environments into which they are introduced. There are essentially three kinds of limitations, those imposed by the current state of the EDP/MIS environment, those imposed by software, and those imposed by practical realities. Let's deal with them separately.

First, the current state of the EDP/MIS environment is such that the application mix contains a mixture of applications that range from three to twenty years in age. As a consequence, the computer programs in these applications may be written in half a dozen different programming languages, employ another half a dozen different access methods and file structures. Most of the applications were implemented on large-scale computers and interface with one another in rather primitive fashion. In their current state, because of their age, they require almost constant modification, and as a result have become unstable and unreliable. The older applications are principally batch, and the newer ones are on-line applications with batch back-end report generation capabilities. More often than not, they are running on the large-scale computers of an overburdened data center. The condition of the data, as far as integrity and accuracy is concerned, is subject to question. In addition, data records are often specified to carry the same information, but because of the instability and unreliability of the applications, this data is inconsistent across the applications and is often not present where it should be when it should be. All these factors mitigate against using small computers to manipulate live data in summarized form from production applications, so that it can be used for presentation to senior managers and executives. In a pristine environment, a small computer would be an ideal tool for performing such a task. Senior managers and executives could use the small computers to query summary databases that contain a combination of historical and current information that has been consolidated from a great quantity of detail data that is resident on a large-scale computer configuration in a data center or computer room. This again is potential, and it is a worthwhile objective. A combined effort on the part of users and EDP/MIS professionals, with the support of senior managers and executives makes this objective achievable. As we all know, this is easier said than done, as achieving cooperation among diverse groups is itself a herculean task. And yet, netting it all out, the potential exists to establish a centralized database on large-scale computer configurations with feeds that facilitate the transfer of summary information to small computers that senior managers and executive can use to manipulate and analyze that summary information. Realization of that potential is possible for senior managers and executives who possess that combination of skills necessary to motivate their subordinates to cooperate in making it happen.

A second limitation of small computers is that imposed by software. There are many products, many varieties of each, and their number is constantly increasing. Even informed and experienced EDP/MIS professionals are hard pressed to make recommendations that are supportable for more than a few weeks. There are at least half a dozen viable operating systems that are universally accepted as reliable and stable; there are tens of communications software products; there are at least ten database management system products that have achieved universal acceptance; and there are numerous versions of interactive and batch compilers of programming languages, such as BASIC, PASCAL, and C. Word processing products abound, and application software options simply cannot be quantified.

Aside from the stable and reliable products (and there is even some debate on these as their quality varies depending on the computer it supports, i.e., XYZ operating system might work well on computer A, and not quite as well on computer B), "what you see is what you get" with small computer software. While most of the products do perform to specifications, users invariably find that specifications can be vague, and the software product is not quite what was expected. The caveat, "let the buyer beware," holds.

The final limitation is that imposed by the practical realities of owning a computer. Owning a computer is like owning any other sophisticated equipment. Again, let's use the word potential. Let's also assume at this point that you've purchased a computer and you take it home or bring it to your office. You may have felt the first tinge of disillusionment when you made your purchase. The small personal computer that you expected to walk away with for $700 has cost you about $1700. You have learned that, in addition to 48K of primary storage and a BASIC board which were included, you really needed a floppy disk drive, a printer, some floppy disks, a couple of cables, some typewriter ribbons, a box of paper for the printer, and a couple of interface cables to hook up the disk drive and the printer. Let's assume the interface cable for the television or monitor was included in the $700 price. Realizing just a portion of the potential of a $700 computer has already cost you an additional grand.

Once you've got the equipment into your home or office, you find that you need three or four electrical outlets (three-prong, grounded), one for the computer, one for the television or monitor, one for the printer, and one for a lamp so you can see what you're doing. If there are a couple of locations in your home or office that you like to use, your neighborhood electrician can fix you up for less than $200. However, electricians can't come right away, so you scrounge up an extension cord with three-prong grounded receptacles on it and a two-prong/three-prong adapter (if your home or office has two-prong receptacles and you get everything powered up).

Within a couple of hours you get everything working by following the instructions in the various booklets that come with the computer, the disk drive, and the printer. The biggest hassle has probably been with the electrical outlets, as most of the booklets provide instructions that are reasonably easy to follow.

After a few days of fooling around with BASIC, you begin to become aware that there is more to it than writing BASIC programs. You want to create some files without having to write a program (a database manager or file utility would be nice), or you'd like to write a report or some letters (a word processing package would be nice). You would like to be able to copy things from one disk to another, and you'd like to have a reference of what is on a disk, something like a table of contents or an index (an operating system and some utilities would be neat). You're also becoming curious about a printer that provides typewriter-quality printer material; the one you got for $400 prints using a dot matrix printing mechanism. It's great as far as speed is concerned, but as far as quality goes, it's marginal.

The phone call you made to the dealer who sold you the computer reveals that for another thousand you can get an operating system and utilities, a database manager, and a word processing package. As far as printers go, you learn that they vary in price from about $800 to over $2000, with the more expensive models being faster and having more features.

At this point, you're at the point of no return. You can try to sell what you've got and probably get back between seventy and eighty cents on the dollar, if you can find somebody who's interested; you can try to get your kids interested, especially if your configuration supports games, or you can make some or all of the additional expenditures and make the transition from mere believer to committed disciple.

Those of you who make the commitment find within a few more weeks that it would be great if you could access the information in the large computer in the data center of the organization for which you work or perhaps have a communications arrangement with others like yourself who have also become committed to the use of computers. You're beginning to see how some of the potential can be realized. Using communications, you can share information and software with others. You call up the computer dealer and learn that for another thousand you can expand your 48K primary storage to 128K, get a modem and a data communications software product that allows you to communicate with a number of other computer types including the one in the data center where you work.

The next day, you contact your EDP/MIS representative in your organization and are informed that you need an ID and a password to get into the computer at the data center, and so you. . . .

And so even though there are limitations, they can be overcome. The small personal and business computers have great potential. Realizing that potential involves overcoming the limitations.

CONCLUSIONS

Small computers are revolutionizing the way we do things. This statement has been heard so often that it is frequently absorbed and accepted, but not understood. Because it is not understood, most people have simplistic and naive notions about computers and what they can or cannot do. In this chapter, we have attempted to show some of the reality of working with computer configurations of all sizes. Computers are not super-intelligent machines, they are not electronic people-replacers, but rather they are tools. They are a powerful potential force. They cannot be ignored and they are going to have an impact on what we do and the way we do it. It is up to us to realize that potential. We can be sure that some are going to realize it, the question is will it be you or will it be someone else?

SUMMARY

In this chapter we have surveyed computer-based operating environments, the places where Murphy's law (If something can go wrong, it will) is in force. Operations is "where the rubber meets the road," whether its a data center with large-scale computers or an office or den with a small personal computer. Early in the chapter, we used an analogy of depots, warehouses, and stores in an attempt to clarify the differences between installations with large-scale computers, those with medium-sized computers, and those with small computers.

We then examined in some detail large-scale EDP/MIS operations, which are often in the form of data centers. We looked at data center resources, the equipment, the software, and the people. Before getting into greater detail, it was pointed out that a data center manager's primary concern is service, a factor that is often overlooked when detailed treatments of data center resources are undertaken. Operations, an equipment-intensive function and software support, a people-intensive function, are found in data centers. Operations includes computer operations, data communications, scheduling, control, and customer service. The software support function is staffed with system programmers who provide for the installation maintenance and enhancement of system software products and technology. Under their care are operating systems, telecommunications products, database/data communications systems, and related products. Software support is also required for the technologies of performance measurement and tuning, interactive/personal computing facilities, distributed systems, and software security systems.

Other data center tasks were explained. These concerns of data center managers are not visible to those outside the data center on a day-to-day basis. The only time they are noticed is when they are neglected by data center managers. Included are the tasks of keeping equipment and software current, providing an acceptable resource billing methodology, maintaining adequate backup and recovery/restart procedures, conducting yearly planning meetings with users to forecast requirements, establishing and maintaining physical security measures, keeping users current on data center equipment and software products, and providing adequate education and training for data center technical staff.

After making some overall observations about data center management, we took a brief look at medium-sized computer rooms, those that are independent stand-alone facilities, and those that serve as nodes in a distributed processing arrangement. Some general observations were also made on medium-sized computer rooms.

The final section of the chapter dealt with small personal and business computer configurations. In this chapter, we described small computers again from a slightly different perspective than the descriptions in Chapter 3. We then went on to indicate their uses and their limitations. Following this treatment of small computers, some overall conclusions were offered.

CHAPTER 9

Why There Are Problems

INTRODUCTION

Information systems technology, it seems, comes equipped with a built-in paradox. Equipment and software vendors, bright, eager young MBAs, and fast-track information systems managers make multicolored slide presentations, complete with some of the latest graphics techniques showing what a sad state the organization is in with outdated technology, and how more current technology can brighten the picture substantially. The presentations are so professional and so well put together that what they suggest appears almost flawless. And yet, some senior managers and executives are beginning to become uncomfortable. They are remembering that they've heard it before. As a matter of fact, they've been hearing it for years, and now they're wondering where it's going to end.

In the 1960s, operating systems and concurrent program execution were going to maximize utilization of the idle resource, the computer.*

*Prior to operating systems, computers were only able to execute one program at a time. Because of relatively slow secondary storage and input/output devices, computer processors spent about 95% of their time waiting for data transfer or input/output operations to complete.

This was accomplished, but only after an extremely costly conversion effort, where all programs that ran on the older nonoperating system computers were rewritten to work on the newer computers. Many organizations found that after a couple of years, they were right back where they were when the conversion began in terms of implemented applications. Only after the conversions were completed could organizations begin to capitalize on the new technology. Those organizations that began new application development immediately on the new computers found themselves saddled with old applications that still had to be supported and run. Extra equipment was needed, and technicians who were satisfied supporting old applications were scarce and commanded high rates. Not a few organizations were still supporting and running these applications ten years later when their cost far outweighed their value. Yet many of them were necessary and had to be kept until their functions were gradually taken over by newly developed applications. New technology is great, but as history teaches, getting from old to new can be costly and time consuming.

In the 1970s, one of the catch phrases was "more bang for the buck." Everyone involved had learned a lesson from the 1960s—no more revolutionary technology changes. In the 1970s it was all supposed to be evolutionary. However, it didn't quite work out that way. While it is true that hardware and software architecture in which programs execute concurrently under the control of operating systems remained fairly constant, other developments made it difficult for the vendors, the MBAs, and the fast-track managers to keep their "more bang for the buck" promises. To be sure, there was more "bang," but there was also a lot more "buck" required to make the bigger "bang" possible. It was during the 1970s that information systems technology began to have significant financial impact on organizational profit-and-loss statements. This impact was not so much in terms of "bang," always difficult to measure, but rather in terms of "bucks," which are relatively easy to measure. Senior managers and executives began to pay attention.

The new developments that were causing the impact were the advances made in data communications and telecommunications, the emergence of database, minicomputers and microprocessors, interactive computing facilities, security requirements, distributed computing, and the so-called office automation phenomenon. In the late 1960s, some of these were leading edge technologies; at various times in the 1970s they made their presence felt. Data communications and telecommunications had passed from state-of-the-art technology to the commonplace by 1972. Minicomputers, used mostly by engineers in the early 1970s, had begun to emerge as commercial application vehicles by 1975. Improvements in hardware, such as virtual storage and billion-byte secondary storage disk devices, had made database a commonly used technology by 1976. The microprocessor had first appeared in 1971, but the real breakthrough had come in 1975. These very small processors had found their way into all kinds of things: calculators, automobile braking systems, and even watches. They had even found their way into what became known as word processors. By 1977 the term *office automation* had been coined. At the time, trade journal articles and seminars had proclaimed a new revolution. However, all that had died down within about a year, when most people became aware that a computer is a computer, whether large or small, and word processing was nothing more than another information systems application. As the 1970s were coming to a close, it had become obvious to nearly everyone that computers had become an integral part of their lives. As the 1980s opened, small personal computers had become affordable to virtually anyone. One hundred dollars could purchase a basic computer with keyboard of sorts that could use a television set as a display screen. Interactive programming facilities were making even large-scale computers more user friendly. Data communications and teleprocessing had made it possible for computers to be interconnected, making distributed computing possible. And just to keep everybody honest, computer security procedures and practices had been developed. However, most of this was extremely expensive and did not seem to work as well as it should have, as many senior managers and executives were aware. The term "dinosaurs in tarpits" was coined. The MBAs who had been supposed to do all kinds of wonderful things turned out to be little more than number manipulators. Their lack of genuine operational business experience made many of their basic assumptions naive, unrealistic, and incorrect.

OK, we've given you the background, now let's try to define the problems. Why doesn't information systems technology live up to its potential? There are a number of reasons, and we are going to attempt to deal with them in an orderly fashion. For the remainder of this chapter, we're going to treat three main problem areas: problems with technology, problems with people, and problems for other reasons. Let's start with the technology.

PROBLEMS WITH TECHNOLOGY

Glitches and Bugs

The terms *glitch* and *bug* are sometimes used interchangeably. Yet, glitch is most commonly used relative to hardware, while bug is most commonly used relative to software. A glitch is a malfunctioning component within a piece of hardware. A glitch is not the same thing as an equipment component failure. When an equipment configuration is working normally and a component fails, processing stops. Repairing or replacing the failing component makes it possible to resume processing. On the other hand, a glitch does not interrupt processing by causing a configuration to fail, but rather causes puzzling results to occur. It involves not the failure of a properly working component but rather a component working but not properly. Most glitches are uncovered and removed by the manufacturer during the fabrication of the prototype. Occasionally one gets through, is built into production models, and is shipped to customers. Isolating and correcting such glitches is a maddening experience for both manufacturer and customer. Fortunately, this type of situation is occurring less frequently as fabrication processes become more mechanical in nature and less error prone.

The term bug usually refers to a malfunctioning module within either an application program or a system software product. Bugs arise in programs that for one reason or another have not been thoroughly tested. In some situations this is totally inexcusable; in others it is understandable. Inexcusable bugs are those introduced into either application programs or system software products by programmers who develop or modify programs or modules and do not adequately test them. Understandable bugs are those that occur in highly integrated applications or software products. In those situations the individual programs or modules can be tested, but as more and more programs and modules are integrated with one another, the probability of testing every conceivable condition that can arise decreases. Therefore, it is taken for granted that elaborate system software products and integrated applications with interrelated programs are going to occasionally have bugs. This understandable bug situation must be accepted as a fact of life and dealt with accordingly. This is one of the reasons for having backup, and recovery/restart procedures. On the other hand, the inexcusable bug situation is something else. While it is impossible to eliminate such bugs altogether, it is possible to minimize them. Sometimes they are caused by a lazy or indifferent programmer. This is a problem within the information systems organization. Other times it is caused by knee-jerk changes that must be implemented overnight. This is a management problem. One of the drawbacks of using information systems technology is that it requires precision, and it does not react well to sudden changes. Senior managers and executives would do well to be cognizant of this when attempting to make hasty adjustments to perceived changes in business conditions. Not only might the adjustment itself not take place properly, but the bugs let loose might infest the application and systems for weeks. A trade-off has to be made. The senior management of an organization ought to be made aware that an adjustment in processing may have undesirable consequences. It is the responsibility of information systems managers, in specific situations, to explain to senior management the potentially unfavorable consequences of a proposed adjustment. This can sometimes be difficult depending upon the personalities involved, but it should be attempted. Senior management may elect to make an adjustment regardless of the consequences, but if they've been forewarned, at least they'll not be completely taken by surprise by the consequences.

Incompatibility of Components

There's a wide range in prices of computer components. It is not surprising then that both individuals and organizations go to some lengths to get as much processing power as they can for as few dollars as possible. This is done by mixing equipment from more than one manufacturer. In organizations with data centers and computer rooms, equipment budgets are sometimes in the hundreds of thousands or even millions of dollars. The differences in prices can result in "on paper" savings of 10 or 20%. The same kind of situation exists in the world of small computer configurations. While the absolute dollar values are significantly lower (hundreds or perhaps thousands of dollars), the percentages may be even greater.

There is a corollary to Murphy's Law which states: "Plug-compatible* devices aren't." To remedy this, we have interfaces. Interface is a generic term that refers to devices that are used to reconcile components that are incompatible.† Despite the corollary to Murphy's Law cited above, there are some truly plug-compatible devices. The point is to make sure that a device is plug compatible and does not require an interface that makes the total cost just as expensive as the original equipment. In addition, it also pays to find out if there are equivalent service contracts available at prices that make using a plug-compatible device an attractive deal financially.

There's a rule of thumb that can be followed here. Generally speaking, the use of plug-compatible devices brings you out ahead in terms of price. As long as everything is running well, you stay ahead. If something goes wrong, it is frequently difficult to determine which component is malfunctioning. If you have a single manufacturer's equipment, you have a single source upon which to call to have the situation at-

*A device or component that can be swapped with a device or component that comes as part of a configuration from a single manufacturer is plug compatible.

†There are also software interfaces that reconcile incompatible software modules or programs.

tended to. If you have two or more manufacturers, it can be quite difficult to have the situation attended to, when each manufacturer's field engineer claims that their equipment checks out. Again, it's a trade-off. On the surface, it appears that identifiable cost savings that show upon the profit-and-loss statement, when less expensive equipment is leased or purchased, are real. Less tangible is the potential extra cost of either wasted time or perhaps lost sales that many be incurred while a configuration is idled because two manufacturers' field engineers cannot or will not cooperate to pinpoint and attend to a problem. As a general rule, a large organization with several configurations in a data center is better equipped to handle a prolonged outage of equipment than is a smaller organization with a single configuration. The larger operation is able to run in a degraded fashion, while the smaller organization is at a standstill. Therefore, capitalizing on less expensive equipment, generally speaking, involves less risk for the larger organization. This assumes, of course, that the less expensive component is not used to perform functions that are essential to the running of the entire data center.

"Ship It"

Tracy Kidder's book, *The Soul of the New Machine*, narrates the process of designing and producing an advanced technology computer that is to give its maker a competitive edge. A fascinating nonfiction book for a number of reasons, it examines both technology and people. One particular character in the narrative is the type of individual who examines the facts, realizes that it's not a perfect world, and makes a decision based on available information. At one point in the story, this individual, made aware that a new machine is almost but not quite ready, says "ship it." That kind of decisiveness is a characteristic of qualified senior managers and executives.

There are other types of individuals in organizations, those with what might be called a more technical mentality. It is almost impossible for them to say "ship it" when they are aware that it is not working perfectly. As a matter of act, in their extreme form, individuals of this type are constantly trying to improve the performance or efficiency of things. If left alone, the product over which they labor would never get shipped.

There is a tension between the two types of individuals just described, and yet both are necessary, first, to get equipment or software designed and built, and second, to get it "out the door." Technology is a process of change, and it appears that the rate of change is accelerating. New hardware and software products are constantly "leapfrogging" over one another so quickly it's virtually impossible to get a fix on things. The technician and the executive, despite the tension, need each other. Technicians are needed to implement the ideas of the executives and to provide them with the information they need to make decisions. Executives are needed to provide vision and direction and to make decisions based on incomplete or even conflicting information. In the real world, there is no total technician or total executive, but only individuals who have tendencies in one direction or another. To put the onus on those in executive or senior management positions, it is suggested that they exercise some patience in dealing with technicians whose skill, unlike their own, is not in making decisions or setting direction, but rather in presenting facts and alternatives.

Change Itself

Change itself and its impact on individuals is a phenomenon that is discussed in depth by psychologists and sociologists. Without going into any kind of heavy sociological treatment of change and its impact, it is possible to highlight some of the difficulties brought about by change in the field of information systems.

Much as they don't like to admit it, information systems professionals are also overwhelmed with the changes taking place in the field. In earlier chapters of this book, we surveyed hardware and software. We distinguished between system software and application software. We described the different types of system software. We indicated that while all computer configurations have the same functional components, the applications of large-scale configurations differ from the applications of smaller configurations. We pointed out that the management of large configurations is different than the management of small configurations. It follows then that information systems is a field of many specializations. In addition, the specializations are dynamic. It is difficult for technicians to stay abreast; it is even more difficult for information systems managers to keep up-to-date on the various aspects of technology.

Most of today's information systems managers have grown up with the industry. Many of them started out as operators and programmers. They began to leave their technical skills behind as they entered the ranks of management. Computer operations and programming were quite different in the 1960s than they are today. And yet, some of these managers, while aware that things have changed, find it difficult to make the transition. Having left the technical, which is a precise trade, and having entered management, which is an imprecise and nebulous profession, they are faced with the classic tension of management. They must leave the black-and-white technical things to the technicians and must devote their energies to the gray area of interpersonal relationships required of managers. This can be a cause of anxiety and insecurity for individuals in times of stress. Confronted with a particularly difficult management situation, they attempt to fall back on their technical know-how and find that it has changed. The behavior of managers in such situations varies all over the place, depending on the type of individual. The anxiety and insecurity can manifest itself in indecisiveness, pigheadedness, glib superficiality, incessant quoting of statistics, anger and frustration, or on some occasions, candor. The point is this, keeping up with the dynamics of the information systems field is a herculean task for managers. In many situations, they are put upon to produce results that are made to look easy by vendors, certain entertainers disguised as information systems gurus, and bright, young fast-track MBAs, who are up on one or two elements of the latest technology. Information systems managers, who are going through an internal struggle with their own competence, are torn between resisting the vendors, gurus, and MBAs and appearing negative or supporting them and going along with something that in their gut they feel uncomfortable with.

Technicians also have trouble dealing with change. They have a tendency to get comfortable with what they know and do well. Change, in the form of new technology, poses a threat to their feelings of comfort and well-being. Attempting to convince technicians who are skilled in the use of or the support of a particular product that a new one should be used in its place is an impossible task. Instead, the approach should be to give it to the technicians and let them play with it for a while and if its better, they'll probably, but not always, go for it.

The reason that change presents a problem is because both information systems managers and technicians are very close to the day-to-day activities necessary to use existing technology to support the requirement of an organization. To them, new technology represents nothing but additional work and problems. While the concepts of information systems are only somewhat complex, and the scenarios of fully integrated database/data communication facilities are rather easy to visualize, their implementation and support are an extremely complicated and multifaceted task. Information systems managers with ten years experience have gone through the introduction of a few minor and one major technological innovation. Those with twenty years experience have twice as much exposure. They view technological progress and change with a jaundiced eye. While they realize that there are advantages, they also view it somewhat pragmatically and see the rewards going to others and see themselves paying the price.

PROBLEMS WITH PEOPLE (POLITICS)

Machiavelli

It has been said that Machiavelli describes things as they really are, as opposed to the way they ought to be. Dealing with things as they are seems to be safer than trying to make things the way they ought to be. Politics is not the dirty word many individuals think it is. It is merely a survival mechanism for some and a way of getting things done for others. Everyone uses politics one way or another to succeed or survive. Some are less hypocritical about it than others.

Every individual likes to think of himself or herself as unique and essentially good. Things begin to become interesting as soon as two or more unique and good individuals have to work together to achieve some common objective. The larger the group of unique and good individuals, the more interesting things become and surprisingly the more vexing it may become to achieve the objective. Sometimes the objective itself becomes somewhat blurred as each individual sees it in slightly different form.

In Machiavelli's real world, there is no right way or wrong way, there is the way that is effective, the way that works. Everything in the real world involves trade-offs. This appears to be a reasonably accurate assessment of the way things are. And yet, there are many individuals who believe or feel that their analysis or proposal represents the right way to go in achieving an objective. Needless to say, that attitude can cause friction in a group of several individuals. The amount of friction increases proportionally with the number of individuals in the group, the number of perceived right ways of achieving the objective, and the magnitude of the differences between the two most extremely variant positions. Politics is the art of reconciling the various right ways of a number of unique and good individuals, so that they can compromise on their differences and agree on an approach to achieve a common objective.

It has been said that a camel is a horse designed by a committee. While there is some truth in that sentiment, it doesn't go far enough. For if a horse is the ultimate, and a camel is the result of compromise, what are the other alternatives? Could a horse have been produced if one individual had been strong enough to convince or force others to conform to his or her will? Yes, but that's also politics. Another alternative is maybe a camel is better than a horse; while another is that nothing was produced except a group of quarrelling individuals who produced nothing except contention and strife. In the former alternative situation, politics actually improved the situation, while in the latter case, the complete lack of politics resulted in nothing at all being produced.

While it is true that some politically motivated arrangements come about as the result of self-serving individuals, the claim that politics is dirty is an oversimplification and a cop-out. Those making such claims are usually inexperienced and immature individuals who become petulant when things are not done the way they perceive that they ought to be done.

What's Good for Me/What's Good for the Project (Organization)

Survival is a basic human instinct. Survival in the grandest style possible is also a human instinct, perhaps not so basic, but definitely human. Improving one's lifestyle often imposes a threat, imagined or real, to the survival of others. Therefore, survival in grand style introduces an element of risk which grows in proportion to the grandness of the style.

There are two types of success an individual can enjoy within an organization. One type is success in completing projects or in achieving objectives. This helps to assure survival of the organization. Another type is the personal and/or professional success of the individual. This helps to assure the survival of the individual. Unfortunately, the two do not necessarily go hand-in-hand.

Organizations are staffed with unique and good people who will let you do anything you want for them. Sometimes they remember, and sometimes they forget. Remember the threats, real or imagined. If their mode of survival is not threatened by remembering what you've done, they'll remember. They'll thank you and perhaps give you public recognition, which of course can contribute to your personal and professional success. If you pose any kind of a threat, they will forget what you've done and may even take credit for it themselves.

The higher individuals move in an organization, the grander is the style of survival and of course the greater the risk. Individuals must determine for themselves what they must do to survive and to succeed. There are no sure methods for survival or success. However, there are some guidelines that may help. Since they may seem to be contradictory, be advised that they are merely guidelines and do not come with a guarantee. Be assured also that some individuals have either consciously put some or all of them into practice and they may definitely be the cause of problems. The guidelines are as follows:

- Decide who it is you want to please and find out how to do it, then do it. There may be more than one individual. It may be your boss, his or her boss, some other executives, or yourself, or all of the above. This can cause problems, because those who can't or won't do this refer to it as brownnosing, and they are offended by it.

- Determine what your professional and personal strengths are and do everything in your power to use them to the utmost. A corollary to this is to determine your weaknesses and do everything in your power to avoid situations where they will be highlighted. To some this is called discretion, others call it cowardice. This, too, can lead to problems.
- Make your own definition of success. Find a few individuals who embody success as you define it and try to emulate their behavior. Avoid fantasies. Use real-life individuals. If you're ordinary in appearance or a little overweight and balding, don't try to emulate some macho image from the movie screen or some football hero. The same goes for those of you who are female. Most of you have neither the poise nor the looks of the modern women of television and magazine commercials, or the superficial exaggerated self-confidence of self-styled feminist movement leaders.
- Get involved in other things besides your "job." Make yourself valuable. If you merely perform in an outstanding fashion in your job and don't allow yourself to do anything else of consequence, both you and the organization you are serving lose out. You lose out, because over time, you'll become insecure, defensive, and hostile. As things change, you won't. You'll want to continue to do what you know how to do, the way you know how to do it. The organization loses out because you won't achieve your potential, and you may even inhibit the necessary changes that need to take place in the organization's procedures.
- Every now and then, take a chance. It's risky, but it's exciting. Otherwise things get really boring.

Misunderstandings

Aside from the somewhat amusing irony in the fact that the acronym MIS can also be used as a prefix that has negative connotations, misunderstandings are a fundamental cause of problems. Misunderstandings among individuals or departments cause an "us 'n' them" mentality to develop that can severely inhibit the achievement of objectives. But there are even more basic misunderstandings that lead to discontent and frustration. These misunderstandings stem from differences between expectations and realizations. Unrealistic expectations exist as the result of advertising and promotions that emphasize potential and also because of the naive belief that computers can solve problems.

Let's clear up the latter misconception first. Computers don't solve problems; people solve problems, and computers execute solutions. Attempting to use a computer to solve a problem will only result in a clearer and more rapid manifestation of the problem. Computers merely highlight our inability to communicate.

The other cause of unrealistic expectations is promotions and advertising that can be downright misleading. While a computer configuration has the potential to do many of the things contained in advertisements and promotions, an impression is also created that it's as easy as getting out of bed. That impression leads to unrealistic and consequently unrealized expectations. Computers and computer technology get a bad name, and nobody wins except perhaps the agency that created the advertising and the promotion.

Operations Versus the World

When an individual buys a small computer, he or she soon finds out what "operations" is all about, on a small scale. Buying the computer is easy, and as the advertising indicates, it is also relatively inexpensive. But then the individual finds that other equipment and supplies are needed. Then the individual has to make it all work. The individual with the small personal computer is the planner, the programmer, the manager, the operator, and to some degree the maintenance person, all rolled into one.

In medium-sized installations, there is a little more division of labor, and in large-scale installations, the division of labor is even greater. In either situation, "operations" is generally the last group to handle everything, and when something goes wrong, they get the grief. They are immediately blamed for any type of malfunction. They are held responsible for their own errors and initially at least for everyone else's. This can lead to the development of a "seige mentality" in the minds of the individuals in operations. These individuals frequently become defensive, sometimes even hostile. They begin to feel that users of computer services are out to get them. In addition to the constant humiliation of acknowledging their own errors when they occur, they frequently absorb the imputed responsibility for the errors of others, since by the time everything gets sorted out and the true cause of an error is determined, enough time has elapsed to make it history. No one cares any longer where the cause of the error really lies, and everyone writes it off as another data center or computer room screw up.

One way to deal with this problem is to attempt to rotate individuals back and forth between jobs in the computer room or data center and jobs in the users' departments. This is not always possible or feasible, but where it is, it should be attempted.

PROBLEMS FOR OTHER REASONS

Economics

Computer technology, both hardware and software, changes very rapidly. It is just not possible to keep completely up-to-date technically. This is true in all situations.

If an individual were to attempt to constantly improve a small computer configuration with the latest equipment in order to capitalize on the most efficient or the fastest or even the cheapest (on a per unit basis), he or she would soon have a garage and attic filled with obsolete or obsolescent equipment and a sorely depleted bank account with very little to show for it in terms of improved performance.

In medium- or large-scale configurations, where some equipment is leased for two or three years, it is not possible to change equipment without breaking a lease. Since there may be a financial penalty for doing that, it may be an inhibiting factor in bringing in new equipment.

There may also be a conversion cost involved in changing over to a new and improved equipment component. For example, a new and improved disk storage device may be able to hold twice as much data and transfer it into primary storage twice as quickly. And yet to capitalize of this advantage, files have to be analyzed and perhaps restructured.

System software products are often subtle culprits in causing hardware costs to increase. With small computers, you might hear about a fantastic new product that has all kinds of capabilities. You check it out and find out that your computer requires another 64K of primary storage to run it. In medium- and large-scale shops, it is even more subtle. In those situations, it is possible to add system software products with only minimal impact being made on overall configuration performance. But as more and more products are added, to enhance, to measure, to help fine tune, and so forth, the next thing you know, more primary storage is needed or perhaps a bigger computer, or maybe more channels. A not commonly known and somewhat disquieting phenomenon that exists in large-scale installations are computer configurations with between 50 and 75% of their primary storage allocated to system software, buffers, queues, and system work space, leaving 25 to 50% for applications. Remember, applications are the reason you bought the computer in the first place. Vendors and technicians quite often seem to discover system software products that you cannot really be without. While it may be true that a product may improve or enhance your organization's information systems capabilities, there's always a cost. Before acquiring such a product, check other installations and determine its true cost.

The Big Picture

Senior managers and executives who are either involved in or serviced by the information systems function ought to take the time to read Lewis Carroll's *Alice in Wonderland* and *Through the Looking Glass* just to get a perspective on the way things are.

The entire field of electronic data processing, computer, data communications, and information systems is so broad in scope and so complex in its various details as to be overwhelming. No single individual can grasp it all. Most people would acknowledge this, and yet there are those who feel that they understand it all and can keep it under control. These individuals manifest some of the characteristics of the Mad Hatter and the March Hare. These types are sometimes found in middle management positions. There are also some technicians who, because they have mastered one particular discipline within the field, believe that they understand it all. Conversations with these individuals includes flawless logic against which no one can argue, the only problem being that things never seem to be the way they describe them. Senior managers who have to deal with such know-it-alls come away with mixed feelings of frustration, intimidation, incredulity, and boredom.

It is our belief that any senior manager or executive who wishes to do so can achieve a level of general understanding of the technology equal to an information systems senior manager or executive within a relatively short period of time. The specifics in the field are changing so rapidly that the task of managing the information systems function is more a task of managing change than it is of managing a specific technology. The individuals in senior management or executive positions within the information systems functions are just as overwhelmed as those outside of it.

What we have in information systems organizations today is a hodgepodge of technology ranging across the very old, the old, the not so old, the recent, and the new, with the percentages of each varying from one installation to another. The variety of the technologies and the percentages of each is to some degree a manifestation of the organization. The task of senior managers and executives both within and outside the information systems function is get the maximum usage out of the information systems resources, not matter what the mix of technologies.

The mixture of very old, old, not so old, recent, and new technology has an impact of the management task. The greater the variety, the more difficult the task. Attempts should be made to minimize the variety. Very old and old technology tends to be expensive, and the older it gets the more expensive it becomes. New technology can be risky. Murphy's Law comes into play with new technology. New technology should be used, but estimates for implementations using it ought to be conservative. A high percentage of not-so-old and recent technology offers the best chance at realizing the maximum utilization of information systems resources. A mixture of 70% not-so-old and recent with 10 to 15% old and very old and 15 to 20% new is probably a realistic target for an organization. Very old technology would be that which is ten years old or older; old would be that which is between seven and ten years old; not-so-old is that which is between five and seven years old; recent is that which is between one and five years old; and new is that which is less than a year old.

This way of measuring technology is merely a suggested guideline we believe would be of some value in improving productivity and efficiency. In reality, most computer applications use several different technology products, some of which may be older than others. In addition to that, there are some old and very old technology products that are still quite efficient in spite of their age. So, a certain amount of discernment and discretion should be exercised in applying these guidelines.

Information Overload on Management

Back in the 1950s and 1960s, college courses, textbooks, trade books, articles, and seminars were advocating that senior managers and executives be provided with more accurate and timely information so that they would be able to make more informed decisions. Since that time, monumental improvements in information storage and retrieval technology have made it possible to provide information in unprecedented quantities and with increasing speed. And yet. . . .

In the 1950s and 1960s, the term *information revolution* was heard, and its connotation was essentially positive. In the 1970s, the term *information explosion* was heard, and the connotation became somewhat less positive, with feelings of alarm and concern creeping in. By the 1980s, the term *information overload* had been coined, reflecting beliefs and feelings that the information available was overwhelming and unmanageable. In making a distinction between data and information, it could be said that by the time the 1980s arrived we were data rich and information poor. We'll pick this particular problem up again in the next chapter.

Interpersonal Communications

If there is any single source of the problems and difficulties that plague us in producing information systems that satisfy rather than alienate their users, it is in the area of interpersonal communications. This is an area of difficulty that is subtle in its manifestation, and therefore, it is often misdiagnosed. No doubt you have heard comments like "what a ding-a-ling that guy Fred Brickburger is!" or "the next time that scatter-brained Winnie Whistlestopper makes a commitment, I'm going to demand it in writing!" While there are some ding-a-lings and scatter-brains around, it is more than likely that Fred Brickburger and Winnie Whistlestopper are reasonably competent individuals. The comments made by individuals who perceive themselves as victims of the incompetence of others, we believe, more often than not, are victims instead of misunderstandings. This is not an attempt to deny the existence of incompetence, lying, sandbagging, or of certain types of political gamesmanship in some situations, but we do believe that these are the exceptions rather than the rules. For if incompetence, lying, sandbagging, and political oneupsmanship are the rule, we may just as well give up any attempt at cooperation and try to get as much as we can for ourselves.

Working on the assumption then that most of the problems and difficulties encountered during attempts to implement satisfactory information systems are the result of misunderstandings or breakdowns in interpersonal communications, let's isolate the causes. In doing so, let's make one further assumption that most of us are basically competent though flawed individuals. There are few geniuses and few total incompetents. Let's look at the failures in communications in terms of our own weaknesses and realize that on occasion we look like Fred Brickburger or Winnie Whistlestopper to others. When we realize we have limitations of our own, it becomes a lot easier to be tolerant of the apparent shortcomings of others. In the next few pages we'll discuss some limitations that we all have from time to time. Let's go through them and from the discussion, perhaps we can crystallize some specific reasons for problems and difficulties that come about as a result of breakdowns in interpersonal communications. We'll look at some reasons why misunderstandings come about and also some suggested remedies.

A major cause of breakdowns in interpersonal communications is the use of jargon. While it is true that jargon is used by individuals in all professions and disciplines, it appears that the creation and use of buzzwords and acronyms that information systems organizations are right up there with the medical and legal profession in establishing and maintaining a mystique, complete with high priests and wizards. As this book attempts to show, there is nothing mysterious about computers and their applications. Granted, certain aspects of the technology are complex, and jargon is extremely useful for technicians as they communicate among themselves, but the use of jargon should be kept at the technical level. There are two recommendations that can be made to senior managers and executives. First, it is your right and your responsibility to insist that explanations of information systems strategy, logistics, and expenditures be given in terms you understand. Buzzword and acronym-filled presentations that appear unclear to you are probably just as unclear to those who are making them. Push for explanations. Someone once said that doing something with a computer should make it easier than doing it without a computer. The fact that this had to be said indicates that some are perceiving it differently. Implementations of information systems require the use of complex technology, but presentations of their strategic or logistic value and their costs should be understandable. As a rule of thumb, if information systems presentations appear nebulous and confusing, and are filled with what appears to be technical jargon, then the explanations of why it's not installed on time or within budget are going to appear nebulous and confusing, and filled with technical jargon. Second, senior managers and executives should make an attempt to learn something about computers and information systems technology. To get where you are, you learned something about marketing, finance, law, accounting, operations, and personnel. There now appears to be another basic business function to contend with, information systems. Begin with this: the concepts are relatively simple, the technology is extremely complex, but its stability and reliability are constantly improving. If you've gotten this far in the book, you're making great progress.

A second cause of breakdowns in interpersonal communications comes about as a result of our inability to listen. In itself, failure to listen can stem from a number of causes. Preoccupation with other concerns, preconceived ideas, or prejudices and interruptions, all have an impact on our ability or willingness to listen.

Preoccupation with other concerns assures that interpersonal communications that are taking place are going to be valueless. If you are preoccupied, you cannot listen. In some situations, you cannot terminate the conversation and you must continue to make it appear as though you are listening. Where possible, make an attempt to terminate the conversation and to reschedule it for a time when you are not preoccupied. Being polite and pretending that you are not preoccupied can be only marginally effective. If the shoe is on the other foot and you detect preoccupation in the individual to whom you are attempting to communicate, endeavor to terminate and reschedule the conversation. Continuing conversations when one of the parties is preoccupied is virtually certain to lead to future misunderstandings.

Preconceived ideas or prejudices frequently lead to arguments, confrontations, and defensiveness. This drawback is best perceived in other individuals. It is extremely difficult for individuals to find prejudices within themselves. Dealing with them in others can be a rather trying experience. Attempts at communication between individuals where one perceives the other as being prejudiced are at best somewhat strained. Listening to a prejudiced point of view, one can either acquiese or resist. In neither case is it likely that fruitful communications can take place. Unless the prejudices or preconceived ideas can be overcome, communication becomes confrontation, and a win-or-lose situation develops. Unresolved win-or-lose situations result in stalemates and periodic flareups. Listening is inhibited by confrontations. Resolutions are difficult to achieve.

Interruptions also inhibit effective interpersonal communications. An office is probably the worst place to have a conversation unless phone calls and other interruptions can be intercepted by a secretary or an assistant. Interruptions sidetrack conversations. After an interruption takes place, several minutes are usually required to get the conversation back to where it was prior to the interruption. Two, three interruptions can completely nullify any effective interpersonal communication. There are no doubt situations where meetings or conversations must be held in an office. However, when not absolutely necessary, meetings can be quite effective when held in conference rooms. One to one conversations do very well over breakfast, lunch, or dinner. Interruptions are minimized and the potential for communication is maximized. Listening is facilitated by relaxed, comfortable surroundings.

CONCLUSIONS

The track record of information systems for the first ten years of its life, assuming a birth date of 1960, was rather spotty. There were many glowing prognostications about what could be done with computers. The term "management information systems" was coined in the 1960s. Many self-appointed experts wrote articles and conducted seminars expounding that computer-based systems capable of retrieving and displaying the kinds strategic information needed by senior managers and executives were within reach. Feasibility studies were performed, gigantic flow diagrams were drawn, specifications were prepared, and programming begun. A few prophetic voices had been heard proclaiming that the grandiose schemes and proposals were suggesting applications and systems that were beyond the capabilities of existing technology. These voices were drowned out in the euphoria fostered by the potential of the technology. What occurred in the mid and late 1960s were a number of well-publicized information system failures, some limited successes, and the emergence of some significant prototype technology. Unfortunately, the well-publicized failures got most of the attention, and the technology took the rap. It was not the technology that had failed, but rather it was the overly ambitious applications to which it had been prematurely put that had caused the failures.

The modest, and consequently less publicized, successes had shown that the technology was sound if not yet far enough advanced or of a sufficient magnitude to handle the massive strategic information systems that the more optimistic designers had thought possible. These modest successes had shown, however, that data communications and teleprocessing applications were possible. Database management prototype systems, while limited in magnitude, contained the logic needed to interrelate data elements from one or more files. While strategic information systems had not been implemented, smaller logistical applications had. These logistical applications contained the computer processes by which the data needed in the day-to-day operations of an organization was captured and stored.

As the 1970s began, there was still something of a lingering information system hangover left from the 1960s. Despite the limited successes, the failures were remembered because they had been expensive and visible. Management information systems had become the acronym MIS. It was being used to identify that organization function charged with designing, developing and supporting information systems using computer or EDP technology. Toward the middle of the 1970s, the introduction of high capacity direct access storage devices (DASD) made secondary storage available in sufficient magnitude to hold large databases. In addition, virtual storage* hardware and software provided a sophisticated processing methodology that simplified the task of developing large applications. It was during the 1970s, that

*Virtual storage is a combination of circuitry and programs giving a computer equipment configuration the capability of swapping instructions, buffers, and other information between primary storage and secondary storage devices, creating the illusion that the configuration has virtually unlimited primary storage. This gave rise to the comment "it's all done with mirrors," a reply given by a virtual storage developer when asked how it was all really done.

things began to change. The logistical applications settled down, they worked and they worked reasonably well. There were problems to be sure, but most of them were operational in nature, the so-called human error. However, the most noticeable change was in the stability and reliability of the technology. The hardware failures were less catastrophic and occurred less frequently. Software products, although much more complicated, were becoming more dependable. Transaction volumes of on-line transactions and numbers of batch job turnarounds increased steadily.

In the 1960s, the advocates of strategic information systems for senior managers and executives had been some farsighted individuals whose vision had been accurate, but beyond the capabilities of the technology then available. As the 1970s ended and the 1980s began, some senior managers and executives themselves began to be aware of the potential of computers in providing strategic information systems. During the 1960s and 1970s, the lament had frequently been heard that without the support of senior management there was no hope of building a successful information system. Well, in the 1980s, it appears that not only is there going to be senior management support, but there is going to be senior manager and executive initiative. The technology is better than ever and continuing to improve. The potential is there. Realization of true management information systems (MIS) using the technology of computers and electronic data processing (EDP) is now possible. However, the implementation of strategic information systems requires a careful and thoughtful consideration of the existing situation. This varies from one organization to another. The preceding chapters of this book have attempted to explain EDP/MIS technology, its strengths and its weaknesses, its simplicity and its complexity. Earlier in this chapter we made the statement "computers merely highlight our inability to communicate." A character in the comic strip *Pogo* once voiced the sentiment "we have met the enemy and they is us." For an organization to build a reasonably successful strategic information system, the individuals designing, developing, and implementing it need to come to grips with the fact that most of the mistakes, screw-ups, and shortcomings are the result of their own limitations and those imposed by earlier implementations. For a host of reasons, some good, some not so good, expediency has a way of winning out. The state in which an existing information systems environment finds itself may be an inhibiting factor in the development of an integrated strategic information system. If individuals in senior management and executive levels, as well as individuals in the middle- and first-line management positions recognize and acknowledge this, there is a high probability that they can use the EDP technology to develop the MIS the organization needs.

SUMMARY

In this chapter, we attempted to crystallize the problems and difficulties involved in putting together a strategic information system. We began the chapter with a little history, laced with some editorial comment. Then we tried to identify and describe the kinds of problems that exist in the technology of information systems. We described bugs and glitches and incompatibilities among components. Also examined was the philosophical tension that exists between the implementer and the technician and how it is sometimes necessary to work with, work around, or utilize a technical component that isn't performing the way it should. We discussed the phenomenon of "change," indicating that "change" itself is accelerating and is likely to continue to do so. This makes decision making risky and difficult.

Then we looked at problems with people, the so-called politics of organizations. The real world of Machiavelli was contrasted with the ideal world envisioned by less-realistic individuals. A basic tension of individuals wanting to survive in the grandest style possible and to do a good job for the organization in which they work was discussed. Some guidelines for success in achieving personal and professional objectives were suggested. Misunderstandings were shown to be more of a problem than politics among individuals and groups who work together toward a common objective. The oft-maligned operations function was discussed as the scapegoat and whipping boy of organizations.

Other problem areas were also reviewed. It was explained that some of the great and wonderful improvements offered by technology may simply be unaffordable, no matter how great their long-term benefits appear to be. The idea of an overall guru was given some treatment. Netting it out, beware of these types; no one can be familiar with it all, for there's just too much for one person to stay abreast of. Information overload was explained as an unforeseen consequence of attempts to provide information to senior managers and executives for the purpose of facilitating strategic decision making.

We then got into the area of interpersonal communications, probably the single biggest source of difficulties and problems when developing information systems. In our conclusion we indicate that we believe that the technology required to produce integrated strategic information systems is now available in sufficient quantity and quality. We also believe that we need to recognize and acknowledge our own limitations, and attempt to overcome them if we are to implement these systems.

CHAPTER 10

Conclusions and Recommendations

INTRODUCTION

The first nine chapters of this book represent an attempt to sharpen the distinction between potential and realized management information systems. To do this, we arranged the book in three sections, an I is for Information section, an S is for Systems section, and an M is for Management section. We started out with the I is for Information section by discussing what information is and how, in the contemporary setting, computer (EDP) technology is used to store, process, retrieve, and display information. The chapters in the S is for Systems section are devoted to explanations of EDP technology. Then, in the M is for Management section, we get into the most intangible part of all, management. And yet, we believe that it is frequently not recognized as such. There exists instead the mistaken notion that the technology is the primary cause of problems and difficulties. It is not the technology, but rather its misapplication that creates problems and difficulties.

Technology deals with "black and white"; bits are either on or off; answers are yes or no, there's no maybe. Managers and executives struggle with the "maybe" and "it all depends" situations. Managers and executives have the freedom to be inconsistent; technology does not. Faced with the same set of facts on two different occasions these individuals can make two different decisions; they can adjust their internal programming "on the fly." A computer cannot do that, in and of itself. For a computer to make such an adjustment, its programming must be modified by an external source. A programmer must change its programming; otherwise, each time it is confronted with the same facts, it will execute the same decision. This major difference between technology and management is essential to realizing the potential of information systems through EDP. It's a two-edged sword. It bestows upon management increased flexibility, but also increased responsibility.

Chapter 9 presented a series of problems or difficulties that beset senior managers and executives and which inhibit the realization of the potential of information systems technology. This chapter is going to offer some suggested courses of action. These suggestions are not to be interpreted as "can't miss" solutions, but rather as informed recommendations. Each of these recommendations is backed up with some explanations and reasoning. If they are in line with a particular situation they can be followed, or perhaps modified somewhat to fit another situation. There's a little prayer that has been around for a number of years now, but the first time I heard it, it came from an executive.

O God, grant me the serenity
To accept the things that I can't change,
The courage to change the things that I can,
And the wisdom to know the difference between the two.

An individual who receives an answer to that prayer can be a truly successful executive.

What Is Management?

Textbooks define it, seminars and courses teach it, degrees are granted in it, and those under it allude to it. Well, since this is the last chapter, we're certainly not going to deal with it in the depth found in textbooks, seminars, courses, and degree programs. Yet, we must describe it in some way. Management, then, is the art of dealing with what is uncertain. Management is a process of making decisions based on incomplete information. It is trying to foretell the future. It is the task of getting individuals to work together in achieving an objective. It is the art of keeping track of materials, subassemblies, and finished goods. Management involves planning for sources and uses of funds and keeping track of income and expenditures. There are levels of management and there are styles of management. Let's define these. Let's look first at levels:

- *First-line managers.* These individuals are usually foremen, supervisors, project managers, and chiefs who implement the policies set down by senior managers. First-line managers also attend to those situations not clearly defined or not covered by policy. These are the "rubber meets the road" managers. They see to it that the stuff gets built and out the door. They assure that the books get closed each month.
- *Technical managers.* These individuals are found in the ranks of both first-line and functional (described below) management. They are found in the laboratories, computer rooms and other technology-oriented functions within an organization. Those in first-line technical management are the ones who get things done. Those in functional technical management do the planning and coordinating of projects, estimate costs and staffing, and justify funding to senior managers.
- *Functional managers.* These individuals are the managers, directors, and lower-level vice-presidents who break down senior management policies into specific objectives and projects that can be achieved by first-line managers. They walk the line between the day-to-day management of specific projects and the more strategic policy-making management function performed at senior and executive levels. The functional managers are often responsible for specific departments within the functions of an organization. For example, within the accounting function, there might be managers or directors of accounts payable, accounts receivable, and general ledger. Functional managers have the additional responsibility of keeping senior management informed about situations in their areas, both internal and external to the organization.
- *Senior managers or executives.* These individuals operate at a level where they are being paid for getting things done strategically. Their superiors are not terribly interested in hearing why things aren't getting done. Senior managers have titles such as president, vice-president, executive vice-president or executive director. They often have responsibility and are accountable for complete business functions such as sales, manufacturing, finance, information systems, or personnel. They establish policy, attempt to set general direction and keep organizations profitable in a world filled with uncertainties.

These are general, loosely structured definitions describing the level of management as they would be found in large organizations. In small organizations, the levels would be compressed. Senior managers and executives would pick up some of the tasks of functional management; the first-line managers would probably pick up the rest. Functional management, as such, is not required in smaller organizations. The same could be said for the technical manager. In smaller organizations, both the senior managers and the first-line managers possess the technical skill required in the organization. Of course, very small organizations may find the senior manager and the first-line manager as one person. The oft-maligned housewife is an example of an individual who performs first-line, functional, technical, and senior management tasks in keeping a contemporary home afloat.

Let's have a look now at management styles:

- *Authoritarian/dictatorial.* Individuals managing with this type of management operate by capitalizing on the fear of their subordinates. They dictate and subordinates carry out. It can be effective, from an organizational perspective, if the dictates of the authoritarian leader lead to profits. The philosophy behind this type of management can be seen in the works of the late Ayn Rand, especially in the book *Atlas Shrugged.* Douglas McGregor defined this as the Theory X style of management.
- *Authoritarian/benevolent.* In the early 1980s several books on the Japanese style of management got quite a bit of attention for a short period of time. They got the attention because of the productivity of Japanese industry. In this style, managers dictate policy, but part of that policy includes taking care of industrial workers and first-line managers from cradle to grave. This policy appears to foster a docile and industrious labor force in Japan. The final count is not in yet as to whether it will work elsewhere. Some United States industries support a similar style; it's called paternalistic. It enjoys success in some quarters.
- *Management by committee.* Individuals who manage with this style make an attempt to manage by consensus. They invite opinions from subordinates and would rather let policy and decision evolve than to issue them dictatorially. Subordinates are given an opportunity to participate in setting policy as well as in carrying it out. Douglas McGregor gave this the name Theory Y style of management.
- *Management by analysis.* Individuals employing this style of management generally build up large staffs of analysts who attempt to make evaluations and recommendations by examining quantitative information from several perspectives. Data is collected, tabulated, sorted, summarized, collated, and correlated. Percentages are calculated, trends are plotted, and deviations

noted. Decisions are made based on the results of the analysis. This style of management is advocated by business schools seeking to place their graduating MBAs. Its effectiveness depends heavily on the quality of the data used.

Each of these management styles has its place. Temper each of them with a little Machiavellian politics, and the combinations are virtually limitless. Authoritarian styles are great when the leaders' perceptions and policies are in line with reality and result in profits. If authoritarian leaders share the wealth either through social benevolence or higher salaries they can be effective. The potential weakness in this style become evident when the leaders are wrong more often than right. If profits go down and social benevolence or higher salaries are not forthcoming, then workers rebel or seek employment elsewhere. Management by committee is good in that it fosters camaraderie, cooperation, and team spirit. Accountability and responsibility are spread, the organization is loosely structured, and since objectives are set by concensus, they are rarely wrong. They are safe and usually benign. Great things do not often come out of such an organization. The potential weakness of this style is that it tends to discourage individual initiative and is slow in reacting when quick decisions are needed. Management by analysis has strength and weakness also, both of which vary in proportion to the quality of the data. If much data is available and the calculations can be performed on the data in a timely fashion, the decision process can be greatly enhanced. The data collection, calculation, and display process is known as modeling. A model that reflects reality and well-researched data represent significant management tools. If, on the other hand, the model does not reflect reality or the quality of the data is substandard, no amount of analysis is going to produce any worthwhile results. One of the greatest weaknesses of this management style is the difficulty in determining the quality of the model or of the data until it's too late.

OK, so that's management. To some it's an art, to others a science, and to still others, it's a mixture of the two. The styles of management that we've just discussed are departure points, that is, it would be difficult to find an individual or an organization that reflected a single style. It is more likely that individuals within organizations would generally lean toward one of the styles, but would manifest attributes of one or more of the others from time to time. Organizations themselves would also generally reflect one style at the expense of the others, but because organizations are made up of numbers of individuals, manifestations of the other styles would also be seen here and there. Success in an organization or with influential leaders depends on one's ability to discern management style and to perform according to what that style requires.

What Does the Information Systems Organization Currently Give to Management?

In most organizations, the current mix is a loosely integrated or interfaced set of applications that generally support the logistical and operational business functions. Finance and accounting get the most support because information systems organizations typically report to chief financial officers. The remaining functional areas that are supported are operations, i.e., order entry, warehousing, inventory, manufacturing, distribution, billing, and accounts receivable, the last two overlapping with the accounting function. Sales and marketing are also supported. First-line and functional managers and their staffs are the beneficiaries of most of what comes out of these information systems applications.

A typical flow of data through a logistical business application includes input, validation, file maintenance, main processing, and output. These applications may be batch or interactive/on-line or a combination of both. The improvements in teleprocessing software and the economy of using CRT devices has made interactive processing commonplace. Contemporary order entry operations use tens or even hundreds of CRT devices to enter and validate orders for merchandise, to inquire as to inventory or customer status, to perform file maintenance, and to apply cash receipts. This type of information systems support is found in nearly all organizations today.

There are complications, however. The various functional systems were probably installed during different time periods and have been modified over the years. Different levels of technology were in use in those different time periods. It is therefore quite possible that a number of the accounting and financial applications are batch-processing oriented and are using sequential files, while the operations systems, which were developed later, make use of teleprocessing software that supports interactive/on-line transactions against direct access or indexed files. Manufacturing and marketing applications may have been the last to be developed, and they were implemented with a database/data communications software product with structured records containing data elements with relationships transcending traditional file boundaries. All three of these levels of technology are essentially incompatible with one another at the physical level. While it is theoretically possible to create an integrated system with all applications having access to a single set of databases, the physical incompatibilities make it necessary to convert to a single technology or to construct physical access method mechanism that would be able to accommodate the various file organizations and record structures. The cost of producing such a mechanism would be staggering, and it is rather doubtful that, if produced, it would even function efficiently. The complexity of producing such a mechanism is comparable to the complexity of producing a universal telecommunications access method that supports a number of different terminal devices. There are, in fact, universal access methods such as these being supported. Their magnitude is such that only equipment vendors such IBM, DEC, Wang, and Xerox can handle the task. The idea then, of an individual organization developing an equivalent access method for a number of different file organizations and record structures is quite impractical. What is an organization to do? Well, there is an answer which we'll see below, but it does involve biting the proverbial bullet.

What Would Management Like To Get From Information Systems Organizations?

First-line managers would like to get applications that were more responsive to the changing needs of the business. Functional managers would like to be able to interact with the applications, to ask questions randomly and receive responses to those questions within a few seconds. Senior managers and executives would like to have models that they could interact with, to ask the "what if . . ." questions. They would like to be able to get at yesterday's sales, first thing in the morning. They would like to be able to generate "P&L's" for each profit center, for each product, or for some other major components of the business. These facilities that the various levels of management would like to have are not unreasonable expectations. The potential exists within the technology, but it is complicated by economics, technology changes, conflicting philosophies, and management styles.

Let's first look at economics. A manager in a functional area should not have to accept "that can't be done" from an information systems technician or manager. The technician or manager doesn't really mean that something can't be done, what he or she really means is that doing it is probably difficult and consequently expensive. In defense of the technicians and managers, they have a tendency sometimes to become defensive and reluctant to make changes and modifications that appear simple to functional users, because their estimates have frequently been second guessed and they've had to implement changes and modifications too quickly. The justification for their apparently lengthy estimates included explanations that "quick and dirty" changes would lead to complications in the future. These explanations were often ignored, and "quick and dirty" changes were implemented. In many organizations the future has arrived, and many applications are populated by the complications caused by the "quick and dirty" changes made earlier. Consequently, when technicians or managers appear reluctant to make changes, their caustic comment "that can't be done" is closer to the truth presently than it was in the past. Many an organization is aware of the high cost of maintaining existing applications. The cost is kept high because expediency has ruled in the past. Expediency is usually justified on the basis of business needs by functional managers and even senior managers. This may indeed be a valid justification, but it adds to information systems costs. How much expediency adds is a function of how often it is used as a justification. It's another one of those things that are difficult to quantify.

There's an inherent conflict between maintaining rapid input/output and processing activity for operational applications and creating up-to-the-minute summary information for strategic management systems. If an organization wishes to minimize the number of terminal devices used for operational functions such as entering orders, applying cash, and so on, it is necessary to develop and implement transactions that execute quickly for the applications supporting those operational functions. Quickly executing transactions require minimal input/output activity. Now, if an organization also wishes that each transaction update some summary database(s) that provides a strategic up-to-the-minute information to senior management, some additional input/output activity is required to update that summary database. That increased input/output activity is going to reduce the speed of the operational transactions. Of course, more terminals, a more powerful computer, and additional secondary storage can be acquired, but that costs.

The conflict can be reduced somewhat by leaving the operational transactions alone and having the strategic summary database updated in batch mode in the evening when the interactive on-line portion of the application is shut down. The management summary data is then a day old. If senior managers and executives can accept that, then the only competitors for computer resources are the operational transactions themselves and the queries entered by the senior managers and executives. The impact is minimal, but the information is not as current. This is another example of the time/money trade-off. This particular issue is a critical one for senior managers and executives to understand. Some kind of policy should be set to prevent conflicts from arising among first-line, functional, and technical managers over which operating philosophy is to be used. With no policy, there will be hybrids; some applications mixing strategic management summary database updates with operational transactions and others going the batch route. This situation results in some strategic summary information being current and other summary information being a day old. It is just such an operating environment that leads all levels of management to believe that the technology is screwing everything up.

Changes in management have a potentially negative impact on the ability of the information systems functions to respond to the needs of all levels of management. Management is made up of individuals, and individuals move on. They get fired or leave a position in an organization and are replaced. They move to a new position within the organization. When a position is filled by an individual, that individual's operating philosophy, to a greater or lesser extent depending on the level of management, fills that position also. At the first-line level of management, individuals attempt to impact the way that the operational information systems applications function. Those first-line managers in a position when an application is being designed and developed have a great deal to say about what it does and how it does it. If those managers stay in that position, they continually refine the application, a situation that is relatively easy for the information system function to accommodate. If the first-line manager leaves the position and is replaced by another individual whose management style is radically different, then a situation arises that is usually more difficult for the information systems function to accommodate. There's a strong possibility that the new manager may want to make major modifications to the way the application functions. He or she may even wish to capitalize on new information systems technology, complicating things even further.

In the area of functional management, the situations just mentioned can be repeated, yet because of the generally greater influence of the higher level of management, the effects of both stability and change can be more sweeping.

Nothing is permanent, but the rate of turnover in senior management and executive positions is somewhat lower than in functional and first-line management positions. Therefore if the information systems function is to design and implement strategic systems, the senior managers and executives ought to set the overall philosophy underlying these systems. To do so they should understand, in general terms, what is currently available and what is apparently going to be available in the near future through information systems technology. There is more to information systems technology than expenditures for technicians and machines to support operational functions. It is now becoming possible and economically feasible to develop true management information systems. It's going to cost and there are going to be problems and difficulties, but the potential can be realized. The technology is basically sound; the equipment is more reliable than ever and promises to get better still. Fundamental software, operating systems, access methods, database/data communications, and teleprocessing programs are more comprehensive and also more reliable. In the near future many of the features of fundamental software, since they are repetitive and unchanging, will be fabricated into more sophisticated semiconductor components. In other words, there is trend toward converting many functions now performed by software into hardware. In the area of applications software, even that is being made more standardized, and it, too, will be fabricated into semiconductor components. Think abut it, how many ways are there to prepare general ledgers or payrolls? Although there are variations from one organization to another, the basic application is the same. It is in these variations that the uniqueness and creativity of different individuals reside. It is these variations that provide the ideas and the concepts needed to realize the potential of information systems. No matter how much fundamental software is fabricated into semiconductor chips, the uniqueness and creativity of individuals will demand some sort of variation. EDP technology has the potential to standardize the repetitive and the mundane; information systems leaves to individuals the potential to realize the exceptions and the unusual.

What Is Available and What Is Coming?

Most of what is available and what is coming has been examined in some detail in earlier chapters of the book. We'll review it here and attempt to project into the near future. We make no claim to supernatural vision. Foretelling the future is a risky proposition. What we do here is based on experiences in the information systems field for the past twenty-five years. The projections into the future are cautious extrapolations based on that experience. We also make the assumption that technology gets better and people generally remain the same. The extrapolations which follow deal primarily with small computers, fundamental system software products, graphics, teletext and videotext, modeling, applications development with fourth generation languages, and the so-called automated office. Following that there is a followup treatment of the problems with technology, people, and other things, that were discussed in the preceding chapter.

Small Computers

It is quite certain that the processing capabilities of computers, that is of CPUs and primary storage, are going to continue to increase, while at the same time, the relative size and price are going to continue to decrease. The prices of input/output terminals and of secondary storage devices are also going to continue to decrease, but not as dramatically. The size of input/output terminals can only be reduced so far, and going beyond that point reduces their functionality. Anyone with large fingers working on some of the contemporary pocket calculators or an individual with vision that is something less than 20/20 using a 5½″ CRT screen can testify to that. The size of secondary storage devices also can be made just so small. Beyond a certain limit, they become little more than impressive gadgets which are too unreliable to be of any real use.

One of the most significant developments involving small computers is the transfer of the performance of repetitive tasks to a function of hardware rather than of software. Certain functions such as compilers and access methods are fabricated into miniature circuits referred to as *read only memory*, or ROM. ROM functions in essentially the same way as primary storage, except that it can only be read from and not written to. Incidentally primary storage is often referred to as RAM (random access memory) to distinguish it from ROM. Modules or tasks that are in ROM form do not take up any space in primary storage. Modules or tasks that are in software form do require primary storage space.

There have been some amusing comments made about small computers. The following are a sample:

- Small computers are the pet rocks of the 1980s.
- Personal computers are solutions looking for problems.
- The best application of a small computer was the one where the seventh grade kid has to write "I must not misbehave in a class" two hundred times. The kid wrote a BASIC program. . . .

There is an element of truth in these sentiments, especially for those who wish to procure a small computer to prepare their income tax or to keep track of their checks. It's easier and less expensive to do these tasks manually. However, electronic worksheet software products such as VISICALC, SUPERCALC and LOTUS 1-2-3 have been able to justify and pay back small computer purchases within a few months. The improvements in the accuracy and the speed with which spread sheet and work sheets tabulations and calculations could be performed probably were responsible for the sale of more small computers than any other single factor.

There are more applications to which small computers can be put. Models and prototype databases are examples. It's another case of potential and realization. If senior managers or executives wish to use small personal computers, they ought to be prepared to invest some of their own time and/or the time of a secretary or assistant in learning how to use it. It has been done. In our own professional experience we've been exposed to the president of the division of a large corporation who developed some BASIC programs to do a break-even analysis for a product manufactured by his division. This individual made an investment of his own time and was so pleased with the results that he ordered several small computers to be used in other functional areas of the division.

In terms of the future, it appears that small computers will be used in networks where they can be given access to a common database. They will be able to function as both terminals and as computers. As terminals they will be able to enter and retrieve data, and as computers they will be able to process that data and display it as information. Again, it must be stressed that this is potential. The technology to do this is available. Yet, for the reasons set forth earlier, realizing the potential is an elaborate management task.

Fundamental System Software Products

System software represents the first step taken in realizing the potential of information system with EDP technology. A computer by itself is nothing but raw processing speed, but even that is only potential. Some basic programming is necessary to get the computer going. The operating system or control program is the most fundamental program or set of programs in any computer. It is the operating system that has the capability of allocating the resources of a computer equipment configuration among the activities that require those resources. The resources are primary storage, secondary storage, input devices, output devices, and channels or buses. The activities requiring the resources are programs, data records and data elements, and transactions and messages.

Integral to or integrated with an operating system are the access methods, those programs which execute the data transfers between primary storage and secondary storage and between a communications control computer (front end) and primary storage. It is these programs that read records and segments to primary storage from files and databases on secondary storage devices or that write records and segments from primary storage to files and databases on secondary storage devices. They also read input transactions into primary storage from the front end and write output transactions to the front end from primary storage.

The next element of system software that we encounter is the database/data communication system. It interfaces with the access methods to store and retrieve data from complex structures. Database/data communications systems have functional components (sets of programs) that facilitate specification of complex structures and their compilation into computer-recognizable form. There are also facilities that interfere with access methods in the storage and retrieval of data. While it is the access methods that perform the physical data transfers, it is the database/

data communications software that extracts specific data from retrieved records or segments, or that combines records or segments into complex structures.

Network management software is used to manage the traffic between the devices and the computers that are on the same communications network. Products in this category are extremely complex. Since there are virtually no universal standards, it appears that it's going to stay that way. Potentially, networking could be a bridge between different devices both locally and remotely located. Network products are announced by all major equipment vendors, but implementations are difficult to find. They are coming, but the competition is going to be stiff, and it'll be some time before the dust settles in this area.

The primary objective of these fundamental system software products is to realize the potential of computers by making them easier to use. From the large mainframes all the way down to the small microprocessor-based personal computers, millions of dollars and millions of hours are being spent to develop software that makes computers easier to use. The catch-word is user friendly. The smallest computers are essentially single-user systems, and most of them require an investment of time to learn how to use them. Medium-sized and large-scale machines can support multiple users in what is called a time-sharing mode of operation. Problem oriented languages, off-the-shelf software products, and turnkey systems are all technologies that are intended to make computers more user friendly.

We've come a long way since the 1950s, when the only individuals who were able to interact with computers were the engineers and scientists who built them. We now have computers with capabilities far exceeding those primitive prototypes built just after World War II. We see them advertised on television. Computers of the 1950s were programmed in machine languages and primitive assembler languages. In the 1960s, problem-oriented languages made their appearance together with operating systems and primitive teleprocessing programs. In the 1970s interactive systems, database/data communications systems and non-procedural programming languages* came into play and teleprocessing capabilities matured. Through software, computers are steadily becoming more accessible to individuals possessing less technical skill.

While it is still necessary to make an investment of time to learn to use a computer, that is not the biggest problem. The most significant

*These languages include facilities whereby much of the logic generally found in programs is found instead in relationships among data elements. Programming, that is, the "processing" part of data processing is simplified, while the "data" part of data processing is made more complex. There are some who would argue with this somewhat simplistic distinction.

hurdle that must be overcome is the reluctance of individuals to get involved with computers. This reluctance may stem from intimidation in some situations; it may stem from commitment to more pressing priorities; it may stem from a lack of interest; or it may stem from impatience. We believe that this reluctance to get involved with computers can be overcome if individuals can be shown that the advances made in the fundamental system software are continually making computers more user friendly. While not yet as good as it can be, it is certainly better than it has been.

Let's look at each reason for reluctance separately. Intimidation is one of the most common reasons for failure to get involved with a computer. Yet most individuals, especially senior managers and executives, don't like to admit this. The best way to overcome intimidation is to go out and buy a personal computer, any kind, bring it home or to your office, read the instruction booklet or primer that comes with it, and fool around with it. Commitment to more pressing priorities and impatience are probably the most valid reasons for not getting involved. However, the problem here is not a problem with software technology, but simply a problem with time. If you are overwhelmed with commitments and simply don't have any time left over for computers or for anything, we sympathize, but we can't help you. We can say, however, there has never been a better time to get involved with computers. Software is at a point where it is still possible to learn the fundamentals of computing. It is still possible to learn enough so that you'll not be completely at the mercy of the technology. Within a few more years this may no longer be possible. Lack of interest if difficult to overcome. However, we believe that computers, through software, are becoming more and more integrated with our day-to-day living. We believe that those individuals, especially those in senior management and executive positions, are missing out on an opportunity to more fully realize the potential of their own functions if they fail to get involved with computers.

The Future Is Now

There are several areas in which computers can be helpful. These areas are what might be considered contemporary technology.* Contemporary technology includes graphics, modeling, videotext, teletext, and word processing.

*From the time that I write this to the time that the book is produced and made available for consumption, about one year goes by. There are some things that technology just can't seem to overcome. But what I write here as contemporary may be commonplace by the time the book is in your hands.

We discussed graphics technology in some detail in an earlier chapter. At this point, we will merely make some comments on graphics technology. The old saying that a picture says more than a thousand words has validity. Graphics quality continues to improve as monitors and plotters with fine resolution and color capabilities are manufactured. What senior manager or executive would not prefer to see a bar or pie chart or plotted trends in several colors rather than a display or report full of numbers. Yet, bar charts, pie charts and plotted trends are primitive when compared to the real potential of graphics. There are a number of applications that could use graphics illustrations. In addition to the CAD/CAM mentioned in an earlier chapter, there is virtually no end to the possibilities of graphics. A Canadian organization, for example, with some governmental subsidies, has developed a package that contains a database with information about recorded music albums. Part of the database is a graphic of the album cover that can be displayed in color on a CRT screen when information about that album is displayed. However, the package with the graphics option is somewhat more expensive than it is without it. Currently, the one drawback to graphics technology is its cost. It is expensive in terms of dollars and in terms of overhead. Computer graphics software, at the present time, requires a considerable amount of computer resources. Microcomputers, with their relatively expensive processors and primary storage components are going to be a significant factor in lowering the cost of using graphics software.

Videotext and teletext are two young technologies that use the combined resources of telecommunications and computers. *Videotext* involves the transmission of text over telephone lines or cable, while *teletext* uses the vertical blanking interval of a television signal (the horizontal black bar that appears when the television picture jumps or rolls). Teletext is one way, while videotext is interactive. Subscribers to a videotext service are able to request information from that service's databases. Various transactional services, such as banking, bill paying, and shopping are available. Revenues come from three sources: (1) customers pay for subscriptions, (2) fees are charged to merchants for advertising, and (3) transactions are charged to customers. Since this type of service is still in the prototype stage, it is still quite expensive. As volumes increase, costs ought to diminish. The technology underlying it is sound and proven. Again, realizing the potential is a managerial task rather than a technical one. Teletext is one way. Using a hand-held keypad, subscribers can "call up" teletext pages (screens) of information which are displayed on their television sets. The teletext information can either be in place of the picture, or it can be superimposed over it as in the case of captions. The service is advertiser supported and transmitted free of charge to those with decoders or teletext-equipped television sets. All homes and offices equipped with a cable service have teletext in some form.

Contemporary computers also lend themselves to data-processing techniques that have been given several names, including modeling, simulation, decision support systems, and "what if . . . analysis." One type of modeling involves the creation of a mathematical formula that is a representation of some organizational function or process, of an entire organization, or of the entire world economic system. The number of variables in the formula increases as scope of the model increases in magnitude. Computers are able to execute the arithmetic of the formula when numeric values are substituted for the variables in the formula. Because of their great speed, computers are able to perform many executions with different numeric values very quickly. The process of doing this is known as simulation. The use of the formula and the numeric values is an attempt to approximate the performance of an organizational function or process, or something of greater magnitude. The formula or model together with the numeric values allows planners and analysts to extrapolate what may happen under certain conditions. It is a valid and useful technique as long as those using it remember that the models and simulations are no better than the assumptions made in developing the formula.

Another type of model is what might be called a data model. This type of model is also based on assumptions, but may serve as a relatively inexpensive way of establishing trends, determining current conditions such as sales and expenses, and forecasting future expectations. No mathematical formula is required. The assumption is made that a subset (some fraction) of all the data can be selected that when processed, can produce results that are close to the results that would be produced if all the data were used. The estimating of the results of elections is a use of this type of model. There are other types of data models that can be developed either with subsets or with summarized information. Armed with computer technology, model and simulation potential is limited only by the practical realities of the amount of equipment available and by the creativity and imagination of the analysts and their managers.

Decision support systems is an example of terminology. The term was probably invented by some astute, enterprising individuals who realized that senior managers and executives might have reservations about management information systems because of the misadventures of the past. Decision support systems are the strategic systems that were envisioned by the early advocates of management information systems back in the 1960s. As we mentioned earlier, the potential of management information systems in the 1960s was beyond the capability of the technology. However, that is no longer the case. In the contemporary setting, the potential of management information systems is inhibited by the diversity and the incompatibility of the technology, but in terms of capability, the technology exists to do the job. Realizing the potential is now a task that requires the combined efforts of senior managers, executives, technical managers, and technicians. Cooperation among groups of individuals of these types with their differing outlooks, objectives, priorities, and personalities is difficult to achieve. Yet the problems are managerial and political, not technical. The technology is available. The technology is potential; if it is to be realized, it is to be realized by people. Furthermore, it is possible. Tracy Kidder's *The Soul of the New Machine* narrated how the potential of technology was realized by a group of individuals, including senior managers, executives, technical managers, and technicians. That narrative showed how these individuals with all their strengths and weaknesses developed a new computer that was designed and built with some of the most advanced technology available at the time. If it can be done with hardware, it can be done with software. Management information systems or decision support systems, or whatever you want to call them are now possible and feasible.

"What if . . . analysis" goes hand-in-hand with modeling and decision support systems. Basically, it allows senior managers and executives to make some adjustments to the numeric values in the models and then to see the results of those adjustments throughout the rest of model. In one of the most primitive but efficient and effective applications, the electronic worksheet products that can be run on small personal computers, the value of modeling and "what if . . . analysis" can be realized. These products provide analysts with a column and row worksheet usually containing 60 or more columns and 250 or more rows. Each field is uniquely identified by a column and row indicator, A1, Q76 and the like. Each field can be used to hold a numeric value entered by an analyst or it can be used to hold a formula which directs the performance of some arithmetic on the numeric values in other fields, A1 * Q76 for instance. If a new value is entered into A1, the value in the field where Al * Q76 is entered, is recalculated. The asterisk denotes multiplication. The advantages of such products over the green spread sheets are obvious. The potential of this particular technology was realized by thousands of analysts and managers and, as we stated earlier, probably stimulated personal computer sales more than any other single factor.

One last observation on an area of technology whose potential is not being fully realized because it is being viewed incorrectly by some senior managers and executives. Word processing is not intended to make secretaries' tasks easier. In contemporary business situations, most senior managers and executives enjoy the benefits of a private secretary. Most middle and first-line managers have to share secretarial help. Middle managers and first-line managers are required to produce more typed material than senior managers and executives. Word processing is a benefit to middle and first-line managers. It results in more accurate documents, and it produces them more quickly. We believe one of the biggest bottlenecks in getting tasks completed is in the area of typing. Documentation, reports, memos, and letters must be dictated or hand-written, typed, proofread, edited, corrected, and retyped. The bottleneck is in the proofreading, editing, correcting, and retyping cycle. Without a word processing facility, each retyped document has to be completely reread. While old errors are corrected, it is possible for new errors to creep in. With a word processing facility, this is much less likely to occur, and material that was originally correct, stays correct. This eliminates the bottleneck, relieves the middle managers and first-line managers from the tedious task of reproofing the same material more than once. It improves their efficiency and effectiveness and gets the typed material finished more quickly. As a by-product of this, is enhances one aspect of secretarial work as well.

DEALING WITH . . .

In Chapter 9, we outlined three problem areas that inhibit the realization of the potential of information systems: (1) problems with technology, (2) problems with people, and (3) problems with other things. In conclusion, we would like to deal with these three problem areas.

Dealing with Technology

There is no doubt that at the "nuts-and-bolts" level, technology is complex. But we believe that the major problems that occur are not with the complexity of individual components of the technology but rather with some of the mechanical tasks associated with implementing the components and also at points where two or more components interface.

It is in these two areas where management skills are required. Technicians are, generally speaking, precise individuals who deal with black-and-white situations. Remember, with computers, it's on or it's off; it's zero or it's one; it's yes or it's no; there's no maybe. And yet, before a black-and-white situation can be seen clearly, it often manifests itself as gray. It is in the gray situations that the performance of technicians degrade and management ought to step in. Technicians have a tendency to evaluate a situation in terms of their own experience and area of expertise. They also tend to make sweeping generalizations based on their own experience and expertise. For example, a system programmer might think that an assembler language should be used for all programming because it is efficient in terms of execution, while application programmers might believe that programs written in assembler languages are too difficult to maintain and that they slow down development work on new applications. In the best-case situations this can lead to some good-natured kidding around, while in the worst case it can result in downright animosity and hostility among groups who have to work together to get a job done.

Technicians such as system programmers enjoy technical challenges. They like to search out and solve difficult problems, apply a fix, and move on to another challenge. They don't like to document what they do, and they abhor administration. It's not that they prefer chaos over order, but they'd just like to let somebody else take care of the details of documentation and administration. There are other individuals with information systems experience and expertise who are less captivated by the technical challenges. They prefer to provide the documentation and to take care of the administrative details. They tend to see the big picture and do not like to spend a lot of effort solving difficult technical problems in one area. These individuals are also technicians, but technicians in a different sense. Included in this group are application analysts, database administrators, and data administrators.

With EDP/MIS organizations, individuals with different skills are very often required to combine their efforts to implement an application. The interfaces of both individuals and technologies is a potential source of friction. The amount of friction increases with the amount of pressure exerted at the time the application is being implemented. It is when the pressure is the greatest that defensiveness and "sandbagging" increase. Senior managers and executives ought to be aware of these varying characteristics of the different types of technicians so that when critical implementations are planned they can be discerning and discriminate between real technological problems and interpersonal problems among technicians.

As far as problems with technology is concerned, there is just one other situation that senior managers and executives ought to be aware of, and that is the one-or-two-day seminar or management briefing at which all the benefits of the latest technology are shown. Many of these seminars are orchestrated by consultants and vendors seeking business. They often begin with the myth of the application backlog, a vendor-inspired ploy, to make attendees believe that their organizations need a whole bunch of new technology to relieve this log-jam of applications waiting to be implemented. While there are improvements that can be made, much of it can be done with careful and systematic planning and analysis. Some new technology is helpful, but in carefully measured increments. Remember, part of the difficulty organizations are now having with their information systems functions stems from the fact that there are existing applications, of varying ages, based on two or more types of technology, awkwardly interfaced with one another already. The introduction of more new technology, unless carefully planned, will aggrevate this situation rather than improve it.

New technology nearly always promises to speed up the process of developing new applications. Depending upon the awkwardness of existing application interfaces, it might be better to slow down application development rather than to speed it up. Some careful planning and analysis may result in consolidations that may well reduce computer equipment resource utilization. Freed-up resources can be used for new development without the expenditure of funds for additional technology. This is not a recommendation of a no-growth, no-new-technology policy, but rather a suggestion that senior managers encourage their subordinates to make a conscientious evaluation of existing applications and resource utilization with a view toward migrating to new technology while consolidating what is currently running. The direction to do this can only come from senior managers and executives, since they are the only individuals whose scope of authority is broad enough. Remember, the presentations made at briefings and seminars are staged and what they portray is potential. Realization of that potential in a real-world environment is possible only after careful planning and analysis. Neglect of the effort required will result merely in greater complexity and quite probably in even greater problems. The new technology works and works well in a pristine vendor-orchestrated environment. Getting it to work in the something less than pristine environment of a real-world organization is a task that requires a combination of technical and management skill.

Dealing with People

Dealing with people is an art. There are some who are attempting to make it a science, but they are doomed to failure. We make no claims to be experts in either psychology or sociology, but we can offer the benefit of our experience. We make the basic assumptions that most of the time, most individuals, unless threatened (perceived threats are as real to the individual perceiving the threat as are actual threats), attempt to perform in a reasonable fashion, take pride in their work and accomplishments, and tend to be honest in their dealings with others. We did say most of the time and most individuals; we're not naive enough to believe that there's no conniving, shirking, and dishonesty. However, when the latter kind of behavior becomes the norm, we can all buy our

.44 magnums and head for the hills. Based on those assumptions, we offer the following suggestions in dealing with people.

It is our belief that many of the problems that occur during implementations of technology products and of applications using them come about through misunderstandings. As we indicated earlier, different individuals with differing perspectives on a situation can easily come up with various interpretations of that situation. That fact alone may lead to a misunderstanding. If we lived in a world of magnanamous, secure, and well-adjusted individuals, then the misunderstandings would be quickly resolved. A phone call would be made or a small meeting would be convened to resolve this issue or issues causing the misunderstanding. However, we do not live in such a world. If we did, almost everything could be worked out between visionaries and technicians; the number of managers required would be dramatically decreased.

A primary objective of middle managers ought to be the discernment and quick solution of problems stemming from misunderstandings before any hint of their existence escalates to senior management. That is what middle managers are being paid to do. When misunderstandings causing problems between technicians, groups of technicians, technical managers, or first-line supervisors escalate to senior management, the result is further misunderstandings, complications, and a significant lengthening of the time it takes to reach a resolution. The escalation process involves formal documentation of the problem, preparation of elaborate explanations that satisfy everybody, translation of what is best expressed in technical terms into terms that senior management can deal with, and worst of all the assuming of defensive postures by the individuals or groups who are the center of the misunderstanding. The real problem is often completely obscured and efforts toward resolution are diluted. The order of the day becomes: "make sure we're covered." Interoffice memoranda increase in volume and intensity. Known as "interoffice hate mail," this correspondence occasionally starts out as a careful, one-sided documentation of "the problem." Each individual or group prepares one. Then as subtle indications in each memorandum hint at technical or managerial difficiencies on the other side of the issue, rebuttal memoranda are issued, and so on. No doubt the scenario is all too familiar. There's little need to describe it completely. But rather, let's attempt to offer some recommendations that can prevent misunderstandings from happening in the first place. These recommendations carry no guarantee, and they are going to cost in terms of time and money, but they have been used with a degree of success in some organizations.

There are essentially two recommendations, and then there is a suggestion.

The first recommendation is something that could be called "The Annual Meeting of Information Systems Middle Managers." It should be presided over or chaired by a senior information systems manager or executive. Other senior managers or executives can be invited to attend also, for the entire meeting or for part, depending upon their availability. It should be a two- or three-day affair and should consist of a series of both formal and informal meetings. It should be held at a site far enough away from the managers' offices so that returning would be impractical. The agenda for the mornings might include presentations by managers, with each one providing an explanation of what's going on in his or her area. Afternoons can include golf outings, tennis matches, softball, or MIS Olympics for the nonsports minded. Dinner meetings can include speakers from outside the information systems ranks of the organization or from outside the organization. Information can be shared among individual middle managers who otherwise might have little time or inclination to talk to one another, as they go about handling the day-to-day activities in their own areas. Not every individual is working with the most recently developed technology or application techniques, and the opportunity afforded by a managers' meeting can benefit both the organization and the individual managers. At best, two or more managers might find out that they are pursuing similar developments in parallel and that they may be able to pursue together for a saving in either equipment or manpower. One manager may find that another manager is trying to locate a piece of equipment that he or she no longer needs. At the very least, some middle managers get a chance to exchange information with their peers.

The second recommendation involves the use of a planning technique that is relatively inexpensive, involves both middle and first-line managers, and provides senior managers and executives with an overall plan for each component within the information systems function. There is a complete description of the technique in Appendix C. Basically, it begins with a detailed calendarization of tasks that need to be performed to achieve specific objectives. Both objectives and tasks are laid out on a long sheet of paper that may be twenty-five feet long and three or four feet wide. The objectives are set based on estimates for tasks that are established by first-line managers and supervisors. The middle managers transfer the objectives to Gantt Charts* which are used to make senior information systems managers and executives aware of the goals for the functional component for the next twelve or fifteen months. These senior managers and executives can summarize further and translate the technological goals into broader objectives

*Gantt Charts are a type of bar chart in which projects can be scheduled and progress measured. Projects go on the vertical axis and time on the horizontal axis.

when they make their presentations to the organization's senior managers and executives.

For best results, this technique should also be practiced at a site away from the normal place of business. Aside from the Gantt Chart preparation, the activities necessary to complete the plan can be completed within two days. It is quite conceivable that it may not be practical to have all first-line managers and supervisors away from an area at one time for a two-day period. If that is the situation, the technique can be modified to handle half the managers and supervisors on one day and the other half on the next day. It may then become necessary to extend the session to three days, but the results should still be worth it. This technique can benefit senior managers and executives in two ways, one actual and one potential. In actual form, it assures senior managers and executives of an organization that the plan they receive from senior information systems managers and executives is based on detailed estimates from the individuals who are charged with meeting those estimates, the first-line managers and supervisors. In potential form, the technique can be used by senior managers and executives themselves to lay out their own objectives and tasks in a disciplined way and to see, while they are doing it, how those objectives and tasks may impact one another. This technique, whether used by first-line and middle management to report to senior managers and executives, or whether used by senior managers and executives themselves, goes a long way toward reducing misunderstanding by getting individuals to work together to produce a comprehensive plan. All who participate in the development of the plan have a reasonably good idea of what the others are doing. This can go a long way in heading off the type of surprises that create misunderstandings.

The "annual meeting" and planning technique just described are recommendations; the following paragraph contains a suggestion that may both improve productivity and employ an otherwise underutilized resource.

In the area of dealing with people, information systems technology provides a way for us to make use of an untapped, frequently overlooked resource, the handicapped worker. The CRT and personal-computer-oriented environment is a natural situation for individuals confined to wheelchairs or to those who have the use of their hands but who have not the use of some of their other faculties. As voice recognition in computer equipment continues to improve, even more opportunities will become available. The field of information systems offer tremendous opportunity for handicapped individuals to be not only self-supporting, but to make contributions as well. We believe that many handicapped individuals are highly motivated and attempt to compensate for their handicaps by putting extraordinary efforts into being productive and communicative.

Dealing with Other Things

In Chapter 9 we mentioned the problem of information overload, indicating that in the contemporary information systems environment the situation often exists where we are data rich and information poor. By data rich and information poor we mean that there are mountains of data stored in our computer systems, which for reasons that have been cited, are difficult to access and manipulate so that they can be displayed as information. Actually, these are two separate problems. Information overload implies that we as individuals and that includes senior managers and executives are being exposed to more information than we are able to assimilate. There is little we can do about this except to become somewhat arbitrary and to dismiss some of the information out of hand. As it turns out, this method of dealing with information systems issues may not be all that bad. Contrary to the belief of numerous opinionated technicians, there are a number of hardware and software products that are equally capable of performing the tasks of a given application. Personal computers and off-the-shelf software products illustrate this. For example, for a typical small computer application, say an electronic worksheet, any one of at least half a dozen personal computers can handle the job. Even if the intended use of a personal computer is beyond those of the electronic worksheet, it is still quite probable that a number of them will be up to the job. Information overload takes place when vendors throw all kinds of irrelevant information into advertising which is intended to make their configuration look "better." Data transfer rates, esoteric architecture characteristics, and other attributes are important when spending millions of dollars for large-scale computers, but this significance is relatively unimportant when purchasing a personal computer for some specific applications. When buying a personal computer, attempt to determine what it is you want to do with it, talk to some people who've already gotten one, think a little bit about future uses, and then find how many configurations will do what you want. After that make your selection based on price, functionality and even whim if that suits your fancy. Avoid the nonessential information, make your choice, and buy one. Also, be aware that the personal computer you buy is going to be obsolete from a technological point of view within a year, but this, too, is relatively unimportant. If it does what you want it to, obsolescence is irrelevant.

Software is another area where a degree of arbitrariness is necessary to avoid the burdens of information overload. There are too many software products to grant an individual or a group an opportunity to evaluate them all. Again, determine what you want to do, find two or three products that will do it, arbitrarily dismiss the rest, and pick the best of the two or three.

Data rich and information poor indicates another phenomenon of the contemporary information systems environment. Ever since the early 1960s, we have continually found new and better ways to collect and store data. We have, at the same time, developed ways to retrieve that data and display it as information. And yet, when senior managers and executives, and even middle and first-line managers make a request to the information systems managers for information, the response is that it will take several days, weeks, or sometimes even months. The reason for this is that no one, not senior managers and executives, not middle or first-line managers, not even the information systems managers and technicians can foresee totally the combinations and formats of future information requests. And yet, there is no doubt that a certain amount of foresight is possible and that the current situation can be improved upon. Realizing the potential of information systems involves establishing the relationships among data elements that make the entire collection of data elements, the database, responsive to the requests for information made by senior managers and executives, middle and first-line managers and by the managers and technicians themselves. As we have attempted to show in this book, the tools are available and the task is a formidable one. Yet it is possible. It requires a great deal of disciplined effort, but it can be done. It is possible to develop an on-line database, but it is expensive. It is possible to distribute a database, but that is more expensive; it is possible to establish a communications network so that virtually every individual in an organization can have access to that database; but that is even more expensive; and at the same time certain data elements and combinations of data elements must be kept secure, another expensive consideration. These expenses manifest themselves primarily in the costs of hardware, software, and people. Despite the claims of vendors and some technical gurus about the efficiencies of database, make no mistake about it, databases take up significant amounts of secondary storage, and the physical storage and retrieval operations require significant quantities of computer and channel horsepower. As computer equipment and software continue to become more sophisticated, the skill of system software technicians becomes more specialized. Where we once had system software technicians that "did it all," we now have database system software technicians, operating system software technicians, data communications and network system software technicians, interactive system software technicians, and performance measurement and tuning technicians. In addition to that, as the logic that used to appear in application programs is transferred to the data element relationships in databases, the additional technical skill of the database administrator can be added to the list. These are the tools, what about implementation? That's the task of the data administrator.

In the past, senior managers of an organization set policy, executives attempted to implement the policy through middle and first-line managers. Some of this policy was written, some was verbal. The actual implementation of the policy was carried out by individuals who performed the tasks that got the product manufactured and got it out the door, or who performed the tasks that supplied the service. Data that recorded those activities, that is, the implementation of the policy, were recorded on paper documents. Data processing of transactions was done manually. Later on, electronic accounting machines made it possible to process transactions where data was recorded on cards, and then in the 1950s and 1960s computers came into use and transactions were processed electronically, and data was recorded on magnetic tape and magnetic disk.

People are more flexible than computers. Policy is usually stated in general terms and individual executives, managers, and those performing tasks are able to make adjustments when confronted by a situation not specifically covered by policy or by a situation where policy just won't work. Designing computer systems and applications with the same kind of adjustment capability has proven to be rather difficult. While people are able to make decisions "on the fly," computer systems or applications can only do what they have been programmed to do. In other words, every conceivable situation that can possibly occur must be built into the system or application, or some kind of default option must be designed in to take care of the unforeseen. And so, we're back to square one, realizing the potential of information systems is the collective responsibility of senior managers and executives, middle managers and first-line managers. Computers only do what they're told to do. Policies and their implementations constitute the makeup of current information systems applications. They reflect an organization. A true management information systems is one which can extract timely, accurate, and meaningful information from an organization's files or databases. Files and databases that are not responsive ought to be redesigned, but only in the light of clearly articulated and implemented policy. To attempt a redesign without this would subject an organization to whim and caprice of the individual or group doing the design.

CONCLUSION

Information systems technology is a tool to be used under the direction and guidance of senior managers and executives, middle managers, and first-line managers in the development of a responsive management information system. An individual or a department can be given the responsibility and the authority to develop a logical database for the organization that meets the management information system requirements as set down in a policy statement. The function with this responsibility and authority is commonly known as data administration. Once the logical database is developed and understood and approved by senior managers and executives, middle managers, and first-line managers, a technical team of database administrators, applications analysts, and system software technicians can be directed to physically implement the database. This process involves selecting a physical mechanism as well as an overall operating philosophy. The choices here require cooperation between managers and technicians. The decisions are a management responsibility, but a technical perspective is required in making those decisions. Which type of database model is best suited to the organization's information requirements and whether databases and computers should be distributed are philosophical considerations. Technicians and technical managers have an obligation to inform senior managers and executives of the relative merits of these philosophical considerations.

When implementations commence, responsibility lies with the technicians and their managers. This is where the technical trade-offs begin and where the inevitable gaps in policy start cropping up. The gray areas are difficult to implement on computers that recognize only black and white. And yet, the tools are available. Gray can always be refined down to its basic ingredients, black and white. In terms of policy, it may involve a complex relationship among several data elements, or it may involve some complex logic on an application program, but the potential for resolution of nebulous policy is available. Realization in this instance comes down to the perseverence of the technician or the data administrator. In any event, realizing the potential of information systems using available technology is possible, but only with the commitment and support of senior managers and executives. Without that commitment and support, information systems and computer technology will continue to function erratically, with a logistical success here and there, but with no harmony of effort, no integration of data, and consequently no unified body of data from which to extract management information. On the other hand, with the commitment and support of senior managers and executives providing a top/down perspective on information systems development activity, there is an impetus to implement applications and systems that in addition to being an important logistical component, are also in integral part of a total management information system.

APPENDIX A

Reconciling Individual and Organizational Success

THERE ARE TWO ASPECTS to successful management: success of the projects being managed and success of the individual managing the projects. They are not always interdependent. This essay raises questions and makes observations about both types of success. There are seventeen guidelines that are helpful to bring in successful projects, which were previously published as an article in the May 1978 issue of the *Journal of Systems Management.** The Machiavellian observations following each guideline have been added to highlight those elements that may separate individual success from organizational success. Both the guidelines and the questions and commentaries reflect my own understanding and discernment of situations; as such, they are subject to change. Readers are free to pick and choose, and to accept or reject what is found here. It is conceivable that my own perceptions may have changed by the time this is being read. Life, among other things, is a process of learning.

Guideline #1

Write it down. I keep a piece of paper handy on which I write the things I feel ought to be done. When I first started doing this, I used to write down

*Walsh, Myles E. *Common Sense Guidelines as an Aid to Project Management, Journal of Systems Management*, May 1978. Used by permission.

everything that had to be done, now I just write down what I expect no one else will remember. The technique is really quite simple. Keep a piece of paper handy at all times, and as ideas become known, write them down. As they get done, cross them off the list. The list that I compiled while working on the 1970 election system was about twenty pages long at one point. The way I do it now, it is never more than three pages. At one point, I began to think that the need for such notes was so obvious, that using it as a management guideline was superfluous, until I noticed a trade journal carrying an article devoted entirely to the subject of keeping such notes.

In addition, I have observed a number of other managers using this technique and in my judgement these individuals are successful managers. I don't mean to say that their success is due entirely to the taking of notes, but I believe it does help. Conversely, I have also noticed that some managers try to keep everything in their heads and do not take notes. It has been my experience that it is these individuals who forget to pass on a piece of information, get involved in conflicting meetings, forget to make a phone call, etc.

This list can also be used for personal commitments as well. If you do not carry it with you every place you go, you can make notes on pieces of paper while you are out and add them to the list when you get back. There are some individuals who may be impressed if you appear to be able to keep everything in your head. If you wish to impress such an individual, then don't take notes in his presence. Keep as much as you can in your head while interacting with him and then try to write it all down when you are no longer in his presence. However, there is a risk involved. If you forget something, you can ruin the impression you tried to make. If you're not good at keeping things in your head, it's better not to try. Even if you fail to make the initial impression you'd like to make, you'll at least get the facts straight and avoid making a fool of yourself by doing a job incorrectly or by constantly returning for clarification.

Machiavellian observation #1

In some organizations, there's an image to keep up, that of the executive who's up-to-date on everything. Taking notes may tarnish that image. It's gamesmanship. No one really cares whether you take notes or not. There are times when taking notes or reading from them is inappropriate. It's up to individuals to determine when the use of notes is to be shunned.

Guideline #2

If you don't understand, say so. Since most people in business speak in a jargon that is peculiar to their function, invariably something will be said at a meeting or in a conversation that you will not understand. If understanding that particular item is prerequisite to understanding what follows, and the work that you are going to do depends on it, you'd better get clarification.

Judgement is required here. When dealing with an individual, in most cases it is a good idea to interrupt to get a clarification. At a meeting, glance around and see how everyone else is doing. If they seem to be following, hold your question temporarily. If there is someone at the meeting with whom you can later check, hold your question. If the meeting goes on and you find that you're lost because you didn't ask the question, then by all means, interrupt and ask the question. If someone else interrupts and asks a question, you might try to tactfully tack yours onto it. If you judge that an explanation can wait till later, don't interrupt a meeting, but make a note to get it later.

If you are dealing with a superior, a client or a user and are getting information with which to do a job, and you do not understand what you are being told, interrupt and ask for an explanation. If you are worried about looking stupid in front of your superior, your client or a user, by acknowledging that you don't understand something, just think of how stupid you'll look if you don't interrupt and come back later with the job done incorrectly.

If you are dealing with subordinates and you can't understand them, interrupt and ask for clarification. If you feel that you have frequent problems in understanding a subordinate, then you should have a talk with the individual and explain to him that it is part of his job to be able to communicate with you. If the problem continues, there's a good chance that he is deliberately snowing you and you'd better get rid of him.

Machiavellian observation #2

There are times when you may be getting thoroughly snowed at a meeting. If asking a pertinent question would prove embarrassing to you, then ask an irrelevant one. The results may surprise you. If your ploy is successful, you may be able to redirect the entire discussion.

Guideline #3

Don't snow others. This is the reciprocal of the above. You can generally tell when you've lost somebody to whom you are speaking. If it is a superior, you have probably made one of the following mistakes.

a. The time you picked to talk about this topic is not right. If so, either change the topic and wait for a reaction or end the discussion and wait for another time.

b. The topic you are presenting doesn't interest him at all. If so, drop it and wait for him to ask you about it.

c. He may not want to appear stupid or impolite to you, but you are losing him by using terminology that he does not understand. If so, try at all times to use a language as simple and as free from jargon as possible.

When speaking to subordinates, be sure that they understand what you want done. If they do not, when time comes when results are expected, and they are not forthcoming, it is your responsibility, not theirs, and it is you who will have to explain to your superiors why the job is not done. It is your responsibility to inform and be informed of project status, so that if misunderstandings have caused problems, you are able to find out early enough to either catch up the lagging work, or push back the target date with sufficient notice so as not to inconvenience those who might be depending upon you.

There is a great deal of attention being given to interpersonal communications these days. On the other hand, there is another phenomenon that is a bit perplexing. There are some individuals who seem to be able to intimidate others because they appear to possess knowledge. They have the ability to rattle off facts, figures, statistics, and quotes from reputable sources, that on the surface seem impressive but only because they are incomprehensible. There seem to be any number of normally intelligent, rational, competent managers who completely lose their ability to communicate when confronted by one of these individuals.

I used to think individuals who practiced this were dishonest, conniving and self-seeking. I have discovered that this is no more true of them than it is of the rest of us. These individuals speak in terms which are familiar to them. They often fall into the trap of becoming enamored with their own technical superiority in one area. Such individuals quite often are either exploited or ultimately ignored. I personally have seen both. In the former case, the individual was used and then jettisoned when his usefulness diminished. In the latter case, a reasonably intelligent, gifted individual got labeled as a specialist and has virtually no chance for advancement. These individuals unwittingly generate snowstorms whenever they speak, and managers do not want snow in the office, only on the slopes.

Machiavellian observation #3

During an interview for a job I did not get, I was told that it was better to answer a question with a random answer than to respond "I don't know." I found this advice to be rather curious at the time, but since then I have seen individuals doing it. Perhaps guideline #3 is not as sound as I thought it to be. The individual who gave me the advice is now a division president.

Guideline #4

Nudge. Invariably on every project, there is a mixture of procrastinators, narrow-minded superstars, good solid all-around people, and a dud or two. Procrastinators have to be pushed gently to get their work done; if not, they tend to wait till the last minute to do things somewhat sloppily and usually at the expense of others. The procrastinators then require more resources, and deprive those who are on schedule of adequate resources to stay on schedule. In this way, the entire project is jeopardized and ill-will is generated among members of the project team.

Narrow-minded superstars can do a lot for you if you keep their morale up, pay them well, and direct them very closely. Care must be taken with these people since the enhancement of their own creations tend to blind them to the goals of the overall project. A well-managed superstar can do the work of two or three men, but the adjective "well-managed" is the key. Uncontrolled, badly managed superstars can hurt the project very badly. If left on their own for too long a time they can become enamored of their own importance, and when they have to be guided or corrected, they can become petulant and trenchant and not perform properly the technical duties required.

Good, solid, all-around people are the kind who will use good sense and channel their efforts for the good of the entire project. They will generally do anything that is asked of them, and occasionally, you get an individual who can be given a relatively free hand to get things done.

A dud can be an individual who is unhappy with what he is doing, or an incompetent in what he is doing. These individuals can cause much damage and waste an inordinate amount of your and everyone else's time. If you have the time, try to find out if they can fit into another area of the project; otherwise, get rid of them.

In large corporations you rarely have as much control as you would like over those working under you. If you can get a staff of superstars, and good, all-around people, you're fortunate. Before getting rid of anybody, check with the Personnel Department.

Machiavellian observation #4

Watch carefully those who work for you; if they look too good, your superiors may find they don't need you that much.

Guideline #5

Keep it simple. In the area of interpersonal communications, try to keep things as simple as possible. Esoteric language, memos and letters make communications more difficult. The more ornate and flowery the language, the more obscure becomes the message. Instructions should be stated simply and precisely. If by necessity the instructions are lengthy, write them.

On two different occasions I attended interpersonal communications seminars where a little game was played. Four men were asked to leave the room. The lecturer then made three simple statements to an individual who had not left the room. One of the four men who left the room was asked to return. The individual to whom the lecturer had made the three simple statements was asked to pass the information to the man who had returned. This process continued as the second man returned and had the statements repeated to him from the first man. The third man returned and was given the statements by the second man. By the time the statements were passed to the fourth man, they were quite different from the original statements. The lecturer's point was: as information is passed from individual to individual, it gets garbled.

Many psychologists have postulated that interpersonal communications are inhibited by the biases and prejudices of the individuals involved. If you are ever in doubt about how well you've communicated to others, ask them to repeat what you've told them.

Machiavellian observation #5

There are times when communications are best when they are left vague. It results in a certain amount of flexibility later on.

Guideline #6

You can't know it all. When I first became a manager, I knew more technically than those working for me. This lasted for about six months. At first it worried me, but I soon realized that to be an effective manager, you have to let your technical ability slide. You must stay abreast of your field at the conceptual level, but you'll drive yourself to death if you try to be both managerially and technically competent. You have to know enough technically to be able to manage a staff of competent technicians. The development of your management skills must have a higher priority than technical. You must rely on the technical skills of your staff to get the job done. When technical problems come up, you must rely on your staff to recommend solutions so that you can decide, after discussion, which solution to apply.

Your job as a manager is completely different. You will be required to submit estimates for getting work done. You, in turn, must rely on your staff to give you estimates for task elements which you must develop into a longer estimate for an entire system. These estimates are then used to make up budgets, for which you must get approval. After your budget has been approved, it is your responsibility to stay within it. If unanticipated costs arise, you have a couple of options available. You can go to your superior and ask for authorization to spend more money. If you can explain the cost increase to him in a satisfactory manner and if there is money available, you may get it. This is the best case. More than likely, you will have to do the best you can with the money you've been budgeted. This can be a rather unpleasant experience, but as the years go by you should become better at preparing budgets. As your experience at preparing and meeting budgets grows, your superiors should give you more responsibility. This is one of many criteria by which you are judged worthy of greater responsibility. Other criteria include who you know and who knows you. To some this might seem purely political. It is, but to those who complain about it, just ask yourself this: When you want to get something done, who do you ask? Somebody you know—right?

Machiavellian observation #6

The higher you go in an organization the more you have to worry about your subordinates than your superiors.

Guideline #7

Do get the routine work yourself and let your staff get on with their own work. The manager should write the memos, not the programmer. Phone calls that are necessary for coordinating activities of a number of people should be made by the manager, not the analyst. If a group of programmers is working hard to meet a deadline, the manager can go for coffee, not one of the programmers. If a piece of hardware seems to be causing trouble, the manager should call the field engineers, not the programmer. If an analyst has a problem and wants to talk, listen to him. In my own experience, many solutions have been found in this way. An analyst, on the other hand, should not be above getting coffee for the boss when he is busy and the analyst is less involved.

Machiavellian observation #7

Some people think management is a science; others think it is an art. If you're trying to impress a scientist, don't behave like an artist.

Guideline #8

If someone else drops the ball, pick it up. There is a disproportionate amount of time spent in organizations, writing memos, arguing between departments, and having meetings trying to pin the responsibility for a mistake on some individual or some department. This type of environment interferes with the performance of all departments and individuals involved. Mistakes will always be made. However, the important thing is not to affix blame, but to recover as quickly as possible and get on with what has to be done. Although politically risky, it is my recommendation that if an error is made by anyone and it is within your power to correct it, do so. Once the show is back on the road, sit down with those involved in the error and try to set up a procedure to prevent that kind of an error from recurring. By getting the job done and showing others that you can be trusted, you can help to establish an environment where things can get done. The risks involved are that you'll be taken for a sucker and others will try to get you to do their work and assume responsibilities that are not really yours. Your ability will be greatly tested if you try this technique. The risks are great, but so are the rewards. A good management is interested in results, not in ability to avoid responsibility for failures by placing the blame on someone else. And yet while you are contributing to the success of the project by helping others, do not neglect to subtly let your superiors know how good you are. Remember not too soon after the completion of a successful project, no one is going to remember who contributed to its success unless they are reminded.

Machiavellian observation #8

When picking up a dropped ball, make sure it doesn't have a fuse on it. It has been said: "If you want to make an enemy, do somebody a favor." Sometimes a ball is dropped deliberately.

Guideline #9

Head off trouble before it happens. Quite often it is possible for you to spot a potential problem before it actually occurs. Being manager of a systems and programming department provides you with knowledge about many of the working functions within your organization and how they interface with one another. If you have systems installed in the different areas, your knowledge is even greater. Generally, the people in the departments are too busy handling the day-to-day activities to be aware of a problem that is creeping up on them. If you notice a problem like this, try to come up with some potential solutions. Discuss it with the working department or departments that are involved. If it turns out that the problem appears to be serious, then a shifting of current priorities might be in order. As uncomfortable as that might seem, it is probably the best alternative. For if the problem is severe and not brought to someone's attention and just allowed to happen, the shift in priorities that will result will probably be even more severe.

There are also other smaller problems that, if not corrected early, can lead to greater problems in the future. The kind of problem to which I refer is the project that begins to fall behind, the late report, the incorrectly keypunched input, and the like. Usually, these problems can be resolved by some dialogue between the parties involved. Use the telephone. Get the facts and try to straighten the whole thing out before the memos start. Try to get the parties involved to live with each other's occasional errors. Good feelings and trust between departments that have to work with one another is essential to a smoothly functioning organization. Many errors that take place are results of misunderstandings and lack of communication. Set up specific individuals who can be called if something appears unclear or out of the ordinary. If you able to successfully anticipate problems and help to solve them before they become serious, you can enhance your own reputation among those with whom you work.

Machiavellian observation #9

The guidelines set down in number nine are a two-edged sword. They are quite useful in maintaining smooth operations and in assuring the individual who practices them a virtually complete lack of recognition. By heading off problems, the consequences are avoided, and those causing them can actually "look good."

Guideline #10

Two heads are sometimes better than one. The best way to play this game is with others. As an EDP manager, you are often called upon to make proposals for new systems or improvements to existing systems. Before presenting your proposal, get a member of your staff, an associate or a manager or supervisor from the department with sufficient knowledge of the project, to try to find holes in it. Quite often, when proposals are prepared, some blind spots creep in, which are carried along throughout the analysis and design phase and are not discovered until the implementation state of the project. These blind spots can cause considerable rework if they affect the logic of the system. Quite often, these blind spots are minor and only require a small amount of rework. It should be emphasized that reworking during the implementation stage of a project coincides with the period of time where the pressure is heaviest, because of an approaching target date, and the coordinating of activities necessary to get the system into production. Using another person to take a look at your proposal in its infancy and plugging a hole or two at that stage is worthwhile to everyone involved. I have often done this, and I sometimes find it difficult when some nit-picking character finds a small fault in a presentation or proposal that has taken me hours to produce. Yet at the same time, I remember that this kind of criticism keeps me honest, and when all is said and done, I don't have to follow the nit-picker's advice if I don't want to.

Machiavellian observation #10

It's all right to ask the advice of others, but at the same time, be prepared to share the credit.

Guideline #11

Avoid distractions. Some tasks require a dedicated amount of concentration for some period of time. Many of us cannot concentrate on one problem for more than ten minutes without our mind wandering. External distractions result in less concentration still. Therefore, some tasks should be undertaken as far removed from external distractions as is reasonably possible. Some managers find that working after hours provides an environment free from external distractions. My own experience has shown that working before hours or at home is much more effective. In working on tasks requiring quite a bit of concentration, I have accomplished more by working for an hour and a half before regular hours than I would if I had worked three hours after normal hours. The reason for this is rather obvious. After a full day of work, a manager is more apt to be tired, tense, and upset. In the morning, there's a good chance that he is rested and refreshed. I have found myself more motivated early in the morning than I am late in the evening.

Working at home, if one's job permits, keeps an individual away from distractions such as random phone calls and people dropping into the office. Additionally, in some cases, a couple of hours of commuting time is replaced by a couple of hours of useful work at a kitchen table at home. Management tasks requiring some degree of concentration are reading or preparing specifications, reading technical material for conceptual content, discussing alternative solutions to a problem with another person, and discussing a personnel problem with the involved individual. The kind of distractions that can really jangle your thoughts or conversation are a ringing telephone, someone entering your office, and radios. Certain types of planning activities can best be accomplished away from the office also. Preparing budgets on detailed project plans can often be done in a hotel suite. Line up three or four important people, reserve a suite for a day or two, and do the job.

Machiavellian observation #11

Doing work early in the day rather than late has one disadvantage. Nobody sees what time you come in, but everybody sees you leave. There are those who work late and who look down on those who don't. Working at home or in a hotel suite may also result in criticism.

Guideline #12

Isolate tasks. Every manager, at some period of time, has been faced with what appeared to be an insurmountable amount of work. When this occurs, stand back for a minute, take a look at what is before you. Break the pile of work into separate tasks. Having done this, try to get the smaller tasks out of the way first. The smaller tasks are usually things like making telephone calls and writing memos or letters. Practicing this idea does not reduce the amount of work, but it does put into clearer perspective the amount of work to be done. At times, the magnitude of the work seems greater than it actually is, until it is organized as separate tasks.

With the arrival on the scene of the third generation of computers, the concept of a modular programming was introduced. The concept was not new, but a great deal of attention was given to it, because of the architecture of the equipment. This concept of modularity of tasks can also be applied to management. If you isolate or modularize the tasks before you, and then concentrate on completing them one at a time, you should be more effective in each of them than if you waded into a conglomeration of unrelated tasks and tended to them in a haphazard manner. Not too long ago, I was introduced to another idea in this area; when confronted with a large number of tasks, separate them into large and small and tackle the ones you judge to be the most important first, regardless of size. In this way there's a chance that some of those considered not so important will not get done at all. If they are really important, they'll keep cropping up; if not, they'll just disappear and you won't have to do them after all.

Machiavellian observation #12

It's incredible how much work withers up and dies from lack of attention. Discerning that which will from that which won't is what makes management an art rather than a science.

Guideline #13

Don't be too quick to call the other guy an idiot. Many times I have come out of meetings and, as the group breaks up and individuals get out of earshot, somebody is heard to say, "Boy, that guy ______ is an idiot. He just doesn't understand the problem." For openers, there's probably a fair-to-middling chance he is saying the same thing about you. If asked, you would probably not admit to being an idiot, so let's assume that the fellow you're talking about is also not an idiot. Or, perhaps the guy is a jerk. Either way, if you're going to have to work with him to accomplish the same goal, you'd better get together with him and talk things over.

If and when the opportunity arises, make an attempt to talk to the individual about the subject you feel he doesn't understand. The worst that can happen is that you'll make no progress at all. However, there is a chance that either you or he will come away from the conversation with a clearer understanding of the subject.

The apparent stubbornness of an individual at a meeting can arise for a variety of reasons. Try to determine the reason before thinking of some individual as an idiot. For example, you may have been closely associated with a subject or a project for years, and the purpose of the meeting is to explain to some legitimately interested people the reasons behind your methodology. Your very familiarity with the subject might lead you to omit some simple basic concepts from your explanation. As your explanation proceeds quite logically, based on what you know, the listeners might become confused. One of them might interrupt with a question, causing you slight irritation. Your answer to the question might reflect the irritation. The questioner might detect the irritation, become a little flustered, and not understand your reply to his question. The progression to apparent stubbornness can proceed from this point on your part as well as his. The above is only one example of many reasons for people coming out of meetings thinking of one another as idiots.

Machiavellian observation #13

There are indeed stubborn, egotistical individuals with fixed ideas. It is extremely difficult to deal with them. Sometimes individuals like these reach positions of power. This feeds their egotism. They become more intransigent. Individuals usually surround themselves with sycophants and flatterers. Great caution must be exercised when dealing with such individuals. The real danger is not from the individual in power, but rather from certain types found within the clique. Read some accounts of the activities of Martin Bormann, Hitler's right-hand man, an extreme case to be sure, but a good illustration nonetheless.

As you advance into management positions, with all their nebulous and vague situations which which you must deal, you can be sure that there will be individuals who believe that you are an idiot. Highly skilled technicians who deal in black-and-white situations are likely to be your most severe critics. A manager learns to live with this, realizing that in some cases the critics are correct in their assessment.

Guideline #14

Be patient—involved problems take time to solve. Many EDP managers were at one time programmers. When they encountered a bug in a program, they sat down with the dump and listing and found it. Some bugs were found in ten minutes. Other bugs took hours and occasionally a day or two to find. Some management problems can be solved in ten minutes; others take longer. One of the differences between management problems and the problems of a program bug is that the management problems usually involve fallible people instead of infallible machines. When a computer "abends" a program, you're off—you've got a bug, a dump (most of the time), and there's no question about it. With people, it's not that clear cut. People problems cannot always be solved with logic, APARS, or within given sets of rules.

Involved problems are not always caused by people exclusively, but people can quite often contribute greater complications to an already complex situation. Yet without people, the problems will not get solved at all. The problems of getting things done with people, where more than one function is involved, is as old as organized enterprise. Generally speaking, the more functions and people that are involved, the more complex a problem appears. Usually some kind of compromise will have to be made to get the problem solved or to get a job done.

Cutting through such bother can be difficult unless you are an extremely forceful person who can present a case without any loopholes. My suggestion is to try patience, and to work with and listen to those who might appear to be rivals or opponents. Quite often, systems managers get the feeling that because their position enables them to get an overview of their company's operations, they can propose systems that can solve a number of the company's problems. In some cases, they are right; in many others they are not. Most department heads do not possess the system manager's overview and must be given time to understand the system manager's proposal. System managers should give their proposals time, discuss the parts affecting individual departments with the heads of those departments and listen to what the department heads have to say.

Machiavellian observation #14

Being patient and practical can bring about good relationships and fairly smooth operations. Being forceful, aggressive, and unreasonable can quite often get things accomplished that would not ordinarily get done. Those who practice forcefulness, aggressiveness, and unreasonableness are generally feared, grudgingly respected, and even occasionally well liked.

Guideline #15

Some thoughts on meetings. A possible method for reducing the amount of time an individual must spend at a meeting would be to try to conduct a *modular meeting*. For example, say two or three individuals must sit through an entire meeting. Three or four other individuals must contribute to or receive from the meeting specific information. These individuals are called in and dismissed from the meeting as necessity dictates. The agenda and presentation of topics should be set up before the meeting so that the individuals who must be called in are summoned only once or twice. If they are called in more often than that, they will be ineffective outside the meeting and might as well sit in for the entire meeting. If information involving these people is discussed in their absence, a meeting's minutes should be published and all those attending any part of the meeting should get a copy.

A meeting should be set up if it has been found that dialog between individuals is inadequate. A good indicator of dialog between individuals being inadequate is when small misunderstandings begin to take place. When people of departments within a group begin to ask for everything in writing (CYA paper), a meeting is in order. Once a meeting has been set up, its purpose should be established ahead of time, and an agenda should be published. Attempt to begin the meeting with agreement on the points that caused the misunderstanding, so that when the meeting has ended, those involved can go back to functioning as an effective group. The meeting should not be a witch hunt.

Another solid reason for a meeting is when a number of departments are working on a common project, but each one becomes so busy with its own work that it tends to lose sight of what the others are doing. A periodic status meeting between department heads can keep the overall goal in perspective by giving each department head the opportunity to find out what the others are doing. While a meeting is taking place, those in attendance are taken away from their jobs. The more people that are attending and the longer the meeting lasts, the more the jobs of those people suffer. The purpose of the meeting should be important enough to offset the loss of time to the attendees' jobs.

Machiavellian observation #15

Meetings are a "net-spreading process." Get enough people together to discuss a situation that appears to be in trouble. In the best case, the problems can be addressed and solved. In the worst case, the net can catch enough individuals so that the cause of the problems can be spread. A suggested motto: "When all else fails, convene a meeting."

Guideline #16

Follow up. I was once called a "noodge" by a fellow who worked with me on the Election Night project in 1970. A noodge is a pest. I was a pest to this fellow because he required follow-up. He did not realize the stake that I had in the success of the project, and therefore virtually everything I asked of him had to be followed up. In addition, this individual was one of those who liked to keep everything in his head instead of writing it down.

Some individuals require more follow-up than others. All individuals require some follow-up, if only to maintain their perspective or interest in a project. Follow-up is a useful technique. If applied properly and thoroughly, it can eliminate to a great extent the need to affix blame on someone who forgot to do something or did something incorrectly. In the context of trying to get a job done as a member of a team, rather than trying to become a "star" at the expense of others, a follow-up phone call or inquiry is much more effective than saying, "I thought George was going to do that" when a project has slipped for some reason. There are some occasions when it is tempting to let something slip so as to make an apparently irresponsible or incompetent individual aware of his shortcomings. One would hope that being made aware of his lapses would prod this individual to improve his performance. It has been my experience that succumbing to this temptation rarely has any favorable impact on an individual's performance. Judgement on quality or competence is quite subjective, and the expectation you have of another's performance is questionable anyway. Netting it all out, it is better to give the other fellow the benefit of the doubt and follow up on those areas which you suspect require it. To facilitate remembering things on which you have to follow up, write them down and keep the list handy, and review it periodically.

Follow-up generally becomes more important when you are dealing with people who are supporting your project or operation, as well as a host of other projects. Those people who have a number of other projects operations to take care of do not have the interest or involvement in your project or operation that you have. This is perfectly understandable. Just as getting your total job done consists of a number of things, so does theirs. Just as you occasionally forget something, so might they. What they may forget is a small task to them; however, it could be quite important to you. Following up assures that the task is not likely to be overlooked. Following up on your subordinates is a matter of judgement. For some, a short conversation once a day suffices. For others, their work occasionally must be checked in detail.

Machiavellian observation #16

The antithesis of follow-up is to slough off. Attempt to sidestep as much responsibility as possible by letting others assume more responsibility. This is an exciting process, especially when others are attempting to do the same thing. Beware of the individuals who telephone you and attempt to elicit your involvement in their problems.

Guideline #17

For lack of a nail. . . . Have you heard the story of the million-dollar computer that couldn't run because the wrong amphenol connector was installed? It's true—I was there. Twenty-four hours of processing was delayed, time was wasted up and down the line making phone calls to locate the proper connector, and a forty-mile drive from New York to New Jersey and back was finally required to acquire it and get it installed. For every project, many little things have to be done. For example: to get an RJE terminal site working, in addition to the big things like electrical and air-conditioning requirements and continuous form paper, one must assume the presence of little things like ribbons. The point I am trying to make here is a simple one. Try to be sure to have someone available to you who looks after details and ties up the loose ends. A technique which is helpful in taking care of loose ends on jobs that are somewhat repetitive is the use of a checklist. Preparation of the checklist can take place before the job is done the first time. Upon completion of the job, revise the checklist and continue to do so until you have one that is complete. Revisions usually are required not to compensate for what you forgot the first time, but for modifications in the form of improvements that become apparent during the actual performance of the job. Revisions can also become necessary as a job expands and takes on new functions. A specific individual should be assigned to pay careful attention to small details before a job is actually started. Revisions can also become necessary as a job expands and takes on new functions. Careful attention to small changes before a job is actually started will sometimes save the job completely, but at the very least will reduce the amount of aggravation and confusion during the performance of the job.

Machiavellian observation #17

The "heroes" of projects are those who are responsible for the entire project, that is, the big things, not the little things. Taking care of little things is important, but generally not vital. The "big money" and the recognition comes with total responsibility including the little things. If you wish to take responsibility for a total project, make every attempt to find a low-key individual to take care of details who gets satisfaction from getting a job done and does not require the "big money" or the glory.

CONCLUSION

Project management and administrative management are very subjective. The higher up in an organization you go, the more interested your superiors become in what you can get done for them and the less interested they are in how you do it. Nobody above you cares about your techniques, be it Theory X, Theory Y, participatory, or autocratic. They are interested in results and in being undisturbed by situations that they're paying you to take care of. They are not interested in your career, because they are thoroughly occupied taking care of their own. Once you've achieved a middle-management position, your future advancement depends on a combination of your effectiveness, your ability to communicate to specific individuals, and your persuasive ability. It's a combination of skills, both productive and Machiavellian. Those who say: "it's not what you know, it's who you know," are copping out. It's both.

APPENDIX B

A Revolution Every Ten Years*

THERE MAY BE SOME argument about the date, but let's put the date for the birth of contemporary management information systems (MIS) at some point in the late 1950s. Conception came about as the result of a union between a maker of large electronic toys and a growing business community. The child turned out to be somewhat different than originally envisioned by the parents. As a matter of fact, the child turned out to be children, a fact that will be explained a little later on. The parents were quite generous with the children, bestowing on them many of the sophisticated toys made by the electronic toy maker and paid for by the business community. These two acted like patrons or benefactors to the MIS kids. The early 1960s witnessed the early childhood of these kids. As is the case with most children of that age, the MIS kids got a great deal of attention and were talked about a lot. They were often described in contemporary literature. On one extreme the titles were impressive. "Master Plan for Information Systems"[1] "MIS—Management's Best Friend,"[2] "Management Information Systems"[3] are a sample. These titles and others like them appeared in numerous trade and business jour-

*A modified version of an article published in the *Journal of Systems Management* titled "Look out Management, Here They Come Again." in July, 1979, by Myles E. Walsh

nals. Seminars on how to raise these kids were sponsored by professional organizations such as AMA and ASM. The contents of most of the journal articles and the seminars were quite theoretical and virtually ignored the practical aspects of raising MIS children. There was also a small group of individuals with a middle view that had some reasonably solid, well-thought-out plans for developing an MIS. Neuendorf's "New Dimensions in Management Information,"[4] was an example. In his paper, Neuendorf suggested a rather systematic, step-by-step approach; setting short-term achievable goals, periodically checkpointing what was done and at the same time reevaluating the overall objectives to make sure that it was still in line with the parents' goals and objectives. Any out-of-line situation would dictate that adjustments be made. At the other extreme there were titles indicating that perhaps there was a darker side to all this. John Dearden's "Myth of Real-Time Management Information"[5] or Samuel Faiello's "The Unsolved Problems of Information Retrieval"[6] indicated this.

The next several years, as most businessmen outside of the MIS profession are aware, witnessed the preteen years of the MIS children. As indicated earlier, MIS was initially intended as an only child, which turned out to be two. The second followed the first, clinging to his heel, so to speak, just as Jacob had followed Esau into the world, as described in the twenty-fifth chapter of Genesis. As an only child, MIS was supposed to be a business function, specifically, a comprehensive system designed to take in, store, and manipulate data, and to display it as useful and timely information for management. This MIS only partially lived up to expectations. The second MIS turned out to be an organization composed of a collection of individuals such as computer programmers, systems analysts, and electronic data processing managers. Just as Jacob and Esau had been given names that were descriptive of their roles, the two MIS kids were also named. The first was called MISFIT, or MISF for short, and the second was called MIST, short for MYSTIQUE. MISF and MIST grew, and as young children do, they consumed much food, ran around a lot, and produced significant quantities of output that was of somewhat questionable value. At the same time, business itself was growing, and the children benefitted from the latest toys, which were quite sophisticated. MISF and MIST were grateful for their toys and made every effort to use them in ways that would please their benefactors. Both children were somewhat gifted, each in a different way. MISF was the one who produced; he was the worker, the "operations guy." MIST was the promoter, the entrepreneur. MIST, with childlike enthusiasm, was running to his benefactors on virtually a daily basis to get funding to develop one of MISF's ideas. Some of these ideas were worthwhile, others were in the form of "solutions looking for problems," while some others were nothing more than narcissistic reflections of MISF and MIST. Yet the benefactors allowed almost all of them to be implemented. Since they were still quite young, the two children were somewhat oblivious to the fact that the benefactors had other things on their minds. MISF kept developing new systems, and MIST kept promoting them. To placate the two, the benefactors kept giving them new toys to keep them busy. As for the benefactors themselves, their main concern was making money; they had little real interest in what MISF and MIST were up to, as long as their green-and-white outputs were reasonably accurate and were delivered on time.

In the late 1960s, the titles of some of the trade journal articles began to indicate that there might be some afterthoughts about the activities of MISF and MIST. By way of example "Are Total Systems Practical?"[7] and "Will the Real MIS Stand?"[8] were two of the titles that reflected these afterthoughts. The benefactors became a little uneasy, but the money was still coming in, so they didn't pay too much attention.

In the 1970s the MIS kids entered their adolescence. They grew in size and complexity, exhibiting that sometimes bewildering combination of child and adult. The outputs produced by MISF began to show signs of diminishing in quantity while increasing in quality. His ability to respond to direct questions improved. His answers were given more quickly and more concisely. MIST, on the other hand, continued to grow but began to become introverted. He began to develop his own jargon and had a great deal of difficulty in communicating with others who did not understand it. Since he was only an adolescent, he was oblivious to this deficiency. As a result of this, and reinforced by the increasing successes of MISF, MIST occasionally manifested periods of arrogance alternating with periods of condescension in dealing with others. These attitudes coupled with the youngster's size and strength (he was big for his age) led the others with whom he was dealing to build a fence around MIST's yard. These same individuals began to make attempts to work with MISF directly without involving MIST at all.

Compounding the difficulties of this time was the appearance in the marketplace of less-expensive and smaller versions of one of the toys that were similar to those currently being provided to MISF and MIST by their benefactors. Neither of the MIS kids seemed to care very much for the cheaper toys. However, some members of the business community, the adventuresome, the economy-minded, and the technically inclined, thought that these less-expensive toys might be just fine. They also felt that if MISF and MIST didn't want to, then someone who would like to play with them could be found. There was some feeling on the part of the large, sophisticated toymaker that the business community, who had collaborated in conceiving and giving birth to MIST and

MISF, was now committing adultery with the smaller toy manufacturers. However, being mature and cultivated, these feelings were not explicitly expressed.

The time frame for all this was the early 1970s. These smaller and less expensive versions of one type of MISF's and MIST's sophisticated toys, namely the CPU or computer processor, became available in great quantity. These toys were called MINIs (short for minicomputers) and they appeared to be a tremendous opportunity for those who wished to get away from MIST altogether and also to find a less-expensive child than MISF to care for, at least insofar as providing toys.

Some organizations committed rather heavily into MINIs; others were more cautious. Whatever the commitment, the consequences were not long in coming. Since MIST was an adolescent, he did have some things going for him in spite of his shortcomings. For one thing, his jargon was the language of an adolescent, which while not perfect, was still a long way from the baby talk needed in communicating with individuals involved with MINIs. As a matter of fact, dealing with such individuals was not unlike what dealing with MIST and MISF had been seven or eight years earlier. Since that time, however, MIST and MISF had developed some enhancements. A number of auxiliary and support functions that had been developed by MISF during his childhood and now taken for granted by the benefactors, were neither transferrable from the large sophisticated toys to the MINIs nor were they available with MINIs. That meant that they would have to be developed all over again for the MINIs. Another shortcoming of the smaller toys was that it usually took several of them to do what the adolescent MISF could do with one of his larger CPUs. Compounding this situation even further was the fact that although there were many kinds of MINIs they could not be connected to one another to equal one of MISF's big CPUs, unless they were from the same manufacturer or unless they used some of the MISF's facilities. This last consideration may have been partially responsible for the popularity of Joseph Heller's *Catch 22* with MIST, who was watching all these developments through the fence in his yard.

Those who committed to MINIs found themselves involved with individuals who bore some striking resemblances to MIST. These individuals, advocates of MINIs technology, were of greater number, and they were not like the dependent child MIST was. They were more like relatives who came to eat and sleep and leave their kids and toys while they visited other relatives and went shopping. For example, when MISF and MIST were kids and were getting all the expensive toys, the large toy manufacturer would send engineers of various types to help put the toys together, and to maintain the toys. This kind of service was often given free of charge. And also, some of these engineers would work closely with MISF and MIST in helping to develop the need for more toys, especially the narcissistic kind. And yet, netted out, these large toy manufacturer engineers provided a "hand-holding" service that was quite valuable at times, even if it did create something of a dependency relationship, with MISF, MIST, and the business community relying on the large toy manufacturer. Initially, when MINIs had first begun to appear on the scene, they were used primarily by electronics engineers who already knew much of the language needed to communicate with MINIs, so the "hand-holding" service that the large toy manufacturer supplied was not needed. When a MINI was delivered, "they slowed the truck down and threw it to you." You were on your own. Of course MINIs were inexpensive. However, some of the more "astute" engineers and benefactors and a sprinkling of opportunists saw a chance to become heroes. These individuals attempted to get operating departments to demand their own MINI, justifying the purchase with the rationale that they could do the job more economically than MISF and MIST. Some operating departments got their MINIs. The opportunists, "astute" engineers, and benefactors moved on to other things, and the department heads were left to implement their system. The manufacturers of the MINIs were often called in to help. Because of their unfamiliarity with MIST and MISF and their rather general lack of interest in the problems of teenagers, these manufacturer representatives were of little help initially. However, some of these MINI manufacturer representatives soon became enamoured by the charms of the business community. In addition to charm, it was also observed that the business community had money. And so, several MINI manufacturers began to make adjustments to make themselves look like the large, sophisticated toy manufacturer. The business community also made some adjustments, and a few rendevous took place. MISF made some adjustments also, but MIST was infuriated. He felt threatened.

It was at this time that some additions were made to MISF's vocabulary. Terms like turnkey system and OEM* (original equipment manufacturer) entered the jargon. It wasn't long before MIST began to mature. He decided to swallow his pride, climb over the fence, and go out and play with the relative's kids. Even if they were smaller and could operate in a less-controlled environment, MIST perceived that he and they did have a number of things in common. After all, a computer is a computer, magnetic tape is magnetic tape, a program is a program. "So what if ASCII isn't EBCDIC and start/stop isn't bisynch," MIST thought, "we can overcome that." MISF did his part by producing "interfaces," that is, common areas of communication between MINIs and his own toys.

*These two terms were used to describe fully developed computer systems (including both hardware and software) that could be purchased by an organization and directly applied to an application within the organization.

When MIST first came out of the yard, the little kids were intimidated by him. Some ran away into the woods where they were eaten by bears. Others, some of the bigger ones, tried to fight him. He reacted in kind. Both sides expended substantial amounts of energy in a series of skirmishes the results of which were inconclusive. Others decided that a competitive, but not openly hostile environment would be a suitable situation. Within a few years, a sometimes uneasy but relatively stable environment resulted. The competition was quite fierce, but there was only an occasional flare-up and open warfare did not break out. Concurrent with all this instability and turmoil, the contemporary literature began to question the legitimacy of MISF. "MIS is a Mirage"[9] was one of the titles. Then, for some inexplicable reason, all the furor died down, and an era of peace seemed to settle over the entire scene. MISF grew and began to develop some MINI expertise of his own. The MINI makers continued to add sophistication to their toys so that they began to look like and to function like the toys that MISF had used and developed in his early adolescence. MIST grew and added to his vocabulary all the words of the little kids. The little kids themselves tried and in some cases succeeded in adding MIST's jargon to their own vocabulary.

As the MINI makers began to develop toys more like the big toymakers' sophisticated playthings, that enterprise in turn began to develop toys similar to those made by the MINI manufacturers. This was done in the spirit of competition. Concurrent with this came an awareness that there were some things better done on MINIs and other things better done with the more sophisticated larger toys. Added to that was the awareness that even with a system of related jobs, there were functional distinctions where some tasks were more suitable to MINIs and others more suitable to bigger toys. This observation has led to the development of what are known as distributed systems or distributed processing, where some tasks were handled by small computers and others by larger computers. This idea of distributed processing was in itself a sophisticated technology, in that there was communication among the small toys and the larger ones. In addition to the complex technology of computers was added the complex technology of telecommunications. As if that were not enough, another toy manufacturer arrived on the scene with an even smaller toy. Let's call it MIKE, short for micro or microprocessor. In the mid 1970s, just about the time that MIST, MISF, and MINI kids were getting reconciled, these toys came on the scene. Their impact was similar to that which the introduction of MINIs had originally had on MIST, MISF, and the big toy manufacturers. Without going into details, which would be repetitious, let's just say that it was unsettling. Whereas MINI makers had been like relatives dropping off a few kids and toys, MICRO makers brought busloads.

What had happened? In the early 1960s, the computer was applied to business applications. Prior to that time computers had been used primarily to perform the large-scale number-crunching calculations required by scientific and engineering applications. Computers are still used for this purpose. However, it was the business community's involvement with computers that led to the conception and coming into the world of the MIS kids. The MIS idea came about as the result of the business community's alleged need for more information and the ability of big toy manufacturer's ability to build toys that could provide more information. By the mid 1970s, the business community was buried in information, MIST and MISF had been born, and together with the computers they were cranking out information faster than anybody could use it. There had to be a better way. The business community, the MIS kids, and the toy manufacturers got together and came up with the conclusion that it was not necessarily more information that was needed, but rather more accurate and timely information. On-line, real-time business systems were born. Small computers had been doing on-line, real-line processing for years and helping manufacturers control processes, and refiners to control mixtures. MIST and MISF became more sophisticated and developed the systems to meet the need of business for timely and accurate information. It was in the early stages of the development of these "strategic" management information systems, that the idea of MIS being the salvation of business was formulated. Two big mistakes were made in the business community. First, the important executives and businessmen ignored the idea. Second, MIST and the toymaker really believed it, and together with some aggressive and opportunistic middle-level executives and managers they attempted to make the idea a reality. The only rub was that it took several years, was quite traumatic, and was extremely expensive. In not a few cases, the resultant timely and accurate information was not what was wanted or needed, though this has rarely been admitted.

Within the past few years, an element of stability has been evidenced in MIS. MIST and MISF have matured. The business community has accepted them as legitimate, even if prodigal sons. The big sophisticated toy manufacturer is making MINIs, and MIKEs as well as big toys. MINI makers and MIKE makers are competing with him, and there is sure to be more turbulence ahead. The distinction between MINIs, MIKEs, and the big computers is beginning to blur. The differences at the extremes are discernible enough, but toward the middle they are not all that clear. Added to this is the fact that computers, across the board, are becoming smaller and less expensive. A number of functions that were once software, requiring the services of a highly skilled and highly paid computer programmer, are now part of the computer circuitry. There are indications that there are again forces at work, and individuals under the control of those forces who again believe that the business community is in need of a savior.

In the 1960s it was information in quantity that was going to save business. In the 1970s it was quality information that was needed to save business. In the 1980s it's called "decision support systems." In the 1960s, computers made a useful contribution, but the technological advances and the grandiose orchestrations put forth by the MIS impresarios turned out to be overlong and sometimes rather dissonant and bombastic. The 1970s were a time when upper management was forced to pay attention, because MIS was causing considerable bewilderment and costing substantial sums of money. In the 1980s, the tools (toys) are up to the task, the question now is: Are the MIS function and management up to it?

REFERENCES

1. Marshall K. Evans and Lou R. Hogue, "Master Plan for Information Systems," *Harvard Business Review*, Jan.–Feb. 1962, pp. 92–103.
2. Richard D. Kornblum, "MIS-Management's Best Friend," *International Business Automation*, Oct.–Nov. 1965, pp. 30–35.
3. J.W. Kovalinka and H.G. Trentin, "Management Information Systems," *Management Services*, Sept.–Oct. 1965, pp. 27–39.
4. Charles W. Neuendorf, "New Dimensions in Management Information," *Data Processing Vol IV The Proceedings of the Data Processing Management Association's 1963 International Data Processing Conference*, Detroit, Michigan, June 25–29, 1963, pp. 42–69.
5. John Dearden, "Myth of Real-Time Management Information," *Harvard Business Review*, March–April 1965, pp. 123–132.
6. Samuel Faiello, "The Unsolved Problems of Information Retrieval," *Systems Management*, March–April 1963, pp. 30–40.
7. Allan Harvey, "Are Total Systems Practical?" *Business Automation*, June 1969, pp. 72–75, 142.
8. Robert G. Donkin, "Will the Real MIS Stand?" *Business Automation*, May 1969, pp. 50–53.
9. John Dearden, "MIS is a Mirage," *Harvard Business Review*, Jan.–Feb. 1972. pp. 10–14.

APPENDIX C

A Simple Yet Effective Planning Tool

INTRODUCTION

"Operations" is that functional part of an organization that always seems to be running in "react mode." Operations is where the action is. After all the plans have been laid, after all the functional specifications have been agreed upon, and after all the simulations, unit tests, integrated tests, volume tests and systems tests have been run, it (whatever "it" may be) is given to operations. Operations has to make it work. Operations may be a manufacturing facility, it may be a fulfillment function, or it may be a computer data-processing center. In any event, operations is "where the rubber meets the road."

Since this book deals with the technology of EDP and MIS, the "operations" referred to here is that of a computer data-processing center. This piece describes a technique for preparing an operational plan that covers a time period of about twelve to fifteen months. It is relatively simple, the tools to produce it cost less than $100,* and the whole pro-

*In October 1977, *Infosystems* published an article that I wrote describing the technique as it was used then. The title of the piece was "The 39.95 Planning Tool." See what inflation can do.

cess of creating it takes less than a week, and that includes typing and drawing the Gantt Charts that senior management uses to monitor progress.

BACKGROUND

The ideas used in this planning technique had their origins at an IBM-sponsored planning session held in Palo Alto, California in February 1977. No doubt, the IBM personnel working with other customers had used similar techniques previously. The attractiveness of this particular planning method lies in its simplicity and in the informal setting in which it is conducted.

The technique, as described here, explains how to plan the activities of a large corporate data-processing center. The assumption is made that some items, such as easels, are available and do not have to be purchased. There are, no doubt, other functions both within and outside of the information systems function that could make use of this planning methodology. It is suggested that the group of individuals, who are to develop the details of the plan, isolate themselves for two or three days at a site remote from their departmental activities. Day-to-day concerns, telephone calls, and interruptions are not conducive to the concentration required in careful planning. The lifecycle for this particular technique may be limited to about four years. Once individuals have participated two or three times in the planning process using this technique, their interest in it begins to diminish. After the third iteration, it is time to either change participants or to change the planning technique. And yet, for at least three years the technique can be quite helpful in preparing an operational plan for establishing reasonable, reachable goals for a period of twelve to fifteen months.

OVERVIEW OF THE PROCESS

Let's first look at the entire process in general. Having done that, we can then examine the details. The overall process consists of three steps: first, initial preparation; second, the process of laying out the detailed plan; and third, the preparing of the Gantt Charts. Initial preparation, in reality can be done in a matter of several hours, but those several hours are spread over a couple of months prior to the two day session. Each of the individuals who are to attend the two-day planning session should be able to spend a few hours during the two months preceeding it formulating some fairly specific ideas about concerns and projects for the coming year.

Generally speaking, the process of laying out the details of the plan involves identifying milestones (completed projects) that are to be reached at specific times during the coming year. These milestones are written on small cards that are attached with masking tape to a long sheet of paper that is subdivided into twelve or fifteen sections, each section representing a month. Finally, after all milestones have been specified and scheduled, they can be used to provide the foundation for Gantt Charts that show each milestone as a project, on the vertical axis. The horizontal axis expresses months. Lines are used to indicate original schedule, adjustments to schedule and actual work completed. The long sheet of paper can be maintained; milestone cards can be moved if rescheduled, or marked with an "X" if completed. The details which follow clarify the overview just described.

MATERIALS

The materials needed for this planning process are:

- Index cards, several colors, about fifty of each color and fifty white or manila for each color used. If four colors are used, 200 white cards are needed.
- A rubber stamp, custom made.
- A stamp pad.
- Several felt-tip pens of various colors.
- A roll of 20-lb. paper, at least 36 inches wide and 25 feet long.
- A roll of 1/2 inch masking tape.
- Two or three flip charts with easels.
- Two packages of 8½ × 11 inch paper for project sheets and Gantt Charts.
- Scissors.

Variations on these materials are permitted. The rubber stamp has the framework illustrated in Figure C.1. This framework is stamped

Figure C.1 Rubber stamp framework.

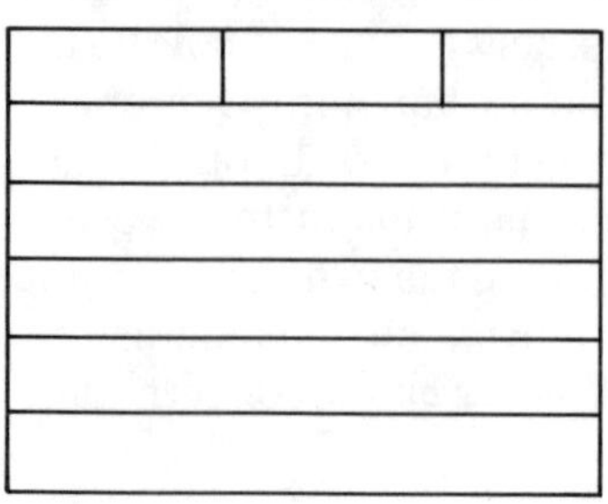

onto the index cards and is then cut out. These make up milestone cards and task cards, the uses of which are explained later. Preparing a number of the task and milestone cards is something that is done prior to the meeting. About fifty of each color together with fifty white or manila for each color should be more than enough. It's a great job for a ten- or eleven-year-old child, and it gives the kid a chance to make a few dollars.

INITIAL PREPARATION

In the months immediately preceeding the two-day session, the participating individuals are able to begin formulating their ideas on concerns about the coming year as well as making a list of projects that they would like to see completed during the year. For a computer data processing center, those individuals whose presence is necessary to make the technique work properly would include:*

- The director or general manager of the data processing center
- The director of operations
- The manager of scheduling
- The manager of computer operations
- The manager of communications operations
- The manager of operations technical support
- The director of software support
- The manager of database systems
- The manager of personal computing systems
- The manager of telecommunications systems
- The manager of operating system support
- The manager of standards and documentation

In addition to those just mentioned, another individual is required to perform the function of moderator and group leader. This role can be played by a staff planner or internal consultant.

One of the individuals in the group is also chosen to be the logistics coordinator of the planning session. Usually there is one who is able to handle the task and is willing to do it. It is advisable to find a hotel or motel about a hundred miles away from the data-processing center. The reason for this is to make it inconvenient for any of the participants to be called away to take care of some emergency. If subordinates cannot keep the data-processing center running for two days, then the planning session should be postponed until they are able to. The logistics co-

*Job titles used here are indicative of the types of individuals required. Such titles vary from company to company.

ordinator deals with hotel or motel staff and makes the arrangements for rooms, meals, the suite in which the meetings are held, and whatever other accommodations are needed. This generally involves a few telephone conversations and one trip to the facility a few days prior to the planning session. The use of the facilities of a hotel or motel increases the cost of the exercise to a sum substantially higher than one hundred dollars. And yet, it is not all that uncommon to hold business meetings of various kinds away from office surrounding. The cost, usually a few thousand dollars, to use the business meeting facilities provided by a hotel or a motel can be justified in several ways. It gets the managers and directors away from day-to-day problems and gives them an opportunity to devote time to planning without interruptions. It gives subordinates an opportunity to fill in for their superiors and to experience some of their superiors' problems. It gives the managers and directors a chance to participate interactively with one another in putting together an integrated plan. Each individual gets the opportunity to see how his or her activities depend upon or impact the activities of others. Adjustments to individual group plans can be made that would probably have been missed, if plans had been made independently.

A suite that is large enough to accommodate the entire group has some advantages over a conference room. This technique is suited to an atmosphere of informality. Continental breakfasts, coffee breaks, and cold-cuts luncheons can be served in the suite. Lounge chairs, coffee tables, and sofas are less formal than the type of chairs and tables normally found in conference rooms. The logistics coordinator assures that everything is in place so that the meeting starts promptly and moves along according to schedule. A schedule of events looks something like that contained in Figure C.2.

For the planning session to begin punctually and stay on schedule, it is advisable for those living more than an hour's time from the hotel or motel to arrive the night before. Some preliminary conversations and comparing of notes can be done over dinner. In that way, the participants will already "be partially up to speed" when the session commences on the following morning.

Since the atmosphere is an informal one, the moderator can begin bringing things to order sometime between 8:45 and nine o'clock. Coffee and buns may be available as the session begins. For approximately two hours, all participants are encouraged to indicate their concerns about the coming twelve to fifteen months. October is a good time to hold the planning session. Projects can be scheduled for November and December and for the succeeding 12 months, that is, the coming year. It is the job of the moderator to crystallize and to record each of the concerns expressed. There may be some discussion permitted as the con-

Figure C.2 Planning session schedule of events.

Day 1

8:30 AM	Continental breakfast
9:00 AM	Statement of concerns
10:30 AM	Coffee
11:00 AM	Statement of projects
12:30 PM	Luncheon
1:45 PM	Review projects Assure that all concerns are covered
3:00 PM	Afternoon break
3:30 PM	Form groups—prepare project estimates
5:00 PM	Break for evening

Day 2

8:30 AM	Continental breakfast
9:00 AM	Groups prepare milestone and task cards
10:30 AM	Coffee
11:00 AM	Begin laying out milestone and task cards on planning sheet
12:30 PM	Luncheon
1:45 PM	Continue layout of plan
3:00 PM	Afternoon break
3:30 PM	Make up project planning sheets
	Break when suitable

cerns are raised, but it is not the objective at this point to address the concerns, but merely to state them. Typical concerns that might be recorded at a data-processing center planning session might include:

- The increases in application programmer productivity is adding to the processing load faster than the data center can acquire equipment to accommodate it.
- The systems software products are becoming so complex and are changing and increasing in magnitude so quickly that maintaining reliability is difficult.
- More attention should be given to data security.
- There don't seem to be enough total resources for testing and development.
- Restart/recovery procedures for the data base/data communications systems are too complex operationally.
- The old job accounting system has been patched up so often, it's

ready to completely break down. One full-time systems software technician is required just to keep it running each month.

- At the present rate of growth, there are not going to be any telecommunications adapters available on the front-end computer by the middle of March.

Mid-morning of the first day marks the end of the process of recording concerns. After a short break, during which the participants discuss the concerns while drinking coffee, the moderator reconvenes the meeting. All of the concerns which had been recorded and numbered on flip charts are hung on the walls of the suite with masking tape.* The list of concerns may number somewhere around sixty.

The next couple of hours is devoted to recording of projects. The functional units (computer operations, scheduling, data base software, telecommunications software, etc.) name their intended projects, one unit at a time. The moderator records the projects on flip chart sheets, numbering them in the process. These sheets are also hung on the suite walls with masking tape. The projects generally number between twenty-five and forty among the functional units, so that upon completion of this part of the process, there may be a total of over two hundred projects. When the projects have been stated, discussed, recorded, and numbered, there can be a break for lunch. Cold cuts, potato salad, cole slaw, beer, soda, and wine can be served in the suite. During the luncheon conversations can begin to determine if all the concerns expressed are covered by the projects that are planned.

The early afternoon is spent correlating concerns and projects. The moderator again directs and controls the meeting. A cross reference sheet is made up in which the concern numbers are listed and next to them are recorded the projects that address the concerns. Unaddressed concerns are those that fall outside the scope of projects. Discussions follow during which unaddressed concerns are assigned to one or more of the three directors. The conclusion of this part of the meeting is in the middle of the afternoon. It is followed by an afternoon break. At this point, the initial preparation for the plan is complete and after the break the detailed planning begins.

LAYING OUT THE DETAILED PLAN

The first step in preparing the detailed plan consists of breaking up into groups. The size of the groups is three or four individuals. Those in the

*Unlike thumbtacks and pins, masking tape does not ruin walls, if removed within 48 hours.

group concentrate on the projects for which they are responsible. Using the flip chart sheets on which their projects had been written by the moderator, the individuals begin to identify the tasks necessary to complete the projects. Projects consist of between two and six tasks. The tasks represent the "things that have to be done" to complete the project. Elapsed time estimates are given to the tasks. The accumulation of the time estimates of the tasks equals the length of the project.

It is the responsibility of the managers to rank the projects according to priority. The directors participate in this. They can move among the groups, advising and giving approvals to priorities. Once this is done, each project is transcribed onto a *milestone card*. The milestones of the various groups are distinguished by color. For instance, green might be used by computer operations, yellow by scheduling, blue by database support, and red by telecommunications systems support. Tasks are transcribed onto the white or manila cards. They are related to specific milestones in two ways: first, they are given a milestone number and they are written with a felt-tip pen, the color of which corresponds to the milestone card color. Tasks are also numbered serially within a project or milestone context. For instance, if milestone number nine had four tasks, those tasks would be numbered 9–1, 9–2, 9–3, and 9–4. The number for both milestones and tasks is generally placed at the upper right of the card. The task estimates are generally written in the upper left of the card. Milestone and task descriptions are written in the body of the card. Figure C.3 contains sketches of milestone and task cards. Typical milestones in a data processing center's plan include:

- Install latest release of the operating system.
- Get the database management system operational as a test vehicle.
- Get the database management system operational as a production vehicle.
- Complete the conversion to the fixed head disk drives.
- Complete the training for interactive programming support function.
- Complete conversion to new communications access method for the manufacturing system.
- Front-end computer configured and delivered.
- Site preparation completed for relocation of software programmers.

This part of the plan preparation requires the most concentration, since it is the most detailed. It begins in the late afternoon of the first day and concludes in the late morning of the second day.

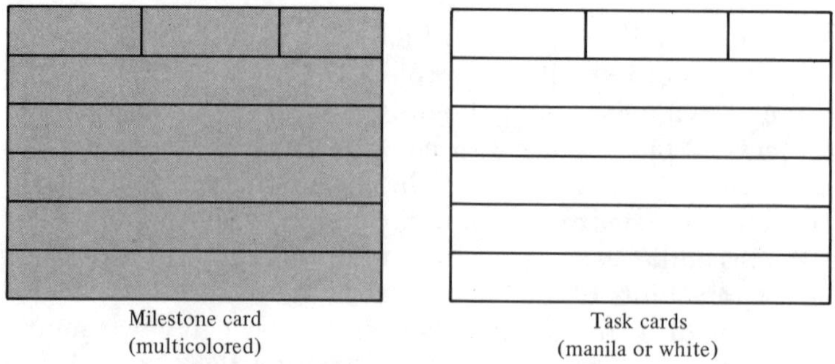

Figure C.3 Milestone and task cards.

After the milestone and task cards have been prepared, the next step is laying out the plan. The roll of paper is used. It can either be hung on a wall or spread over several tables. Sections of the paper can be marked off to delineate months. If the meeting is being held in October, the first month on the paper would be November, the second, December, the third, January, and so on. Twenty-four to thirty inches can be used for November through April; eighteen inches is sufficient for the remaining months. See Figure C.4. When using this technique, the details of projects are usually quite clear and precise for the first six months. As the plan projects further into the coming year, the details become less precise and more sketchy. The allowance of more space for the earlier months is merely a practical one. Since more detail is known, there is a strong probability that more cards are used requiring the additional space.

The process of placing the cards onto the planning sheet by month runs from late morning until the middle of the afternoon. This time frame includes two breaks and a luncheon. The masking tape is used. Small strips about two inches long are cut from the roll and formed into loops with two sides of adhesive. These are used to place the milestone cards and the task cards on the sheet. To get the project plan completed, the task and milestone cards are placed on the sheet. For a given project, a start date is chosen. The first task card is placed at that point. The next task for that project is placed in line horizontally with the first, a

Figure C.4 Layout sheet.

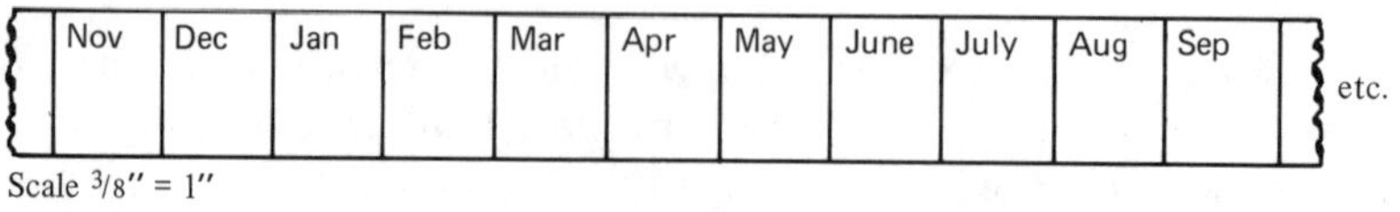

distance equal to the estimate of the length of time required to complete the first task. This process is repeated for all task cards, and finally the milestone card is placed in the same horizontal line at a distance equal to the estimate for completing the last task. All the projects are handled the same way. When they are all completed, it is generally found that there are some conflicts. Dependencies that had not been determined appear. For instance, the manager of data base systems had scheduled a new release of a software product to be installed in June. The only problem was that the product required a feature of an access method that was not scheduled to be installed until August. Or the manager found that projects were scheduled so that in March there was a three-week stretch in which there was work for five people and there were only three in his staff. The whole purpose of laying out the projects on the calendarized sheet of paper is to highlight what's going on, when it's going to occur, and to find conflicts and discrepancies and to correct them. The conflicts and discrepancies can be reconciled by merely changing the locations of some task and milestone cards.

Upon completion of the layout, the approval of the plan is given by the directors. The remainder of the day is given over to the preparation of detailed planning sheets in handwritten form. These sheets (a copy of one can be seen in Figure C.5) which are subsequently typed provide back up for the Gantt Charts which are prepared for senior management so that they can monitor the progress made against the plan.

PREPARING THE GANTT CHARTS

The Gantt Charts are used to provide a summary of the plan that is laid out on the big sheets of paper. Figure C.6 shows the form that is used. Each project occupies a position at the left. In all there are approximately two hundred projects, around one hundred and fifty from the software group and another fifty from operations. So all told, there are between twenty and twenty-five of these sheets prepared for senior MIS management. Each entry, or project is backed up by a detailed planning sheet. As originally prepared, the Gantt Chart contains the entry for the project and a heavy solid line indicating beginning and ending dates for the project. There is an arrowhead at the completion date end of the line. When work begins on a project, a dotted line is used to indicate progress. If the start dates or completion dates change, a thin solid line is used to indicate the new dates. An explanation can be provided to the right for projects that are changed. Typically, Gantt Charts are updated on a quarterly basis.

Figure C.5 Project control form. Courtesy of CBS, Inc.

CBS PROJECT CONTROL

GROUP	DIVISION	PROJECT NUMBER	PAGE OF

PROJECT TITLE

PROJECT DESCRIPTION

TASK NO.	TASK DESCRIPTION	ASSIGNED TO	EST. MAN DAYS	START DATE	COMPLETION DATE	
					INITIAL	REVISED

STATUS AND COMMENTS

PREPARED BY	DATE	PROJECT RESPONSIBILITY	APPROVED BY	DATE

CORP 2653

Figure C.6 Project development schedule form. Courtesy of CBS, Inc.

CBS CORPORATE MIS PROJECT DEVELOPMENT SCHEDULE

SECTION | DATE

PROJECT NO.	PROJECT	DIV.	1983			1984												COMMENTS
			10	11	12	1	2	3	4	5	6	7	8	9	10	11	12	
			OCT.	NOV.	DEC.	JAN.	FEB.	MAR.	APR.	MAY	JUNE	JULY	AUG.	SEPT.	OCT.	NOV.	DEC.	

CORP 3909B REV 6/80

LEGEND: – – – – ACTUAL PROGRESS ——▶ PLANNED COMPLETION ——> REVISED COMPLETION

CONCLUSION

"Any fool can plan, it takes a true executive to leap from crisis to crisis." Although offered in jest, this statement reflects an attitude that often results where there is little or no planning aside from the preparation of the budget. Planning in a hectic operational environment is looked upon as an unachievable luxury. And yet the technique offered here does not heavily interfere with keeping the day-to-day operations going. For an investment of two or three days on the part of several people, the return is a clearer and more manageable set of tasks and projects. The technique has been used, and it works, despite the limitation that it can only be used two or three times by the same group of individuals.

APPENDIX D

Musings of an MIS Director

THIS APPENDIX IS OFFERED for whatever it is worth. It represents the meanderings of the mind of an individual who has spent nearly thirty years working in a variety of jobs. Among those jobs were routeman, warehouseman, tab operator, computer operator, computer room supervisor, computer programmer, manager of systems and programming, and director of information systems in several different organizations. Occasionally, one gets an opportunity to reflect and perhaps philosophize a bit. The following thoughts are independent in the sense that they occurred at different times, but dependent in the sense that they have come about as the result of contacts made with numerous other individuals. Therefore, no claim is made for originality. My only hope is that they stimulate some thought and perhaps direct us all toward finding solutions rather than creating problems.

1. Information systems is potential, realization of that potential is the Pilgrims' Progress of computer technology. The problem is this, if we allow complete freedom in the realization of the potential, the clever and the opportunistic among us will usurp all the power and leave the cautious and the creative with the scraps. And so we must put restrictions on the potential to in-

hibit the clever and the opportunistic, and in doing so we create a bureaucracy that frustrates the cautious and stifles the creative, while at the same time stimulating the clever and the opportunistic to find better ways to bypass the restrictions. And so it goes, further restrictions are imposed to inhibit the bypasses, causing further frustration on the cautious and stifling the creative. The clever and opportunistic again concentrate on getting round the restrictions, and so on.

2. It is always possible to find some kind of valid objection to any proposal or proposition. If you can't come up with a real objection—make one up. Generate enough smoke and you can distort anything. It ensures that nothing gets done.
3. We have a continuing ability to consume resources faster than we can fabricate them—the rate of consumption is increasing exponentially.
4. As application developers and users get tired of dealing with temperamental programmers, they will welcome high-level languages and machines, which while impersonal, are not temperamental (at least initially).
5. When new products are introduced, attitudes in individuals go from complete credulity when they are announced to almost total dismay when they fail to perform according to the unrealistic expectations produced by the announcement. This happens again and again with the same individuals who never seem to get any wiser from past experience and disappointments. People believe what they want to believe.
6. Be cautious of trying to impress senior management with your "good" ideas; they may want you to implement them.
7. IBM can always roll out the reserves when necessary. IBM reserves the right to make final judgement on what constitutes necessary.
8. In large organizations, in many, but not all situations, nobody is "in charge."
9. MIS is constantly changing. It is a process that everything goes through cycles—birth, childhood, adolescence, early adulthood, maternity, middle age, senior citizen, old age, death. It happened to Jimmy Brown, it's happening to MIS. During this cycle, there is new birth—out of the old comes the new. While MIS was maturing, it was also giving birth to new technology, to new ways of doing things such as storing and retrieving information. MIS, in conjunction with other forces, helped to usher in changes in the ways things are managed.
10. Database requires that data elements be interrelated. This can be done by means of pointers (most hierarchical and network

systems) or by physical adjacency (relational models). Realizing the potential of database management systems requires that data element relationships be specified ahead of time, so that when retrieval requests are made, the control blocks contain the information relating the data elements. To design the ultimate database, anticipate all the requests. WOW!!!

11. Those who complain about politics haven't gotten ahead because they are unable to deal with other people. These complainers usually refuse to compromise and prefer sandbagging to cooperation. Politicians are those who are able to bring together a number of essentially self-serving individuals and get them to work together toward a common objective that would never be reached if these individuals continued to strive independently.
12. Some functional managers act like first-line managers and then complain when they don't advance.
13. Could it be that IBM's strategy or architecture SNA is so big and incomprehensible that no one notices when Big Blue makes a 180-degree turn in its strategic direction? Could it be that strategies of other organizations are similar?
14. Do not be too eager to impress your superiors, it might lead to more questions.
15. Be inconsistent; then they can't predict what you're going to do. For example, write a book; put summaries in some chapters, but not in all.

INDEX